Family, Political Economy, and Demographic Change

Life Course Studies

Family and the Female Life Course: The Women of Verviers, Belgium, 1849–1880
George Alter

The Ageless Self: Sources of Meaning in Late Life
Sharon R. Kaufman

Family, Political Economy, and Demographic Change: The Transformation of Life in Casalecchio, Italy, 1861–1921
David I. Kertzer and Dennis P. Hogan

Family, Class, and Ideology in Early Industrial France: Social Policy and the Working-Class Family, 1825–1848
Katherine A. Lynch

Working Parents: Transformations in Gender Roles and Public Policies in Sweden
Phyllis Moen

Family, Political Economy, and Demographic Change

The Transformation of Life in Casalecchio, Italy, 1861–1921

David I. Kertzer
Dennis P. Hogan

The University of Wisconsin Press

The University of Wisconsin Press
114 North Murray Street
Madison, Wisconsin 53715

3 Henrietta Street
London WC2E 8LU, England

5 4 3 2 1

Printed in the United States of America

Library of Congress Cataloging-in-Publication Data
Kertzer, David I., 1948–
Family, political economy, and demographic change.
(Life course studies)
Includes bibliographical references.
1. Casalecchio di Reno (Italy)—Social conditions.
2. Social change—Case studies. I. Hogan, Dennis P.
II. Title. III. Series.
HN488.C288K47 1989 303.4′0945′41 89-40259
ISBN 0-299-12190-9
ISBN 0-299-12194-1 (pbk.)

In memory of

Morris N. Kertzer
Michael H. Hogan

Contents

Illustrations and Maps

Illustrations

Maps

Figures

Tables

Preface

The coming together of social history with other social sciences over the past two decades has unleashed a great wave of enthusiasm, a sense of new possibilities. For those with historical interests, this movement promises a better understanding of what life was like for the majority of peoples of the past and how changes came about. For anthropologists, sociologists, economists, and others, the systematic study of historical materials and historical problems has added a crucial dimension to the understanding of social processes and given a stimulus to theory construction and generalization.

This book is a product of this movement and these enthusiasms. As a collaborative effort by an anthropologist-historian and a sociologist-demographer, it also represents something of an experiment, both in research approach and in content and style. Indeed, with all of the emphasis on interdisciplinary work in the fields of family history and historical demography, it is striking how few empirical studies are jointly authored by scholars from different disciplines.

Such collaboration, as well as the attempt to address a variety of disciplinary audiences, means that settling on the best style of presentation is not a simple matter. Fighting disciplinary training that often rewards the technical and the obscure, we tried as best we could to make this book tell a story, or rather, a series of stories that could be read by a broad academic audience. More technical discussions are relegated to footnotes and to the appendix. Yet, we have tried to take advantage of the full arsenal of research tools offered by our disciplines to shed light on the problems before us. The result is that most readers are likely to encounter sources and methods that are new to them.

Work in Italy with the archives and all work with the Italian primary and secondary literature were the responsibility of Kertzer. Hogan had primary responsibility for the technical demographic and statistical analyses. We tried as best we could to integrate our different perspectives in all phases of analysis and in the writing itself.

The origins of this book lie in work initially begun in 1978 by Kertzer and Andrea Schiaffino, a historical demographer at the University of Bologna. Four years of funding by the National Institute of Child Health and Human Development (Grant HD13415) allowed for much progress in the creation of the demographic data base, the work for which was under the daily supervision of Schiaffino in Bologna. For this phase of the research, thanks are due to Amedeo Angelelli, Giancarlo Bernabei, Marisa Corazza, and Beatrice De Leonibus for their expert assistance in working with the manuscript materials and coding the data. All of this work, as well as subsequent work in the Casalecchio town archives, benefited from the generous support of the mayor of Casalecchio, Floriano Ventura, and other town officials. Indeed, the project would have been impossible without this support.

In the midst of the data-base construction, in 1983, Kertzer and Schiaffino decided to work independently. At that time, Kertzer and Hogan were both fellows at the Center for Advanced Study in the Behavioral Sciences, in Stanford, California, and had had many conversations about the Italian project. The result of these discussions was a collaborative effort which has ultimately led to this book. We would like to express our thanks to the Center for its role in getting this collaborative effort going.

Subsequently, supported by a grant from the NICHD (HD18976), we were able to add new archival materials to the data base—most notably the annual household tax and the conscription data—and to do additional historical archival work. This was also a period in which intensive work was done to correct errors in the original data base and to fill in lacunae.

In addition to the NICHD support listed above, the work on this project and the efforts that went into writing this book were supported by a variety of other sources. Kertzer's work from 1986 to 1988 was made possible by a grant (BNS85-19319) from the National Science Foundation's anthropology program. Hogan's efforts were aided at critical junctures by PHS Biomedical Seed Grant funds from the Division of Social Sciences at the University of Chicago. In addition, research assistance and computer facilities for the final year of the project were provided to Hogan by the Department of Sociology at Pennsylvania State University. The preparation of maps and figures by the Deasy Cartographic Laboratory was supported by the Population Issues Research Center and the Institute for Policy Research and Evaluation at Penn State.

Two of our collaborators merit special attention here, as this book is in no small measure a product of their own work as well as ours. Nancy Karweit, of the Center for Social Organization of Schools at Johns Hopkins University, designed the data-base management system employed in this project. Given the great complexity of our longitudinal data base, this was an immense and challenging task. We are pleased that one result of her work is a data-base management system that is increasingly being used by other life-course researchers around the world.

Massimo Marcolin, an Italian historian in Bologna, collaborated for several years on the qualitative historical archival work for this study. An expert on nineteenth-century Italian social history, his work has helped add a crucial dimension to this book.

We would also like to thank numerous other people who have worked on this project. At Bowdoin College, Joel Richardson and Shawn McDermott provided able assistance as computer programmers, while Roger Bertsch and Monica Carioli worked on data entry and data cleaning. Julie Hodgkins and Jean Lee provided excellent secretarial assistance. At the University of Chicago and Penn State, a number of very capable graduate students provided research assistance. We thank Terry Bryll, Lynne Casper, Jeremy Cattani, Amy Eiden, and Richard Flory for their efforts. Thanks, also, are due to Scott Eliason for his help with computer analysis.

Finally, we would like to thank those colleagues who have helped advise us in this research. On the Italian side, we are grateful to Marzio Barbagli, Franco Cazzola, Arturo Parisi, and Carlo Poni for their support. In the United States, we would like to thank Douglas Anderton, Clifford Clogg, and Michael Massagli. In addition, we thank George Alter, Donald Bell, and Massimo Livi-Bacci for their helpful comments on an earlier draft of this book.

Although none of the chapters of this book has appeared in print before, the book does incorporate some material we have previously published in the following places: "Longitudinal Approaches to Migration in Social History," *Historical Methods* 18 (1985): 20–30; "On the Move: Migration in an Italian Community, 1865–1921," *Social Science History* 9 (1985): 1–23; "Migration Patterns during Italian Urbanization," *Demography* 22 (1985): 309–25; "The Social Bases of Declining Infant Mortality: Lessons from a Nineteenth-Century Italian Town," *European Journal of Population* 2 (1986): 361–86; and "Childhood and Industrialization in Italy," *Anthropological Quarterly* 61 (1987): 152–59.

Family, Political Economy, and Demographic Change

1 Demographic Transformation and Social Change

Of all the changes in people's lives that have taken place in the West over the past two centuries, the demographic revolution is among the most significant. Before this historic decline in mortality and fertility, continuous childbearing marked most women's lives from the time of marriage to the time they were no longer fertile.[1] This affected the entire family unit: both men and women spent most of their married lives rearing dependent children, while children grew up in households with siblings ranging over a broad span of years. Parents could anticipate having at least one child die in infancy and perhaps another in childhood. This whole pattern, which marked European family life for centuries, changed radically in a short period of time. It is this period of demographic change, and the social transformation that accompanied it, that we focus on in these pages.

Historians continue to argue over just which was the crucial period that ushered in modern society in the West. With candidates ranging from the Reformation through the Ages of Discovery and Reason, from the opening up of the New World to European exploration through the French Revolution, champions of the sixteenth, seventeenth, and eighteenth centuries all have ample ammunition. Indeed, even the roots of capitalism and industrialization, which hold center stage in our own narrative, can be traced to these earlier centuries. Yet, for most of the West, it was not until the nineteenth century that the modern transformation of political, economic, and social arrangements truly began, along with the movement toward what was to become the modern demographic regime of low mortality and fertility.

Italy provides a good example of just how pivotal this period was. The nineteenth century began in Italy with the Napoleonic occupation and the undermining of the centuries-old power of the Church and of the political and economic order identified with it. After a brief attempt at restoration of the *ancien régime,* the convulsions of the Risorgimento brought about a new, unified nation in the 1860s under secular, largely bourgeois rule. In the decades that followed, the decades that we examine in these pages, Italian society was radically transformed. This transformation was especially acute in the northern portion of the country that we focus on here. Bologna, the northernmost outpost of the papal states, had been under archaic ecclesiastical rule until the Risorgimento swept the clerics from power. The advent of the new Italian state entailed a whole series of changes commonly identified with economic, social, and demographic modernization. Public schools were established and attendance made compulsory, resulting in skyrocketing literacy rates; public health measures helped bring epidemic diseases under control and once-high infant mortality rates fell dramatically; a society long rooted in a semifeudal sharecropping economy saw the spread of rural capitalism and industrialization; the city of Bologna itself, having suffered a long period of decline, was invigorated and began to expand. Nor did political changes end with the establishment of the new Italian nation, for the six decades we examine (1861–1921) also saw the expansion of the electorate from a small elite of property owners to universal male suffrage. Even more dramatically, these were the years that saw the rise of a powerful socialist movement, and the emergence of one of the most famous "red" regions in the capitalist West.

We here scrutinize this modern transformation process of demographic and social change, as seen in the Italian experience. We focus on one town in which these changes were especially evident in these years, Casalecchio di Reno, lying just beyond the rural outskirts of the commune of Bologna itself. Long dominated by sharecropping agriculture, Casalecchio became the site of a large textile factory in the mid-nineteenth century. In succeeding decades, other factories opened. Once cut off from Bologna by the formidable medieval city walls, Casalecchio became increasingly connected to the city by train and tram lines in the latter part of the nineteenth century, a process accelerated with the tearing down of the city walls in the early years of the twentieth. This was also a period of major demographic changes. The town's population rose as increasing economic opportunities became available, and as an expanding rural population from elsewhere in the province sought an outlet. At the same time, steady declines in mortality and fertility ushered in a modern demographic regime. We examine this community through years of massive changes, from the infancy of the new Italian state in the 1860s to the aftermath of the First World War, when Mussolini was about to bring in a new phase of Italian (and European) history. Yet, as we shall see, these were years that showed remarkable continuities as well, especially as reflected in the lives of the hundreds of sharecroppers who continued to live on the farmland of Casalecchio.

The Transformation of European Family Life

We try to shed light on the transformation of an agrarian society—one dominated by antiquated sharecropping arrangements and large, multiple-family households—to a society that was increasingly urban and industrial. In doing so, our aims are more than descriptive, for we use this Italian case to examine some of the major generalizations and theories that have been advanced regarding the social and demographic transformation of Western society. Our primary focus is on changes in family life, especially as these are seen in the lives of children, the nature of marriage, and childbearing. However, we are interested more broadly in the changing context in which family behavior took place, leading us to pay particular attention to the question of transiency: the extent to which people moved and the patterns of these movements.

Much scholarly attention has been devoted to these topics in recent years and considerable progress has been made in sketching out some of the contours of the massive changes that took place in the West in this period. Yet some of the heady sense of scholarly accomplishment in the initial boom years of the "new" social history has now faded as what were earlier seen as major discoveries have been subject to attack and, not uncommonly, abandoned by their original champions. Scholars are no longer so certain what impact industrialization had on family life, how the spread of capitalism affected the lives of children and women, or just how and why fertility began to fall. We will be using Italian evidence to shed new light on each of these issues.

To date, Italy has not figured prominently in these debates, which have been dominated by students of British, French, and American history. The Italian case, however, is instructive for a variety of reasons. In some important respects Italy is more typical than Britain, where industrialization began so early, or France, where modern declines in fertility preceded the rest of Europe by many decades. Moreover, the Italian archival sources are superior to those found in Britain, France, or the United States in allowing us to examine the lives of people of the nineteenth and early twentieth centuries. Many of the data limitations that have hampered a full understanding of economic change and its human impact in northwestern Europe are not barriers in post-Unification Italy, where population registers and a variety of local-level tax and other records provide a treasure chest of individual-level information.

Finally, the portion of Italy under study here offers an especially intriguing site for examining theories regarding the impact of "modernization" on family life because of the long-time predominance of a multiple-family household system. Earlier theories of family change, which focused on the nuclearization of the family and household, became unfashionable in part because of the growing belief that large, multiple-family households were never common in western Europe. As we shall see, the Italian case reveals the fallacy of overgeneralizing, and raises anew the question of the impact of industrialization and social change in the context of life in complex-family households.

The approach we take in this book is to examine changes in family life and demographic behavior by relating changing economic and political arrangements to the actions of individuals and to the changing uses made of family arrangements. In doing this we employ a wide variety of historical sources and methodological tools. This book is based on many years of work with the Italian archives. Most notable is the creation of a data base which traces the lives of the nineteen thousand individuals who lived in Casalecchio from 1865 to 1921, bringing together information from a variety of sources: the population register, church and civil vital event registers, manuscript censuses, annual household tax registers, state conscription registers, and other official records. In addition, we have pored over a variety of other archival sources, often not lending themselves to computerization or quantification—such as reports of factory directors, town, provincial, and state authorities, and medical investigators—to shed light on the processes of change.

Anthropologists, sociologists, demographers, and historians should all recognize something of their methods in this work. We have tried to take advantage of the analytical power offered by some relatively sophisticated statistical techniques without allowing our narrative to become clogged with unintelligible coefficients and indecipherable prose. The challenge has been to contribute to a broad audience of scholars and students interested in the social and demographic transformation of Europe. We hope what follows will do so.

To set the stage for our account, we begin by briefly reviewing some of the accepted wisdom on the modern transformation of Western family life, and on the rise of demographically modern societies in the West. These are both broad and active areas of current research, yet each is embroiled in major controversies concerning the processes that led to modern Western societies.

The Family in European Modernization

Just what impact the forces of modernization—the spread of capitalism, urban expansion, the proletarianization of the rural population and the growth in factory labor, the spread of education and rise in literacy, and the extension of suffrage—had on European family life depends a great deal on just what family life was like before these forces took hold. The image of the peasant past, in which people were reared in large, complex-family households, long held the popular and scholarly imagination. A corollary of this scenario was the presumed breakdown of a tight family structure with the rise of modern capitalism; modernization was thus equated with family nuclearization. Some viewed this process as disastrous, destructive of the moral fabric of society and symptomatic of the evils of capitalism and modernity, while others hailed the same development as marking the liberation of the individual from the shackles of family obligation.[2]

This familiar portrait came under mounting attack, beginning in the 1960s, as scholars found evidence in Britain and elsewhere that no such nuclearization of household arrangements occurred in the nineteenth century. Indeed, many proclaimed that nuclear family arrangements had long characterized preindustrial society and hence industrialization could not have transformed the basic family arrangements. Building on Laslett's (1965, 1972) earlier work, Wrigley's (1977) comments illustrate this line of thought: "The industrial revolution period is full of apparent paradoxes. In a period of rapid and radical change in most aspects of economic and social life, it is odd that in many ways the West European family should have changed so little" (80). More directly, Hareven (1976) argued that "historical demographers have established the continuity in nuclear household structure in western Europe and in the United States over the past two hundred years. Such findings seriously challenge the earlier view that industrialization caused the emergence of nuclear households" (194).[3]

Wrigley (1977:76–83) and others have taken this argument further, speculating that since nuclear family organization preceded industrialization and the rise of modern capitalism in Europe, the European family may have been especially suited for the development of the modern economy. Hence, rather than industrialization explaining changes in the nature of the European family, the peculiar characteristics of the European family might account for the rise of industrial capitalism in Europe.

In this context the situation we find in the Bologna area is especially intriguing, for here the large, complex-family household was common in the rural areas for centuries preceding industrialization. Indeed, partially in recognition of this Italian family pattern, Laslett (1983) has recently revised his earlier generalizations about the nuclear Western family to exclude Mediterranean Europe.

We argue that preindustrial family life and the impact of the forces of modernization on individuals in nineteenth and early twentieth-century

Europe do not fit the simple generalizations that have been made in the past. Certain forces do, however, govern changes in family life and demographic behavior. Among the most important of these are economic forms of organization and the relationship of the family economy to the larger economic system, political developments and the intervention of the state in family life, and cultural norms regarding appropriate family behavior.[4] That there should be important differences between the Italian situation and that found in northwestern Europe should hardly be surprising in light of variations in these factors. But we also show that these factors affect family and demographic behavior among subgroups within populations and that this is true even in such a geographically limited population as Casalecchio. By so doing, we reformulate the question of the impact of industrialization and urban expansion on people living in the complex-family households of the European past.

Demographic Change in European History

This book is also about demographic change and its relation to social history. Such critical life experiences as choosing a mate, having children, deciding where and with whom to live, and death (of parents, a husband or wife, or children) are demographic events. A hallmark of most demographic research has been its treatment of these vital events in the lives of people as mathematical properties of populations.[5]

Such population research has provided a good deal of information about the demographic changes that took place in Europe during the nineteenth and early twentieth centuries. However, we believe that demographers have relied too heavily on discredited theories of social change to interpret the relationship between demographic processes and the social and economic changes in people's lives. Aggregate studies of population processes, though valuable, lack the kind of information needed to develop a coherent account of the changing demographic behaviors of individuals that together produce societywide demographic change.

We seek to enrich our understanding of the demographic revolution of the last two centuries by relating changing economic and political arrangements in a single community to the actions of individuals and families that determine patterns of marriage, fertility, coresidence, and mortality. In focusing on the community of Casalecchio di Reno, we hope to fulfill many of the criteria that Levine (1977) has suggested for studying the demographic and social transformation of Europe:

> I should like to see further research programs which utilize detailed records so that it will be possible to have a multidimensional approach to the issues of early capitalism, protoindustrialization, and demo-

> graphic change. Ideally it will be necessary to select for study a large community where there were several sectors—peasant farming, capitalist farming, agricultural labor, and protoindustry. (149)

Only by using individual-level data can these issues be addressed effectively.[6] This study uses such data, and our analytic strategy is guided by a life-course perspective. This perspective involves not only inquiry into the changing nature of various life stages, such as childhood, and life transitions, such as marriage, but also examination of how historical changes affect individuals differently depending on their life stage, and how earlier experiences affect later events in the individual's life. Thus, for example, a life-course perspective on migration involves investigation not only of differences in migration behavior by age, but also of how earlier experiences—such as the length of time since last migration—affect propensity to migrate. Or if we take the case of the rise of factory labor and the decline of service, we ask not only what impact these developments had on the nature of childhood, but also what impact these new childhood experiences had on such later life events as choice of residence following marriage.[7]

Thus, we seek to combine an appropriate research perspective, unusually rich data on the members of the population of a strategic community at a critical juncture in its social history, and appropriate statistical techniques to advance our understanding of the relationship of demographic change to European social history. This research builds on the findings of aggregate population research and on recent theoretical developments in understanding demographic change in social history. For this reason, we emphasize the demographic importance of the family economy and intergenerational wealth flows, the factory employment of women and children, the political mobilization and secularization of the population, and cultural values about patterns of family and coresidence over the life course.

The demographic consequences of the social, economic, and political changes that occurred during the late nineteenth and early twentieth century varied by social class. In examining this variation, we distinguish among social classes on the basis of source of income and whether the labor contract encompassed all members of the household or each individual separately. Accordingly, although neither group owned land, we distinguish between those who were bound by sharecropping contracts and those engaged in wage labor.

Economic changes, sometimes affecting only certain classes directly, had ramifying effects on demographic behavior and family life. For example, as factories opened in Casalecchio there were increased employment opportunities for the children of wage-earner families, leading to the virtual disappearance of service as a life stage. The initial effect was that the rate of migration declined, the children of the wage earners lived at home longer, and they contributed more directly to the family income.

Members of the Casalecchio elite were early leaders in the mortality and fertility declines. Sharecroppers, who, compared to the daily wage laborers, had relatively secure incomes and better living conditions, also enjoyed substantial declines in infant mortality during the nineteenth century. In contrast, infant and child mortality among wage-earner families was extremely high. This was associated with the poverty of this class, the difficulties of breast-feeding infants whose mothers were factory workers or who worked in distant fields, and the unsanitary living conditions in the town of Casalecchio. The infant and child mortality rates of the wage-earner families did not converge with those of the sharecroppers until state intervention brought about the improvement of wage earners' living and working conditions.

Compulsory education and laws limiting child labor eventually reduced the economic value of children for wage-earner families, and they began to limit their fertility. The value of sharecropper child labor remained unchanged, however, and sharecroppers continued to have large numbers of children and to live in large, complex-family households well into the twentieth century. Over time, there was a decline in complex households in Casalecchio, but this change was principally associated with a decrease in the percent of the population that was engaged in sharecropping, rather than with any change in household patterns within each economic group. Yet, despite the primacy of economic considerations, the effects of cultural values favoring complex households can be seen even among the wage earners: sons frequently continued to live with parents for at least a time after marriage, and very few old or unmarried people lived alone. Remarkably, in spite of these social, economic, and demographic changes, marriage patterns changed little during this period.

Casalecchio

While no single community can be taken as representative of a whole nation, Casalecchio demonstrates a number of features that make it of historical and theoretical interest. Indeed, in some of these respects it is not an average Italian community, for many of the social changes that were to transform Italy economically, socially, and politically were felt more acutely and earlier in Casalecchio than elsewhere. While this may make Casalecchio less typical of all of Italy for these years, it makes it more historically and theoretically interesting, a harbinger of things to come.

Proud local historians trace settlement in Casalecchio back to the Etruscans, with a community identity going back over a thousand years. Yet, lying just a few kilometers beyond the southwest gate of the walled city of Bologna, Casalecchio has long been closely tied to the fortunes and caprices of the city of Bologna. As one Casalecchio official put it, "If Bologna sneezes, Casalecchio catches a cold" (Zazzeri 1982:17). While this proximity had a profound effect on Casalecchio, it did not undermine the sense of community found there, at least until the changes that came in the wake of the Second World War. Town officials continually struggled against the power of the nearby city, a struggle culminating in the 1930s with the town's successful resistance to an attempt by Bologna to annex Casalecchio to the city.

At the same time as the city's proximity tended to accelerate historical developments in Casalecchio, its location at the edge of the hills rising southwest from Bologna tended to protect it from some of the impact of the proletarianization of agriculture. The most rapid development of large-scale, capitalist agriculture took place, instead, in the plains to the north-east of the city. Thus, as Casalecchio began to industrialize it continued to have a sizeable contingent of traditional sharecroppers.

In 1871, over a third of all males in Casalecchio lived and worked in sharecropping households, with another 14 percent working as agricultural wage laborers (*braccianti*). Yet, alongside them almost a third of the males had jobs as nonagricultural wage laborers, working in factories, on construction, and in many other proletarian occupations. Casalecchio's population more than doubled – from 2,810 in 1871 to 5,990 in 1921 – with much of the growth occurring after the turn of the century. By 1921 almost half the males were in nonagricultural wage work. This growing wage labor sector, along with a growing contingent of artisans and merchants, absorbed most of the labor-force growth that occurred in these years.

Casalecchio experienced these major economic and social changes while lying in a part of Italy known for its multiple-family household system. In 1871, over half of its population lived in complex-family households, that is, households containing kinsmen beyond the nuclear family. Indeed, 40 percent of the residents lived in households containing at least two nuclear family units. The sharecroppers, meanwhile, lived overwhelmingly in such complex households, as they did throughout the decades under study.

In 1861, two-thirds of all men and four-fifths of the women were completely illiterate. Following the advent of universal elementary-school education in this period, though, illiteracy rapidly declined. Few other than the elderly were wholly illiterate by 1921. This was a period of dramatic demographic change as well. The crude death rate (deaths per 1,000 population) sank from a level of 35 in the 1870s to oscillate around 10–15 by the second decade of the twentieth century. Meanwhile, the chances of surviving infancy increased dramatically, as the proportion of babies dying in their first year dropped from 23 percent in the early 1870s to just 7 percent in the years preceding the First World War. Finally, fertility levels declined as well, although more gradually, with crude birth rates (births per 1,000 population) slipping from 36 in the 1870s to 29 in the first decade of the twentieth century.

These were years, too, when people's political involvement increased tremendously and a once quiescent rural population was at the forefront of one of the most successful socialist movements in the late nineteenth- and early twentieth-century world. The women workers of Casalecchio's large hemp factory formed a league and the factory workers repeatedly went on strike. Other workers' leagues and other strikes followed, some tied in with national socialist organizations. The Casalecchio town government, long dominated by the absentee landowners—many of whom bore noble titles—was taken over by the local socialists in the early twentieth century. The resulting left-wing euphoria came to an abrupt end with the Fascist march on Rome.

The story of Casalecchio in the years from Unification to the advent of fascism is thus the story of many of the major changes that shook European society in the nineteenth and early twentieth centuries. While a single town cannot be taken as a microcosm of a country, much less of a continent, we believe that this examination of Casalecchio provides new insight into larger historical and theoretical questions of family life, demography, and social change.

Overview

To understand the changes that engulfed Casalecchio in the late 1800s and the early twentieth century, we first need to understand the larger field of economic and political forces. We thus begin by devoting chapter 2 to the broader historical context of which Casalecchio was a part. Special attention is paid to the sharecropping economy that dominated this agricultural region for centuries, and to the family relations characteristic of the sharecropping system. The rise of an agricultural proletariat in the nineteenth century is discussed, and the implications of rural proletarianization for family life considered. This was not simply an agricultural zone, however, and we therefore examine the historically changing role of the city of Bologna, from its decline as one of Europe's premier industrial cities in the seventeenth century to the rebirth of industry in the late nineteenth and early twentieth centuries.

We turn in chapter 3 to major social historical developments in Casalecchio itself, beginning with the changes associated with the introduction of factory labor and the demise of ecclesiastical rule in the middle of the nineteenth century. We examine patterns of landownership, as well as the development of public education and the skyrocketing of literacy rates; we also investigate the rise of socialism and workers' leagues.

In chapter 4, we describe the effects of these social arrangements on the working and living conditions of sharecroppers, agricultural day laborers, and the growing nonagricultural proletariat. We also look at the multiple-family household system that characterized Casalecchio and at the changes in household dynamics that accompanied industrialization. Finally, we discuss the declines in mortality that took place in these years and how these declines differed among segments of the local population.

It has commonly been thought that industrialization and urbanization are associated with increases in population mobility. In chapter 5 we show that this is not the case for Casalecchio, and that the traditional wisdom on this relationship is misleading. We look at the extent of migration within the agricultural sector—rural-rural migration—as well as the two-way mobility between Casalecchio and the city of Bologna. By using population-register data, we are able to follow individuals from their entry into Casalecchio through their exit to other communes; thus, we are able to examine differences in the propensity to emigrate based on age, sex, occupation, geographical origin, and kinds of household arrangements. By looking at where immigrants come from and where emigrants go, we are also able to evaluate the relationship between industrialization and urbanization and migration patterns.

One of the major debates over the impact of industrialization on family life concerns the lives of children. In chapter 6, we consider some well-known arguments that historians have advanced in this regard, some decrying the pernicious, family-destroying impact of industrialization and others heralding its liberating effects. We examine the evidence about childhood in Casalecchio to assess these theories. We consider the major declines in infant and child mortality that occurred in this period and the differences among occupational groups in these declines. We ask how children's family situations changed in this period of proletarianization and urban expansion, and how these experiences were conditioned by the large, complex families in which children typically lived. These changes are closely linked to the history of service, for this was a period in which service declined from being a common feature of many children's lives to a rarity. Finally, we examine the lives of children who worked in the factories of Casalecchio and how they were affected by national legislative attempts to regulate child labor.

Some prominent scholars have recently heralded a distinctive Mediterranean marriage pattern, and, indeed, north-central sharecropping Italy has been cited as its epicenter. In chapter 7, we examine Casalecchio in light of these generalizations. We examine related questions of marital timing, celibacy, widowhood, and remarriage. We also look at the extent of marital homogamy and at the degree to which marriages were constrained by the occupation of the bride and groom. Bridal pregnancy, too long ignored in studies of Italian marriage, is investigated. In chapter 7, we also examine patterns and changes in patrilocal residence, the long-cherished practice of sons bringing their brides into their parental home.

The first decades of the new Italian state present one fascinating episode in the history of marriage in Europe that we also examine: the battle between Church and state over the marriage ceremony. With the Church refusing to recognize the validity of civil marriage, and the state refusing to recognize the validity of marriages performed in church, marriage itself became a political and social battleground in the nineteenth century. In chapter 7, we look at the way this struggle was played out in Casalecchio.

In chapter 8, we describe the changing reproductive behaviors of the Casalecchio population and show the ways in which these changes differed by social class. The elite were early leaders in fertility reduction, and family economic circumstances were of primary importance in the reproductive behaviors of the rest of the population as well. Changes in child labor and compulsory schooling of children reduced the economic value of children for wage earners at a time when infant and child survivorship was showing marked improvement. In contrast, children continued to be of considerable economic value for sharecroppers. We investigate the consequences of these changes in the family economy for the reproductive behaviors of the different economic groups. We also consider whether increased education and secularization of the population played a role in the "rationalization" of reproductive behaviors and thus led to the population's fertility declines.

Finally, in chapter 9, we consider some of the lessons of our investigation of Casalecchio for an understanding of Italian and European history. We use the Casalecchio case to rethink some of the recent accounts of the nature of the demographic transition in Europe and, by extension, theories of demographic behavior more generally. This leads to our final conclusions regarding the nature of social change and the processes through which modern urban, industrial societies have arisen.

2 The Political Economy of Bologna

Few nineteenth-century political arrangements in the West were as retrograde as those found in Bologna. Until the revolt of 1859, when the national unification movement—the Risorgimento—swept through the northern half of Italy, Bologna was part of the papal states, ruled by the clergy. This anachronistic political structure had its economic counterpart in the sharecropping economy. A small number of landowners, many of them titled nobility, owned the great majority of arable land. Living for the most part in the city of Bologna, they made periodic forays to their rural villas to confer with their agents about their holdings. On such visits, the landowners occasionally paid calls on the heads of their sharecropper families, who lived in fear of the power of the *padrone* to evict them from their farm. Not only did the sharecroppers have to bow and scrape before their masters, but they also had to make regular offerings of chickens, eggs, and their own labor for the landowner's personal uses, all without any direct compensation.

Although this society had been subject to outside influences for centuries, and can hardly be described as unchanging before national unification in the mid-1880s, its course of change did not follow the unilineal model commonly associated with European "modernization." Indeed, the Bologna area had been more closely bound to an international industrial economy in the seventeenth century, when it was famous throughout Europe for its silk and hemp products. The city's industrial backwardness at mid-nineteenth century was the result of backsliding, while in the nearby countryside the traditional sharecropper-*padrone* relations could not mask the rise of a rural proletariat that would soon make this area one of the most active centers of rural revolt in the West.

In this chapter we examine Bolognese society during the unprecedented social and economic upheaval of the late nineteenth and early twentieth centuries. We describe the prevailing economic and political arrangements and identify the forces of change at work, including the expansion of the city and the impact of more modern transportation connecting city and countryside. In this way, we set the stage for an examination of the social and demographic changes that took place in Casalecchio during these years.

The Agricultural Economy

Emilia-Romagna, which became one of the regions in the new Italian nation, had previously been divided into separate states. Most of Emilia, the western half of the region, had been ruled by various duchies of greater or lesser independence from foreign forces. Bologna, in the extreme eastern portion of Emilia, with Romagna to its east, represented the northern limit of the papal states. Although briefly brought together during the Napoleonic occupation in the early years of the nineteenth century, Emilia-Romagna was again torn apart with the Restoration that followed. The region stretches along the Po valley, bordered on the south by the Apennine mountains. Consequently, Bologna, like most of the provinces of Emilia-Romagna, is divided into three topographic zones: plains, hills, and mountains. The city of Bologna itself is found just at the foot of the hills, where the highlands meet the plains. Casalecchio di Reno, bordering the southwestern rural outskirts of the commune of Bologna, lies where the hills begin to rise from the plain (see map 2.1).

People in the mountains faced the harshest environmental conditions in the region, not only because of the weather, but also due to poor soil and inadequate transportation. It was in the mountains that peasants often owned their own small parcels of land, yet these generally afforded them inadequate subsistence, and outmigration toward the hills and plain, as well as seasonal labor migration, had long been common. In the hills and the plain, on the other hand, peasant proprietorship was rare, with almost all land owned by the elite, who lived primarily in the city of Bologna. Landowners delegated supervision of their holdings to agricultural agents or simply gave the land to leaseholders who paid them an annual fee and managed the properties directly. Some of these holdings were huge, especially in the plains, but often landowners owned collections of smaller properties scattered over various parts of the province.

The richest land was found in the plain, where cereals—wheat, corn, and rice—were grown as well as some industrial crops, especially hemp. By the nineteenth century many of the larger farms in the plain were worked exclusively by wage labor rather than parceled out to sharecroppers. This was particularly true with the introduction of rice on a large scale in the

Map 2.1. The Environs of Casalecchio

wake of various land-reclamation projects of the eighteenth and nineteenth centuries. In the hills, where the land in general was good but less fertile than the best watered plains, sharecropping predominated. Here the farms were smaller and cereals were the primary crops.

By the mid-nineteenth century, then, the province of Bologna had both a strong, traditional sharecropping sector as well as an expanding proletarian sector consisting of large-scale capitalist agriculture. On the eve of Unification, almost half of the agricultural population in the mountains owned their own farms, but just 6 percent of agricultural households in the plains and 14 percent in the hills worked their own farms. In the plains, wage laborers headed 57 percent of the agricultural households, with sharecroppers heading 33 percent. In the hills, sharecropper households outnumbered those headed by agricultural wage laborers by 49 percent to 31 percent (Bellettini 1971:174).

One of the striking features of this period was the tenacity with which sharecropping held on, despite the popularity of theories proclaiming the inevitability of its decline with the rise of capitalist agriculture. One of the major reasons why sharecropping proved so tenacious is that the landowners recognized the revolutionary proclivities of the agricultural wage laborers and viewed the sharecroppers, bound in traditional patron-client relations with the landowners, as their best insurance against land expropriation and strikes.[1]

The sharecropping system has a long history in Italy and had dominated central and parts of northern Italy for many centuries. Indeed, it is striking how similar the contracts of the late nineteenth and early twentieth centuries are to the sharecropping contracts of the thirteenth century. It is a system where the land is owned by a landowner but all the labor is provided by the sharecropper family. The unit of labor is the entire sharecropper household, whose members are jointly bound by the contract. Virtually all produce is divided, half given to the landowner and half kept by the sharecroppers. Of special importance is the fact that these contracts ran for one year only, from November to October, and the landowner could expel a sharecropper family with but a few months notice if he was dissatisfied with its performance. This gave landowners tremendous power over their sharecroppers since, especially by the nineteenth century, there were many more people eager to get sharecropping contracts than there were farms available. Moreover, there was little mobility of sharecroppers into the ranks of the landowners, for the price of land was high and the ability of sharecroppers to accumulate capital very limited.[2]

Household Economy and Family Relations

Economic forces had a major impact on the nature of household organization and relationships among kin. To understand the changes in demographic behavior of the people of this area, some understanding of household economics and family relations is necessary. Here we focus on the two most important occupations found in the rural population: sharecropping and wage labor.

For centuries, sharecropping households formed the backbone of the rural population in Bologna. Although often referred to as peasants, they lacked the commonly cited peasant characteristic of owning their own piece of land. Yet, like peasant proprietors, their household was the unit of production as well as consumption. Indeed, in some respects, sharecropper households were a purer unit of production than peasant proprietors, since the latter were free to send family members out to find work off the farm, whereas sharecroppers were not.

Any examination of sharecropper household organization and family relations must begin with the sharecropping contract, which bound the entire family unit to the farm and gave formal authority over the household to the male head. Members of the household were not even allowed to marry without the owner's permission, for landlords discouraged marriages that took household members from the farm and thus diminished the work force.

Landowners sought, within certain limits, to maximize the adult work force on their farms, since they took a simple percentage (customarily one half) of the crop and were little concerned about the problem of diminishing per capita return of additional farm labor. This led to a system in which adult sons were encouraged to bring their brides into their parental sharecropping home, forming patrilaterally extended households. Unlike the practice found elsewhere among the European peasantry, there was no specification that just a single son should bring his wife into the parental home and that the others should leave at marriage. The striking characteristic of the central Italian sharecroppers is that two or more sons commonly brought their wives into the parental household where they lived together.[3]

Families lacking such an extended membership were vulnerable to eviction in favor of larger, complex-family households. However, since most landlords owned more than a single farm, there was a certain amount of paternalistic moving of families around in order to match their size with the size of the farm. Larger families were in general eager to get as large a farm as they could, since the larger the farm—other things being equal—the more their half of the produce would be. These kinds of calculations lay behind the considerable geographical mobility of sharecroppers, who moved in family units, typically within a very limited geographical range.

The head of the sharecropper household, called the *reggitore,* was responsible to the landlord for the entire household membership. The head was ideally the senior male in a household composed of his wife, married sons and their wives and children, and his unmarried sons and daughters. At marriage, a daughter was to move into her husband's parental home, assuming that her husband was himself from a sharecropping family. Lines of authority were, in theory, strict, with the *reggitore* making the decisions and the others carrying them out. However, the senior female, the *reggitrice,* also had considerable authority, especially over the other females in the household, and she made many of the decisions affecting domestic household affairs. All household members worked on the farm, including the women, who, in addition to being in charge of household activities, worked in the fields from March to October, doing all but the heaviest labor. All except the youngest children were called upon to help with the chores around the farm, from minding the animals to bringing water out to the adults working in the fields. The elderly, too, were given tasks to perform when they were too weak to work in the fields, from making brooms and baskets to guarding the household and adjacent land from thieves.

Although the sharecropper household has long been branded patriarchal in both popular descriptions and in the scholarly literature, this is a misleading image. Not only were men undoubtedly influenced by their wives' advice, and not only did women control important aspects of the household, but the pattern of authority among the men was often less hierarchical than indicated by the formal norm. Maintaining household harmony was an important aspect of headship, and a head who acted autocratically was asking for trouble. Decisions were most often based on consultations among household members. This is especially true in the many situations where the head had adult brothers in the household, for the multiple-family households did not necessarily break up upon the death of the father, and married brothers often continued to coreside with their families.

Of course, sharecropper households sometimes did divide, as was inevitable over the course of generations where there were two or more sons in each generation. Yet the general practice was to do everything possible to keep the patrimony intact, for without the basic minimum capital—in the form of farm equipment, animals, and other property—it was difficult or impossible for the newly divided family units to find sharecropping positions. As part of these efforts, daughters were provided with dowries and not with rights to the agricultural capital goods.[4]

Throughout the nineteenth century, sharecroppers who lost their contracts and were unable to convince a landowner to give them a new one generally became *braccianti,* agricultural wage laborers. They thus joined the growing proletariat of the countryside so often blamed by the landowners for the ills of rural society—theft of crops, laziness and unreliability, and incipient rebellion. Yet the *braccianti* constituted the reserve labor pool that not only made possible the expansion of the rural capitalist sector, but also helped support the sharecropping system itself by providing seasonal labor to supplement that of the sharecropping households.

Although some *braccianti,* those dubbed the *obbligati,* had more permanent ties with a single employer which could be renewed from year to year, the great majority had no regular employer and were constantly in search of a day's or week's employment. Many towns (including the city of Bologna itself) had a central piazza where, early each morning, *braccianti* gathered to wait for the proprietors' agents to come and select the day's work force. Unlike the sharecroppers, who were provided with housing on the farm, the *braccianti* had to find their own quarters, generally in cramped and unhygienic apartments in rural town centers or other clumps of squalid buildings.

The *bracciante* household was not a unit of production, and each member was on his or her own in finding work. Both men and women served as *braccianti,* and occasionally children as well. However, a common solution to the lack of resources for supporting children and to the absence of any productive labor for them at home was to put the children into service. They were placed in the homes of sharecroppers, where they generally worked in the fields, or in the households of merchants or artisans, where they helped with the store or craft, or with the elite, where they worked as domestic servants. One of the significant effects of industrialization, as we shall see in chapter 6, was the decline in this pattern of service, with child labor absorbed by factories, permitting the children of *braccianti* to remain at home throughout their childhood. With low wages—even lower for the women than for the men—and an uncertain number of workdays during the year, the *braccianti* lived precariously, rarely well nourished or well clad, and fearful that illness would reduce them to complete penury.[5]

Although the *braccianti* were economically much less secure than the sharecroppers, and ate less well and lived in much worse housing, some younger adults may have preferred the independence of life as a wage laborer to life as a dependent in a large, sharecropper household. Most sharecroppers did not become household heads (or wives of heads) until they were in their forties. There was therefore some attraction to young sharecroppers of striking off on their own, and this meant giving up sharecropping and taking up the vagaries of wage labor. Yet, given the economic disadvantages of this move, especially before other nonagricultural possibilities opened up in the twentieth century, not many sharecroppers made this change willingly.[6]

Proletarianization of a large segment of the rural population in the preindustrial period places in a new light the common thesis that industrialization led to the breakdown of the solidary peasant family. When Merli (1972), for example, refers to the new industrial work force as having "broken their bond with the land and with the patriarchal world" (264), we must realize that in much of this area, including Bologna, the bond to the patriarchal world of the past had been broken well before industrialization. Although undoubtedly some individuals went directly from the bowels of the multiple-family sharecropper household to the factory production line, more commonly it was the already proletarianized rural laborers who sought industrial employment. For them, the family had never been a unit of production, and the relationship of the family to the economy did not essentially change. Indeed, a long-standing characteristic of the *braccianti* was their willingness to take on any wage labor they could get. It was of little moment whether the jobs available were in the fields or in digging irrigation canals, constructing roads, or sweeping streets. The major distinction in the rural areas was not between the agricultural sector and the nonagricultural sector, but between the sharecroppers and the wage laborers.

Industrialization, Deindustrialization, and Reindustrialization

As one of Europe's preeminent exporters of textile products in the sixteenth and seventeenth centuries, Bologna was especially known for its silk scarves and for processing the large amount of hemp grown in its hinterland. However, after a century of slippage, various developments in the mid-eighteenth century led to the collapse of the Bolognese industrial market. In the early nineteenth century the impact of French protectionism and other Continental impediments to the importation of textiles, together with increased competition within Italy, led to a final crisis. Between 1806 and 1811 the already reduced number of workers in urban industry was cut in half, and the population of the city began to shrink. Indeed, in 1808 the population within the walls of Bologna was less than it had been in 1581. With the ravages of the Napoleonic disruptions and the return of pontifical rule in the second decade of the nineteenth century, the failing industrial economy gave rise to a spiral of poverty. Further hardships produced by a typhus epidemic and poor agricultural harvests in 1817–1819 led to thirty thousand "idlers, vagabonds and beggars" being counted among the city's population (Marcolin 1985:5).[7]

Recent studies elsewhere in Europe have shown that industrialization often developed in areas where a good part of the population was no longer agricultural, but rather engaged in home production through a putting-out system. Hence the simple image of a peasant society transformed by the advent of factory labor is, in many cases, misleading. Bologna had a history of protoindustrial labor in the countryside, but its development had been hampered by restrictions that the city had been able to impose on its hinterland until the beginning of the nineteenth century. Thanks to the urban guild protectionist system, for example, hemp processing had been forbidden outside the walls of the city. But by the nineteenth century, protoindustrial production picked up, in part due to the demise of these laws and in part due to the increase in the rural population. However, landowners were quick to forbid their sharecroppers from engaging in such work, for fear it would take time away from their agricultural duties. Hence, other than the common weaving done to make clothes for household members, protoindustrial production was largely limited to small peasant proprietors in the mountains and to agricultural wage-laborer households. Yet here too the pattern was strikingly different from that found in parts of northern Europe, for only women and children engaged in this work, never men or whole families. Casalecchio was typical in this regard. In 1886, there were eighty domestic looms operating seasonally there, ninety days per year, mostly in the winter when other work was unavailable.[8]

At the time of Unification, Italian industry was still in its infancy, much behind developments in northwestern Europe. The bulk of industrial activity involved textiles, continuing an earlier Italian specialization. Much of this early industrial development was concentrated in the northwestern triangle formed by Milan, Turin, and Genoa, magnifying its social effects. Rather than encouraging a more even distribution of industrialization throughout the peninsula, Italian unification had the opposite effect, as the industrial triangle continued to develop disproportionately (Cafagna 1976; Zangheri 1969).

Bologna was at the edge of these developments, with only slow growth in the modern industrial sector. Indeed, Casalecchio was at the forefront of Bolognese industrialization, the site of the largest factory in the province. Through the first decades of Unification, industrialization, particularly in the textile sector, continued to shrink. From 1876 to 1897 the number of workers in the textile industry in the province declined from 12,500 to 7,400. This reflected a more general economic stagnation, for the annual rate of increase in national income in Italy from 1863 to 1897 was close to zero. Yet an economic boom finally came at the end of the century; from 1896 to 1913 industrial output rose nationally by 6.7 percent per year.[9]

At the end of the century, the province of Bologna continued to feel the effects of the long-term crisis in the textile industry, but it began to enjoy the expansion of industries tied to food products and to metal. The city of Bologna was primarily a market and service center, but it also had a significant industrial work force. In the first decade of the twentieth century, the proportion of the city's work force engaged in industry (broadly defined, to include such categories as transportation workers) rose from 27 percent to 32 percent. In that same period, the proportion of industrial workers in the provincial work force rose from 17 percent to 21 percent.[10]

One of the most salient characteristics of nineteenth-century factories—and especially of the textile industry—was the high proportion of women and children in the work force. In 1876, for example, the largest industrial employer in Italy—with 200,000 workers—was the silk industry; less than 8 percent of the silk workers were men, while 60 percent were women and 32 percent children. In the linen and hemp industries nationally, women constituted 47 percent of the work force and children an additional 18 percent.[11]

In the Bologna area, child labor was especially common, involving 24 percent of the work force in manufacturing in 1903, compared to the national average of 14 percent. In Emilia-Romagna, 70 percent of the labor force in the textile industry consisted of women. But even the adults in the industrial work force were disproportionately young. A 1903 inquiry in the Milan area, for example, concluded that the productive period for factory workers was from ages 12 to 39. Few factories of the time exhibited remorse in firing workers who showed signs of slowing down with age.[12]

Agricultural Crisis and Proletarianization

Beginning in the eighteenth century, a rising rural population in Bologna was largely accommodated by an increase in agricultural wage labor. Especially in the plains, a variety of land-reclamation projects led both to periodic employment bonanzas on public-works projects and to new positions for agricultural wage laborers. The sharecropping sector of the economy, meanwhile, was largely stable, not directly affected by these developments. The once-clear predominance of the sharecroppers in Bolognese agriculture gradually gave way as agricultural labor came increasingly to be put on a wage basis.

In the early 1880s, the advent of a Europe-wide agrarian crisis ushered in more than a decade of economic hardship. The crisis was the product of new international competition arising beyond Europe. The precipitous lowering of transportation costs in this period—due to the expansion of railway systems and the opening of the Suez Canal—led to stiff competition on the continent from American and Russian wheat, Indian rice, and silk from China and Japan. From 1880 to 1885, for example, the price paid for wheat fell by a third, with the price of corn and hemp falling even more drastically. From 1889 to 1893, the resulting deep depression affected virtually all sectors of the economy, both rural and urban, and led to a large jump in transoceanic migration in many parts of Italy, although not in the Emilia-Romagna area. Around Bologna the agricultural wage laborers found getting work even more difficult, while the sharecroppers were hard hit as well, driven into debt by the lower prices they were receiving for the share of their crop going to the market.[13]

The long-term impact of the agrarian crisis, which can roughly be dated 1883–1896, was the further undermining of the sharecropping economy and the increased proletarianization of the rural population in Bologna. This population expanded rapidly throughout the nineteenth century, with births outpacing deaths and virtually no migration out of the province. Indeed, not only were the agricultural wage laborers reproducing themselves, but the high fertility in sharecropping households ultimately resulted in many young sharecroppers becoming wage laborers, for the amount of land in sharecropping did not increase after Unification. Although loath to leave the province, these rural laborers were by necessity highly mobile, due to the difficulty of finding daily work. When public-works projects appeared, laborers from many parts of the province converged, only to be dispersed at the project's end.[14]

The years between the end of the agrarian crisis and the onset of the First World War saw considerable economic development in Bologna, as elsewhere in northern Italy. Industry finally began to grow at a sustained pace, especially with the expansion of the food industry. Meanwhile, the use of more modern technology in the agricultural sector (including heavier reliance on mechanical equipment and the introduction of chemical fertilizers) led to gains in productivity.[15]

The Impact of the City of Bologna

The historical influence of the city of Bologna on the surrounding rural area can hardly be overemphasized. This was not simply a matter of division of labor, with the city serving as the center of industry and marketing and the countryside serving as the source of agricultural production. For centuries peasants had been making regular forays to the city, where the largest markets were to be found. Indeed, there was a great variety of markets—daily, weekly, and the special fairs held annually. All power lay in the city, and the senate of Bologna passed laws protecting the interests of the city at the expense of the residents of the rural zones. Indeed, from the 1300s, the massive walls of the city of Bologna served as a social and economic barrier, with all goods coming into the city subject to taxation. The city gates were closed at night, sealing the city off from the countryside on which it fed. It was only with the reforms of the Napoleonic period that this system of protectionism was undermined, although the political and economic control exercised by the city-dwelling elite continued undiminished.[16]

The commune of Bologna consists of the walled city surrounded by the *suburbio,* or rural belt encircling the city. Until the latter part of the nineteenth century the *suburbio,* though part of the commune of Bologna, was little different in nature from other rural areas. The population of the city remained remarkably stationary for the three centuries leading up to Unification, at about 70,000. In this same period, though, the rural population of the area around Bologna grew, slowly throughout the first 150 years and then with increasing velocity in the eighteenth and nineteenth centuries. For example, in the period 1759–1853, while the city population grew modestly from 68,900 to 74,400, the population of the surrounding diocese of Bologna (excluding the city) jumped from 197,900 to 323,200. This was typical of urban centers through much of the Italian peninsula, for it was only near the end of the nineteenth century that they were in a position to begin to absorb the excess population of their rural hinterlands.[17]

If the urban population remained stationary in size, this does not imply any lack of population exchange between city and countryside. Indeed, the city of Bologna was chronically reliant on immigrants from the rural hinterland in order to make up for a natural decrease in population caused by an excess of deaths over births. Even through the nineteenth century, when mortality levels were declining substantially and population growth booming in the area, the city failed to replenish its population through reproduction. This was partially due to the greater proportion of unmarried adults found in the city, linked to an excess of women over men.[18]

Although the city had been intimately linked with its hinterland for centuries, the nature of these ties changed markedly in the years following Unification, as part of the larger campaign to modernize transportation and communication systems in the new Italian state. This is seen most strikingly in the construction of a railway of which the city of Bologna became the regional center. Railroad construction in the period 1860–1890 took Bologna from an antiquated transportation system that had changed little for centuries to a system of railway links to major urban centers not much different from that found today. In conjunction with the beneficial effects on internal trade links of the unification of Italy, this gave Bologna a new importance within the region. The city was not only linked on a north-south axis to the industrial triangle on the north and Rome and the central and southern cities, but also became the node for links between the Tyrranean and Adriatic seas.[19]

One of the implications of developing railway connections with other Italian cities was the undermining of the old concept of the fortress city. Throughout northern Italy construction of railroad stations meant making cracks in the old walls enveloping the cities, hence beginning to open them up more directly to their hinterland. This eventually catalyzed urban sprawl, the expansion of the urban population beyond the well-marked boundaries erected centuries before. Hand in hand with this development was the creation of a network of trams, first drawn by horses, but, by the latter part of the nineteenth century, powered by steam. Most affected were those parts of the hinterland lying near the city, like Casalecchio, for by the 1880s the tracks of the tram line ran directly through such places, undermining their isolation. Indeed, Casalecchio became one of the principal points on the tram line that ran through the city of Bologna, linking Vignola on the east to Budrio on the west.[20]

The dramatic end of Bologna's long history as a fortress city came at the turn of the century when, in 1902, after considerable controversy and delay, the demolition of the city walls was begun. With the exception of the old gates and a few isolated sections of wall, serving as remembrances of a medieval past, the wall was gone within a few years' time. During the period of economic growth that followed, the absorbing power of the city vis-à-vis the hinterland began to be felt. After three centuries of stagnation, the fifteen years following the destruction of the wall saw the population of the commune grow by almost a third.[21]

These developments had a major impact on Casalecchio, which, though long affected by its proximity to the city, had remained somewhat isolated by the lack of speedy transportation and the walls which cut it off from Bologna. Casalecchio straddled one of the major roads into Bologna from Florence, important for tying the city into various outlying agricultural centers. It was along this route that a railway opened in 1864, halving the twelve to fifteen hours of travel time that had previously been required to go from Bologna to Florence (a distance that today takes under an hour and a half by train). By 1888 this time was cut in half again. This same rail network tied Casalecchio, with its new train station, both to Bologna and to other neighboring rural communities, including Praduro e Sasso, Borgo Panigale, and Zola Predosa, the areas from which many of the hemp factory workers came.

It was in this setting of expanding connections with both the city and the neighboring agricultural area that the steam tram line opened in the 1880s, replacing the horse-drawn carriage. Twenty-two daily trips linked Casalecchio to the center of the city, which was now just a half hour away. At a cost of 20 cents (i.e., 0.2 lira) per trip, some of the better-paid wage workers could afford to commute by public transportation for the first time. However, since most workers earned less than two lire per day, the round trip remained expensive, and most *braccianti* and other wage workers continued to travel by foot or, increasingly by the first years of the century, by bicycle. It was at this time, too, though, that Casalecchio's hemp factory began to subsidize tram lines for its own work force, thereby expanding the geographical range from which it could draw workers.

These were years of major social, economic, and political change in northern Italy, and in many ways Casalecchio was at the forefront. In the midst of an ancient sharecropping economy, a large factory opened its gates. In a community long run by the nobility and other wealthy landowners, a socialist movement gained strength and eventually took over the local government. Formerly part of the papal states, with authority closely identified with the Church, Casalecchio experienced a rise in anticlericalism, along with the emergence of both agrarian and nonagrarian workers' leagues. In a community where literacy had long been the mark of the elite, the advent of universal public education led to the spread of literacy throughout the population. Just how these and other major developments of the turn of the century affected life in Casalecchio is the subject to which we turn in the next chapter.

3 Economic and Political Change in Casalecchio

Although Casalecchio had not always been a separate political entity, records of settlements there go back a long way. Located on the agricultural periphery of the city of Bologna, the area was long involved in exchanging population with the urban center. Casalecchio began to take on special importance to the city in 1191, when Bolognese engineers dammed the Reno river there in order to run a canal through the city. The canal, which eventually ran for 37 kilometers, powered many of Bologna's mills and provided water to the urban residents. Initially owned privately, but later passing to municipal control, the canal remained an important source of power for Bologna in the early twentieth century. Casalecchio's early position as the site of large industry in the mid-nineteenth century can be credited to the construction of the canal there seven centuries earlier.[1]

By the eighteenth century, as part of the pontifical polity, Casalecchio was placed under the authority of the congregation of neighboring Borgo Panigale, also an agricultural outpost of the city. In 1781 Casalecchio was reported to have had a bountiful harvest of grapes, in addition to cereals and fruit. Other than a local arms maker who had acquired some regional fame, industry in the town consisted of a variety of small artisans plying their crafts.[2]

By the time of Unification Casalecchio had already changed substantially from the string of hamlets that had comprised this almost entirely agricultural community in the eighteenth century. It was now a distinct commune, and alongside the predominant sharecropping economy stood the largest textile factory in the province, known as *la Canonica.* In the years to follow, this economic transformation gathered steam as better transportational links led to closer ties to the city of Bologna. The following is a thumbnail chronological sketch of the period under study:

1856	The Canonica hemp factory opens; it soon becomes the largest textile factory in the province of Bologna.
1859	As a result of the Risorgimento, Italy's unification movement, Bologna secedes from the papal states and joins the new Italian nation.
1860	Elementary schools, previously run by the Church, are now taken over by the secular state. Communes like Casalecchio are directed to provide two years of elementary education.
1861	Military conscription is introduced by the new government; the parish priest in Casalecchio refuses to cooperate with the civil authorities amid widespread opposition to the draft.
1864	A railroad station opens in Casalecchio. Bologna's first station had opened six years earlier.
1869	The new grist tax on milling flour is introduced by the government, spurring peasant protests throughout the Bologna area and throughout much of the rest of Italy.
1877	Public schooling is made obligatory for children from ages six to nine.
1880	A new steam tram links Casalecchio to the city of Bologna, replacing horse-drawn carriages over the next few years.
1882–1883	The first workers' party and the first socialist rural leagues are organized in Italy, but not yet in Casalecchio. The first socialist is elected to parliament (from a Romagna district) following expansion of the franchise from 9 percent to 24 percent of the adult males.
1883	Following two years of declining grain prices, the agrarian crisis begins.
1887	The Ronzani brewery, employing 35 workers, opens in Casalecchio.
1888	New national welfare laws take effect, including a law mandating free medical treatment for the poor, to be provided by the town physician of each community.
1895	At a clandestine national congress, held in Parma (Emilia), the modern Italian Socialist Party is founded.
1897–1898	With the end of the agrarian crisis, a period of sustained economic development begins. A wave of urban and rural strikes throughout Italy is met by government repression.

1898	A new national law mandates industries to insure workers against industrial accidents.
1900	The Rappini toy factory opens in Casalecchio, relying heavily on child labor.
	The demolition of the walls surrounding the city of Bologna begins, to be completed over the next few years. This catalyzes a housing boom around the urban periphery.
1902	Women workers of Casalecchio's hemp factory found the League of Resistance and hemp factory workers go on strike.
1904	Obligatory school attendance is extended to age 12; Casalecchio adds upper elementary-school grades.
	A *bracciante* league is formed in Casalecchio.
	Casalecchio workers join a one-day national strike.
1905	Influenced by the socialist movement, Casalecchio's bricklayers form their own cooperative.
1906	Casalecchio's *braccianti* go out on strike, winning better wages.
	A new national law mandates that communes provide free pharmaceuticals for the poor; other new social legislation takes effect.
1908	After a half century of rule by the landlords' conservative coalition, local elections with an extended franchise result in a socialist-controlled town council and a socialist mayor in Casalecchio.
	Electric lamps are placed on Casalecchio's main road, replacing gas lights.
1913	Virtually universal male suffrage is introduced.
1915	Italy enters World War I; Casalecchio's industry begins to be transformed for war production, and the call-up of hundreds of young men begins. Forty-eight Casalecchio residents will die at the front, 32 more will die of illness, and 11 will die in prisoner-of-war camps.
1918	The War ends, but rising political tensions result from economic dislocations, the lack of faith in the national government, and the conservative reaction to the rising power of the socialist movement.
1919	Casalecchio elects a left-wing socialist as new mayor.

1920 Following the electoral victory of the left-wing socialists in city elections in Bologna, Fascists attack Bologna's city hall, deposing the municipal government. Fascist violence and socialist response spread fear and disorder throughout the province of Bologna.

1922 Mussolini becomes prime minister, ushering in two decades of fascism. Casalecchio's socialist town government is replaced.

Population Growth

Casalecchio emerged as an important commune in the Bologna suburbs as it developed into a center of industry. Its importance was accentuated by its burgeoning population (see fig. 3.1). From 1865 to 1880 Casalecchio grew from 2,468 to 2,842 people (at an annual rate of 0.9 percent). The rate of population growth increased to 1.1 percent annually from 1880 to 1905, resulting in a 1905 population of 3,776 persons. As Casalecchio became an increasingly important industrial center, the population grew much more rapidly. From 1905 to 1921, the population grew at an annual rate of 2.7 percent (to 5,764 persons by 1921). Although natural increase was an important component of this population growth, two-thirds of the twentieth-century population increase was a result of net migration.[3]

Even though the population of Casalecchio more than doubled during this period, the age and sex composition of the population changed

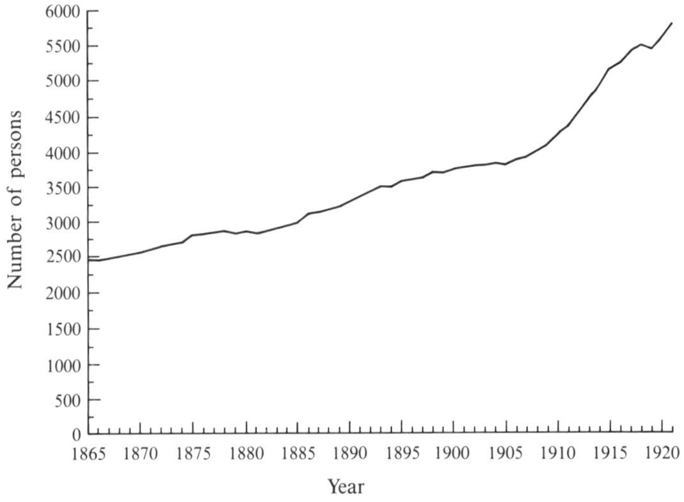

Fig. 3.1. The Population of Casalecchio, 1865–1921

little. The number of males exceeded the number of females by 5–10 percent from 1865 to 1894. This slight excess of males disappeared over the next five years, and the number of males and females were in almost exact balance from 1900 to 1916. From 1917 to 1921, the number of females exceeded the number of males by some 2–4 percent, as a result of the military service obligations of many young men from Casalecchio and wartime casualties. The percentage of the population who were children (ages 0–11) decreased slightly from 28 percent in 1865 to 24 percent in 1921, but the number of persons who were old did not change (remaining at 10 percent in 1865 and 1921). Thus, Casalecchio's "population boom" did not result in a substantial increase in the proportion of the population that was dependent on persons of working age.[4]

Agricultural Life in Casalecchio

As shown in map 3.1, the commune of Casalecchio had been formed from three and a half parishes: Casalecchio, Ceretolo, Tizzano, and a part of Moglio. The parish of Casalecchio, lying on the Reno river nearest the city, was to become the center of industrial development and the site of the major concentration of residential housing, as well as the location of the municipal offices. The other three parishes were almost entirely agricultural, with most housing consisting of the sharecropper residences scattered across the countryside.

At the time of Unification, Casalecchio contained 1,550 hectares of privately owned farmland, one-quarter of which was left uncultivated (as pasture primarily). Of the remainder, 30 percent was planted with wheat, 10 percent with corn, and 10 percent with leguminous fodder plants, with 12 percent being vineyards and 12 percent left fallow. Only small amounts of hemp, barley, oats, potatoes, and other vegetables were grown. A traditional crop-rotation system was employed, with a winter crop of wheat interspersed with a corn or fodder summer crop. It was an intensive system that demanded the use of fertilizer, and hence it was figured that for each hectare of farmland there should be three-quarters to one full head of large livestock on the farm. The farms, run by sharecropper families, did not exceed ten hectares each.

In 1879, Casalecchio's livestock consisted of 779 bovines, 329 pigs, 22 horses, and 59 donkeys, distributed among about one hundred sharecropper households. The importance of the animals in this period was heightened by the absence of mechanical means of traction on the farms. The first two threshing machines appeared at the end of the country, and in 1920 there were still no mechanical plows in use. Due to the abundance of *bracciante* labor, landowners felt little need to mechanize, and the re-

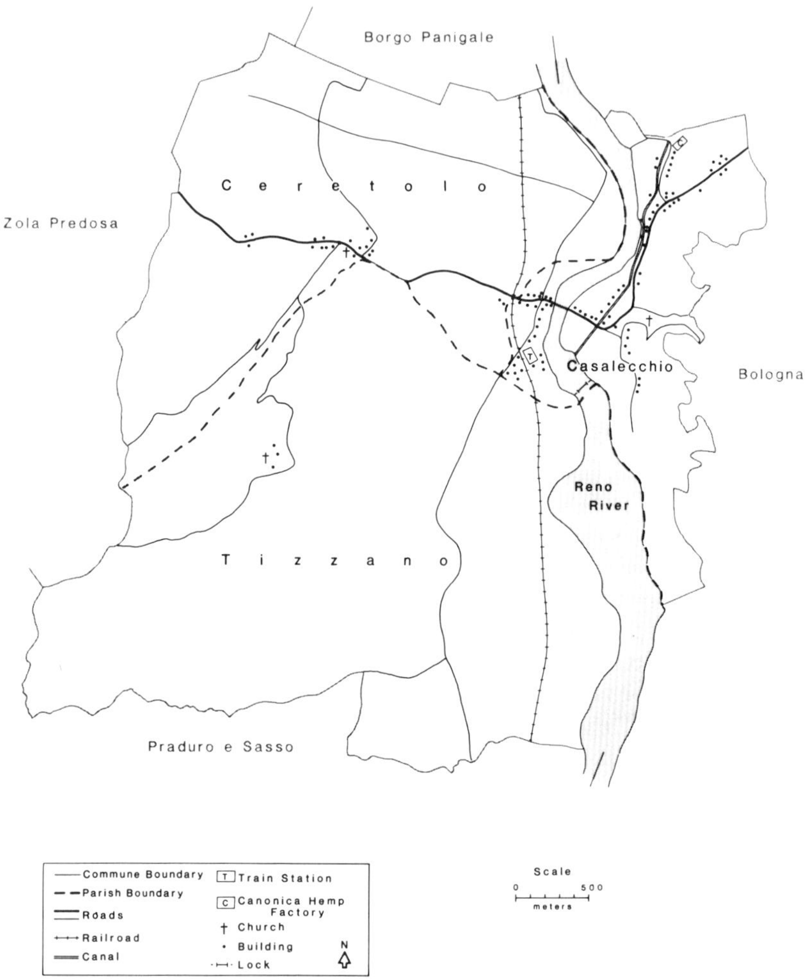

Map 3.1. Casalecchio

sult was a stagnation of local agriculture. Productivity increased only marginally from the mid-eighteenth century to the end of the nineteenth century. A spurt in productivity finally came at the beginning of the twentieth century with passage of land from the old nobility to a more entrepreneurial bourgeoisie. There followed changes in contractual arrangements with the sharecroppers and laborers, as well as the introduction of new parasiticidal agents, fungicides, and synthetic fertilizers.[5]

When the new land cadaster was inaugurated in 1835, there were 58 landowners listed for Casalecchio. These included 18 aristocratic families who owned three-fourths of the agricultural land. Indeed, just four of them accounted for almost half of the agricultural land. Aside from five small pieces owned by various charitable organizations, the rest of the land was owned in small holdings by bourgeois landowners. Throughout the nineteenth century there was a remarkable stability in landownership.

Only eight of the landowners actually lived in Casalecchio in 1879, with the rest living in the city of Bologna. However, about half of the owners kept summer villas in Casalecchio, even though overseeing the sharecroppers was mostly in the hands of agricultural managers hired for this purpose. While some of the landowners rented out part of their holdings, the lessees did not themselves do the farming but rather gave the land out to sharecroppers to farm. Eight of these lessees resided in Casalecchio in 1879. Sharecropping remained virtually the exclusive agrarian contract in Casalecchio in the nineteenth century, with 95 sharecropper houses scattered within the commune.

The sharecroppers themselves did not form a homogeneous economic grouping, for there were considerable differences in wealth among them, with some teetering on the brink of financial ruin and, with it, eviction, and others having built up substantial agricultural capital. The annual communal livestock tax roll of 1883, for example, shows that some sharecroppers owned virtually no livestock, while others owned 15 or more head.[6]

Sharecroppers were provided with substantial houses on the farms as part of their contract, but the other major segment of the agricultural population, the *braccianti,* was not. Instead, they lived in cramped, miserable quarters, generally in larger apartment buildings housing several proletarian families. These were especially concentrated in the parish of Casalecchio, from which the men and women would go each day in search of work either on the sharecropped farms of Casalecchio, on farms of neighboring communes, or wherever a day's wage labor might be found.

The Industrialization of Casalecchio

In the 1850s, on the site of ancient ruins of a fortress along the Reno canal in Casalecchio, there arose one of the largest hemp processing factories in Italy. Dubbed *la Canonica,* for the historic site on which it was located, the new factory was chartered in 1851 and owned by a group of Bolognese entrepreneurs, some of whom were also aristocrats.

Located just five kilometers from the walls of Bologna along the canal bordering the rural outskirts of the Bologna commune, the plant was continuously enlarged in later decades of the century, with stories added up-

Casalecchio di Reno, "La Canonica" Hemp Factory

ward due to the lack of lateral space. On the location, and absorbed by the plant, was an old paper mill.

Management of the mill was always in the hands of foreigners, beginning with the Englishman John Dyer (referred to as Giovanni Dejer in the municipal records!) and including a variety of other Britons and Belgians. Indeed, this was a rotating group of foreign technocrats, who moved among the various hemp factories in the country. Most of the processed hemp was sold domestically; for example, of the one million kilograms produced in 1872, 30 percent stayed in the province of Bologna, and most of the rest remained in northern Italy. However, some of the product was sold to a variety of European countries, and this rose to one-quarter of the output by the turn of the twentieth century.

The work force of the hemp factory grew quickly, from just 150 in 1856 to 350 in 1857 and over 500 by the 1880s. As was characteristic of this industry, the bulk of the workers consisted of women and girls. In 1872, for example, of the 450 employees, 250 were women and 80 were children, mainly aged 10–12. By 1896, of the 503 workers, 276 were women and 70 were children under age 15. Less than half of the adult workers were from Casalecchio itself, with the majority coming from neighboring communities. In 1862, for example, officials of Casalecchio listed 121 of the 277 Canonica workers as residents of the commune, and by 1886 the director of the factory arranged for special tram-line services for the workers commuting from neighboring communities and from other parts of Casalecchio. On the other hand, many of the young girls lived at the factory (particularly in the earliest years of the plant) in quarters provided for them. Indeed, a report to the Paris industrial exposition of 1867 notes that 104 girls "are under the supervision of a respectable woman and are furnished without charge with both school and religious instruction." Moreover, "to maintain their family ties they are sent to visit their relatives at regular intervals."

During most of the nineteenth century, the workday at the hemp factory was twelve and a half hours (excluding breaks) for men, women, and children. With an hour-and-a-half break for lunch and a half hour for supper, the workday actually ran over fourteen hours. In June, when the canal dried up, work was suspended for two weeks. In 1883, most daily wages ranged from 1.5 to 3 lire for men, and were about one lira for women. Children were paid 0.55 lira daily. The lower end of this wage scale, which is what the majority of workers received, was similar to the wage paid to agricultural wage laborers, who, however, had less job security.[7]

While reports from plant managers regularly contained glowing descriptions of hygienic conditions at the factory, the Canonica had many of the health hazards typical of textile factories in this period. In the combing rooms, for example, people worked regularly in clouds of dust, resulting in diseases of the eyes, throat, and lungs. In the areas where the hemp was bathed, high humidity led to a variety of other health problems.[8]

Two decades after Unification, in the 1880s, there remained little industry in Casalecchio outside the Canonica. In all there were about thirty artisans' shops, as well as a fair number of self-employed artisans. Of the 216 residents reported to be employed in the artisans' sector in Casalecchio in 1883, 105 were self-employed, 32 were family members working with them, and just 79 were wage earners working under them. However, these figures do not include residents who worked in the city of Bologna. Jobs included textile weaving, butchering, tailoring, washing, cobbling, furniture making, coopering, bricklaying, carriage making, and blacksmithing.[9]

The first truly industrial enterprise to open in Casalecchio after the hemp factory was the Ronzani brewery, which moved there in 1888, following a dispute over taxes in its previous Bologna location. Located in the *capoluogo,* near the dam, the brewery employed between 28 and 38 men who worked seasonally at the factory and found work in the fields as *braccianti* in the off-season. The men were paid between two and three lire per day, and were given a daily food ration of wheat and corn, as well as a minimal amount of salted herring and a more generous (1.3 liters) daily allowance of beer. Workers were allowed six days of paid vacation per year, at a time chosen by management. In the case of illness, no pay was given the first two days, followed by two weeks of full wages and two weeks of half wages before the worker was let go. As for the fate of older workers, the regulations of the factory, issued in 1914, were clear: "The worker who due to old age or for any other disability becomes unable to work will be let go, without the right to any compensation."[10]

At the turn of the century the Canonica and the brewery were still the only significant local industries in Casalecchio, with only three other enterprises employing more than ten workers. These included the flour mill, employing 13, the cement works, with 14, and the Rappini toy factory, with 25. The improved salaries of male workers are evident in the 1906 wage scale of the toy factory. Men were being paid 2.5 lire per day, although women were still receiving just one lira, with children getting from 0.40 to 0.75 lira depending on age and sex. From 1906 to 1919 the typical workday was ten hours.[11] In addition, there were 25 small artisans' shops, consisting mainly of family labor. This situation was not to change until the second decade of the twentieth century, when a few other small factories were established.

With the building of the tram linking Casalecchio to the city of Bologna in the 1880s, the town became a small center of "tourism," with urban residents coming out for fresh air on Sundays. This led, in the latter years of the nineteenth century, to a boom in tourist-related services in Casalecchio. By 1901, there were 5 cafés, 15 taverns, and 3 pensions in a town of 3,700 inhabitants. In addition, there were 7 small hotels with 52 beds for overnight visitors. The only important seasonal residents were the Bolognese landowners who spent summer months in villas on their property

Downtown Casalecchio in the Early Twentieth Century

in Casalecchio, a practice which members of the emerging Bolognese bourgeoisie began to mimic in the early years of the twentieth century.

The war had a major impact on the people of Casalecchio, and a large portion of the young men were conscripted. By 1918, these conscripts included 120 men from sharecropping families, 91 who had been *braccianti,* and 378 from other sectors of the wage labor force. To compensate them for their lost labor, the 2,142 remaining members of the families of these conscripts were provided with regular subsidies by the government. In the meantime, the demand for labor in Casalecchio was high, as factories were converted to wartime production.[12]

Occupation and Change

From 1871 to 1921, in the space of a half century, the proportion of the Casalecchio male labor force employed in agriculture dropped from one-half to just over one-quarter. In the same period, however, the size of the population doubled, so this decline did not entail any reduction in the number of men employed in agriculture in Casalecchio. Indeed, despite the substantial economic, political, and social changes that had transpired during this period, there remained as many sharecropped farms at the end of it as at the beginning. The nonagricultural sector of the population, however, increased markedly. This sector grew not so much because of the increase in the number of factory jobs available in the commune, but rather because the new links to Bologna and to the neighboring rural communes permitted access to industrial and urban jobs elsewhere, and encouraged the development of marketing and various service activities.

As can be seen in table 3.1, in 1871 a third of the males in the work

Table 3.1. Occupational Composition of the Labor Force by Sex: Census Years (by percentage)

	Male				Female			
Occupation	1871	1881	1911	1921	1871	1881	1911	1921
Sharecropper	35	29	25	17	52	52	29	23
Agric. wage laborer	14	16	15	10	1	3	7	7
Servant	7	6	2	1	7	7	8	8
Other agric. worker	1	2	1	2	0	2	0	2
Elite	5	4	6	8	3	2	5	6
Artisan/Merchant	9	7	17	15	6	4	15	14
Construction worker	7	7	11	12	0	0	0	0
Hemp. indust. worker	12	13	1	1	25	18	8	7
Other wage worker	10	15	22	33	6	12	27	33
N	(1,028)	(1,050)	(1,635)	(2,063)	(534)	(523)	(648)	(909)

force were sharecroppers, with an additional 14 percent working as agricultural wage laborers. This sizable agricultural population lived alongside a substantial number of nonagricultural wage laborers, the largest group in 1871 consisting of the 12 percent working in the hemp factory. Given the fixed number of sharecropped farms, the absolute number of sharecroppers remained largely the same over the years, while the number of *braccianti* actually increased. The latter development can be attributed to the movement of unemployed *braccianti* and others living in rural areas further from the city toward rural areas like Casalecchio where they worked as agricultural wage laborers while seeking urban employment.[13]

With the demolition of the walls of the city and the consequent frenzy of construction around the urban periphery in the early twentieth century, many workers displaced from the overcrowded rural areas found jobs as bricklayers. Meanwhile, with Casalecchio's role as a tourist and market center increasing, the artisan and merchant population expanded considerably.

The occupational history of the female population is more difficult to trace, since officials were seldom systematic in recording women's occupations. This is especially true of the women in *braccianti* households, most of whom worked in the fields for wages but were generally not considered to have an occupation by census takers and other governmental officials. Reliable figures are available, though, for women in sharecropping and in factory labor. All adult women in sharecropping households were considered sharecroppers; indeed, their labor was explicitly committed in the sharecropping contracts. Half the women considered to be in the labor force in the 1870s and 1880s worked as sharecroppers, with this proportion, following that of the men, falling by half by 1921. Again, however, the numbers remained constant. Of special interest is the fact that the proportion of women in the industrial labor force was already about a third by 1871, increasing to 40 percent by 1921.

The proportion of women officially classified in the nondomestic work force varied markedly by age. In 1921, for example, 73 percent of all girls of ages 15–19 were employed, while only 35 percent of women in their thirties and 19 percent of women over age 40 were considered employed. Factory employment was primarily limited to younger women.

While men remained in the formal labor force throughout their adult lives, they did not always keep the same kinds of jobs over their life course. Before we consider some actual life-course patterns of individuals, it is worth taking a look at the differences in men's occupations by age in 1871 and 1921 (table 3.2). In accordance with the sharecroppers' contractual obligation, the children of sharecroppers went to work on their household farms. Other young men sought work outside their parental homes. Many

Table 3.2. Occupational Composition of the Male Labor Force by Age: 1871 and 1921 (by percentage)

	15–19		20–29		30–39		40+	
Occupation	1871	1921	1871	1921	1871	1921	1871	1921
Sharecropper	45	19	29	14	31	17	33	14
Agric. wage laborer	4	3	13	3	10	7	21	16
Nonagric. wage laborer	29	46	35	58	36	51	25	37
Artisan/Merchant	6	14	9	14	12	15	11	14
Elite	0	2	5	7	7	8	7	11
Other	16	16	10	3	4	3	3	8
N	(124)	(263)	(232)	(461)	(183)	(418)	(394)	(868)

spent their adolescent years working as agricultural servants (*garzoni*), primarily in sharecroppers' households or as domestic servants in other households ("Other" in table 3.2). Others sought other forms of wage employment; factory work and certain other types of wage labor (e.g., in construction) were especially geared for younger men. Many of these men came from *braccianti* families: they often returned to wage work in the fields after they lost their more secure nonagricultural jobs.[14]

For those who remained any length of time in Casalecchio, we can get some idea of the sorts of occupational paths that were followed in this period. Three brief examples give some sense of what men's occupational careers were like.

Clodoveo Medici was born in 1856 in Casalecchio, where his father worked in the newly opened hemp factory. By the time he was five his older sister, aged 13, was already working at the hemp factory. By the age of 15, Clodoveo was working as a bricklayer, but then found work in the fields as a *bracciante*. By the time of his marriage, at age 31, to a woman who worked in a factory, he had taken a job back at the hemp factory working as a stoker. Two years later he left Casalecchio and moved to the city of Bologna.

Vincenzo Barilli was born in 1865 in neighboring Zola Predosa, where his father worked as a *bracciante*. The family moved to Casalecchio when Vincenzo was 10. By the time he was 16 Vincenzo found work as an assistant carpenter, while one of his brothers worked for a cobbler and another worked as a farm guard. At age 27, Vincenzo, still in carpentry, married a woman from a sharecropping family. He was to remain a carpenter throughout his life, and by 1921 he and his wife had five children living with them. The two older daughters worked as seamstresses and his older son was an electrician. The youngest three children were still in school.

Evaristo Farnè was born in 1885 in the nearby mountainous commune of Monte San Pietro. He moved to Casalecchio at the age of seven with his family, and his father found work as a *bracciante*. Evaristo himself worked as a *bracciante* as a young man and was still a *bracciante* at age 29 when he married a woman who worked in a factory. However, during the war he was able to obtain a job in the rail yards. He still held this job in 1921 when he was 36 years old.

While these examples provide some indication of the relationship between the occupations of fathers and those of their sons, a more systematic view of the intergenerational transmission of occupation in Casalecchio in the latter part of the nineteenth century is provided by the conscription register (*lista di leva*). At age 19 all males were required to register for the draft, and, from 1862 through the end of the century, they listed not only their own occupation but also that of their father.[15] In all, we have information on 736 young men who registered in this period and whose fathers were alive with an occupation noted.

We analyzed the matrix of father's occupation by son's occupation using log linear modeling methods for the analysis of occupational mobility.[16] The results show a strong association between fathers' and sons' occupations, due primarily to the tendency of sons to take up their fathers' occupations.[17]

About one-third of these youths had fathers who were sharecroppers, and, of these, over 97 percent listed themselves as sharecroppers. This in part reflects the fact that the son of a sharecropper could not remain in his parental household without himself becoming a sharecropper. It also supports the view that, in this period, few youths from sharecropping families struck out on their own, both because of their subservience to family authority and because more attractive alternatives were not available. It is likely that those who left sharecropping did so at a later point in their lives, in connection with their marriage, the splitting up of their multiple-family household, or the loss of their sharecropping contract.

In contrast, just half of the 181 sons of *braccianti* worked as agricultural wage laborers at age 19, with the remainder evenly divided among those working as agricultural servants, those working for artisans or merchants, and those employed in nonagricultural wage labor. On the other hand, the 195 youths whose fathers were nonagricultural wage laborers largely shared in this employment (72 percent), with some (12 percent) finding jobs with artisans or merchants and some (10 percent) doing agricultural wage labor.[18] Thus, across generations of Casalecchio men in the second half of the nineteenth century, the sharecropping sector tended to be self-perpetuating, while there was considerable movement from the agricultural to the nonagricultural sector. The latter came mainly from the already displaced *bracciante* population and not directly from the sharecroppers. Few sons of nonagricultural workers became agricultural workers.

In order to assess occupational change over the life course, we selected men who appeared in both the 1871 and 1881 censuses or the 1911 and 1921 censuses. This provided information on occupational change over a decade for men initially aged 15–49. During the 1871–1881 period, a minimum of seven percent of the men needed to change jobs because of changes in the distribution of jobs held by Casalecchio residents. This doubled to 14 percent between 1911 and 1921, reflecting the expansion of labor-market opportunities. If there had been no occupational persistence over the life course, fully 83 percent of the men would have changed jobs during each of these periods. This, of course, did not happen; 26 percent changed jobs between 1871 and 1881, and 34 percent changed jobs between 1911 and 1921.

Pooling the occupational matrices for the earlier and later periods, log linear models indicated that the over-time career association was statistically significant,[19] and mainly attributable to men keeping the same job.[20] There were no statistically significant changes in the likelihood that a man would keep the same occupation between the 1871–1881 and the 1911–1921 periods, once the greater changes in the twentieth-century labor market are taken into account.[21]

Thus, the picture of the Casalecchio labor market that emerges from these analyses is one of considerable personal stability during periods of rapid economic change. Sharecropping continued as a key element of the Casalecchio economy. Sharecroppers and their sons continued their ancient professions in the face of economic changes surrounding them. Those men who were forced out of sharecropping became agricultural wage workers.[22] The *braccianti* provided a ready pool of workers for the enlarging factory, trade, and service industries. Young men often started as servants or as workers in the hemp factory, but moved on to other wage work as they became adults.

The Rise of Literacy and Public Education

In the half century following Unification, one of Italy's most remarkable social changes involved the rapid spread of literacy, along with the creation of a mass public-school system. In 1866, 60 percent of all men getting married and 79 percent of all brides in Italy were illiterate. The situation was even worse in Emilia-Romagna, where just one in three men and one in six women could even sign their marriage certificates. Yet, by the end of the first decade of the twentieth century those able to sign their own name on the marriage certificate in Italy had risen to 74 percent for the men and 62 percent for the women. The rise of elemental literacy took place at a faster pace in Emilia-Romagna, where by 1909 almost 80 percent of the grooms and 72 percent of the brides could sign their names.[23]

The rise in literacy was one product of the introduction of public education, as can be seen in the case of Casalecchio. Under pontifical rule, Casalecchio's schools were privately run, generally by the churches. Just before Unification, there was a nursery school, a boys' elementary school, and two girls' elementary schools. In 1860 the church schools were closed, pending governmental clarification regarding which schools would be permitted to continue. Although one of the girls' schools was allowed to reopen, under the direction of the parish priest of Ceretolo, it closed permanently in 1878.[24]

Casalecchio, like the rest of Italy, came under the jurisdiction of the school regulations of the Piedmontese state, now extended to the entire kingdom of Italy. In fact, the law governing schooling (known as the Casati law of 1859) was not much different from the law that had been in effect in the papal states. It called for a lower level of elementary instruction consisting of three years, followed by an upper elementary level of two years. Children entered the first grade at age six, and were expected to attain some measure of literacy by the end of the lower elementary level. Those who completed the higher elementary level could then go on to various technical institutes and schools or to teachers' training colleges or secondary schools of classical education, the latter permitting access to the university. The communes were to be responsible for the elementary schools, with the province and state being responsible for all higher levels. Throughout the nineteenth century, Casalecchio offered only the lower elementary level; continuing beyond the third grade meant going to Bologna for instruction.

One element that did differentiate the new state school system from the papal-state elementary education was its broader curriculum. Under the Church, elementary education focused on religious education, along with instruction in reading and the rudiments of writing. In the state system, upon completion of the first three years the student was supposed to know how to read, write, do arithmetic, and have some basic knowledge of geography.

In 1860 the commune of Casalecchio operated three schools, a boys' school and a girls' school in the *capoluogo* and another girls' school in Ceretolo. None of the schools had its own building, and often all three grades had to be taught together due to a shortage of teachers. It was only in 1876 that the first school building was erected, by adding a wing onto the municipal building. In 1877 a new law on elementary instruction was passed, calling for obligatory school attendance between ages six and nine.[25] The rationale given for this law was that previous legislation had not been successful in meeting the objective of training the younger generation to be literate. One result of the new law was that schooling was provided for the first time to the children living in the outlying rural portions of Casalecchio.

Casalecchio made an evaluation of the effects of the new school law in 1887 and concluded that it was largely being followed, with notable implications for the increase in literacy among the young. The commune found that just 13 percent of the children aged six to nine failed to attend. At that time there were five teachers, four of whom were women. This pattern of schooling continued until 1904, when obligatory school attendance was extended by law to age 12 and Casalecchio was forced to provide education for children aged 10 through 12.

The sharp rise in the proportion of Casalecchio residents who were at least minimally literate reflects this advent of mass schooling for children. Although Casalecchio authorities made occasional efforts to provide adult literacy courses, few attended them and they never lasted long. The spread of literacy can be seen in table 3.3. The increase in school attendance led to an age-graded pattern whereby illiteracy came to be characteristic of the older cohorts. Note that in 1861 this was not the case, with young and old exhibiting relatively similar, low levels of literacy. In 1861 male literacy rates ranged from 27 percent to 40 percent in the different age groups, with female literacy considerably lower, ranging from 13 percent to 27 percent. The substantial difference between males and females declined only in the twentieth century, when minimal literacy became virtually universal among the young.

Literacy was not equally distributed within age and sex groups; it was associated with the elite, as would be expected, and with the nonagricultural population, who lived in town near the schools. Thus, there was not

Table 3.3. Percentage Literate, by Age and Sex: Census Years

	Male				Female			
Age	1861	1871	1881	1921	1861	1871	1881	1921
10–19	29	55	63	96	27	44	66	98
20–29	33	50	70	97	25	27	44	96
30–39	30	40	53	93	24	20	31	91
40–49	40	35	42	90	14	17	22	81
50–59	33	36	34	71	17	24	22	61
60+	27	30	28	54	13	14	20	43

Table 3.4. Percentage of Males Literate, by Occupation and Age: Census Years

	1861		1871		1881		1921	
Occupation	%	*N*	%	*N*	%	*N*	%	*N*
Sharecropper								
< 30	26	(117)	42	(177)	50	(140)	91	(147)
30+	18	(168)	23	(185)	27	(161)	72	(185)
Agric. wage laborer								
< 30	17	(36)	20	(41)	48	(56)	87	(39)
30+	13	(108)	15	(106)	24	(140)	51	(185)
Servant								
< 30	13	(77)	15	(55)	14	(50)	77	(13)
30+	20	(20)	14	(14)	20	(15)	55	(11)
Elite								
< 30	86	(7)	100	(12)	88	(8)	95	(41)
30+	87	(31)	90	(41)	97	(30)	97	(125)
Artisan/Merchant								
< 30	68	(25)	94	(32)	94	(16)	99	(111)
30+	63	(59)	68	(65)	78	(54)	91	(186)
Nonagric. wage laborer								
< 30	30	(95)	65	(134)	86	(178)	96	(412)
30+	43	(117)	41	(164)	48	(198)	84	(522)
Total								
< 30	28	(357)	48	(454)	62	(448)	95	(763)
30+	32	(503)	36	(571)	41	(598)	79	(1214)

a simple relationship between wealth and literacy. For example, the sharecroppers, who were in an economically more favorable position than the factory and construction workers, were nonetheless considerably more likely to be illiterate in the years before literacy became almost universal (see table 3.4). This was because even quite small children contributed to the sharecropper household labor force, and hence sharecropper parents were reluctant to send them to school.[26] The artisans and merchants showed considerably higher levels of literacy than the wage laborers.

Thus, through the early years after Unification the Casalecchio population was differentiated not only by economic position, but also by literacy. Women were more often illiterate than men, and those in agriculture—both sharecroppers and *braccianti*—were more often illiterate than those working in the nonagricultural sector.

Politics and Rural Revolt

By the time of the Risorgimento the landowners of Emilia-Romagna were already concerned about the expansion of a mass of proletarianized rural dwellers who were beyond the paternalistic control of the *padroni*. Indeed, they had good reason to be worried, for in the decades that followed, this population of *braccianti* would be at the center of a major rebellion against the political and economic status quo, a rebellion that involved all manner of political activity, from strikes and occasional torching of town halls and the villas of the *padroni* to the systematic building of rural socialist leagues and a socialist party.

Tied to the old, pontifical order, many of the elite blamed these developments on the decline of religious authority and, with it, a decline in the authority of both civil officials and landowners. The *braccianti* were also blamed for widespread theft of crops in the field and were regarded by the elite as squandering their money on drink and gambling. Unlike the sharecroppers, whose lives revolved around their homes and their farms, the *braccianti* were accustomed to working with different groups of people at different times in different places. It was much more common for *braccianti* to while away their time with their comrades at *osterie,* or taverns. This provided a social mechanism for the spread of socialist ideas and facilitated political organization among the disenfranchised.[27]

At the same time, the sharecroppers, too, were the object of landowner concern, although they were seen as a greater force for stabilizing the social and economic order in the countryside than were the *braccianti.* The Bolognese landowners, in fact, established a commission in 1875 to investigate the problem of theft of crops by sharecroppers, which they blamed primarily on the younger family members. This, in turn, was attributed to the greater worldliness of the young sharecropping men who had recently experienced the larger, urban world through military conscription. Indeed, conscription was frequently cited as a cause for the decline of patriarchal authority and the authority of the landowners.[28]

Rural revolt was directed both against the state and against the landowners. No sooner had the new Italian state been formed than a series of antigovernment demonstrations, provoked by new tax laws and military conscription, arose in the countryside. Attempts by the Italian state to draft the first cohort of young men in 1861 led to widespread resistance in Bologna. The Church came to play an active role in this resistance, since state agents asked to use the parish baptismal registers to determine who was to be conscripted. In Casalecchio, as in a number of other communities, the parish priest refused this request and was consequently reported to the civil authorities.[29] This was simply one more battle in the Church's war against the new state, which was regarded as an illegitimate usurper.

In 1869, the state imposed a grist tax (*tassa sul macinato*), a tax which had to be paid every time people had their cereal milled into flour. This tax hit the agricultural population directly and triggered great popular anger; local disturbances spread throughout Bologna in 1869. In one commune of the plain the uprising involved a crowd of 4,000 people who moved on the central piazza, sacked the municipal building and the police station and shouted "Down with the king, viva Pius IX!" Throughout Italy, 257 people died and 1,100 were injured in the protests.[30]

Continuing rural unrest, which state authorities blamed in part on the machinations of the clergy, provided the background for the spread of various anarchist and socialist movements throughout the countryside of Bologna in the 1870s. In the spring of 1874, Andrea Costa, later to become Italy's first socialist member of parliament, proclaimed that a social revolution was imminent, and both government officials and conservative forces lived in fear of an uprising. Indeed, later that year a band of 150 armed revolutionaries, led by the visiting anarchist Bakunin, attempted to march from the nearby city of Imola to Bologna with the intent of taking over the city and sparking a rural revolt. With the arrest of these rebels, hopes (and fears) of an imminent insurrection diminished, and a new phase of socialist organizing began.[31]

One of the notable aspects of the rise of socialism in this area famous for the early strength of its socialist movement was that it was in the countryside, rather than in the city, where the left-wing movement was strongest. There was, certainly, urban unrest and organizing of urban workers as well, but it is a curious fact that the impetus to much of the most militant resistance in the city of Bologna was provided by *braccianti* who had moved to the city from the surrounding hinterland. Not only had they been schooled in class struggle in the countryside but, as recent immigrants, they were less apt to be tied into old networks of patronage in which the urban artisans had long been bound. Many of the strikes in the early years of the twentieth century that involved the nonagricultural population in fact tied together city and rural dwellers, including the construction workers' strike of 1902 and the general strike of September 1904, which the workers of Casalecchio joined.[32]

Although the sharecroppers occasionally took part in public protests organized by socialist forces, they were not by any means at the forefront of the socialist efforts in the nineteenth century. Indeed, there was a certain amount of hostility between the socialists and the sharecroppers in this period, since the socialists regarded sharecropping as feudalistic and a means whereby landowners co-opted the working class. Early agrarian-league attempts to recruit sharecroppers into the *bracciante*-dominated organization failed miserably. The Marxist-inspired program of transforming the feudalistic sharecroppers into more "modern" wage laborers held no allure for the sharecroppers of Emilia-Romagna.[33]

The sharecroppers were also discouraged from political organization because of their economic position. First, they worked in family units largely in isolation from others. Second, they were involved in paternalistic ties with their *padroni* and hence could not strike out either against landowners in general, as could the *braccianti,* or against some distant, impersonal group of owners, as could factory workers. Perhaps most important, from the sharecroppers' perspective, engaging in a strike was suicidal, for they stood to lose not only a few days' or weeks' wages, but all the product of their year's labor. In addition, of course, they realized that they could easily lose their contract, meaning not only loss of a job for an individual, but loss of work and loss of a home for an entire multiple-family household. Moreover, landowners held the threat of calling in the sharecroppers' accumulated debt at any time, a powerful incentive against incurring the landowner's ire. In this setting, it is not surprising that the sharecroppers remained more politically isolated and cautious than the proletarianized workers around them.[34]

The rise of the rural socialist leagues and urban unions and the rapid spread of workers' cooperatives coincided with the advent of church-affiliated rural leagues designed to compete with the socialists. Thus, Emilia-Romagna was perhaps the most highly politicized region of Italy at the time the First World War began. Although Casalecchio was not among the handful of localities—found in the plains—most famous for such developments, it followed a very similar course.[35]

In fact, there is no record of any formal socialist organization in Casalecchio before the twentieth century. However, it is clear that socialist ideas had long been spreading through the population, especially at the hemp factory. Indeed, the Bolognese socialist newspaper, *La Squilla,* claimed in an article in December 1901 that five workers had been fired from the Canonica as a result of their socialist sympathies. At a meeting held in March of the following year, the women workers of the hemp factory formed a League of Resistance, with monthly dues.[36] This had been preceded by a less institutionalized agreement of solidarity between the women spinners and 50 workers threatened by layoffs. The women employed by the factory later walked off their jobs to protest the firing of these workers.

In September 1902 various meetings were held at the Camera del Lavoro of Casalecchio—a recently established branch of the city's Chamber of Labor—to draft demands for improving working conditions at the factory. As a result, the following month the workers presented a list of requests to the management. These included modest increases in wages (women were to be paid 1 lira per day, for example) and a reduction from the current twelve-hour workday to one that was just ten hours: in the winter from 7 A.M. to 6 P.M. with an hour's break in the middle; in the summer from 6 A.M. to 6 P.M. with two hours of break. They also called for the rehiring of the fired workers. When the management rejected these requests out of hand, a strike was called, which lasted for months. In the end the workers were defeated, returning to the factory under the old conditions.

Yet this defeat did not slow the pace of workers' organization in Casalecchio. In September of 1904 the women's League of Spinners and Weavers at the Canonica, together with the bricklayers and the *braccianti* of the commune, joined in the national general strike called by the Chamber of Labor. Both a formal bricklayers' cooperative and a Casalecchio league of *braccianti* were constituted locally. Thus, the factory workers, the construction workers, and the agricultural wage laborers each had their own socialist-inspired organization. In their first action, in the spring of 1906, the *braccianti* of Casalecchio struck, succeeding in improving their wages and reducing their work hours to a maximum of ten hours per day.

In 1907, two years after the factory was sold to a Milan-based conglomerate, a new system of speeding up the work was introduced at the combing section of the Canonica. The women combing workers responded by walking off their jobs, and they were soon joined in strike by the other 360 women and 60 men working at the factory. Symbolic of the times, the new accord, reached a week later, included a day off for May Day. Growing worker solidarity was also evident the following year when the workers at the toy factory in Casalecchio went on strike. During the four-month strike, funds for subsistence and other support were provided by the bricklayers' and *braccianti* leagues, as well as by the Canonica workers.

But the workers were not always successful. In the last strike at the Canonica before the war, in 1909, the workers demanded a reduction of the workday from ten and a half to ten hours, along with wage increases. But management refused to give in, complaining that wages had already been raised 30 percent over the previous three years of agitation. After two months of strike, the owners announced that the factory would be closed permanently unless the workers returned under the old conditions. Two months later, the strike ended in defeat, with the 12 strike leaders fired and the league left in disarray.[37]

Local Government in Casalecchio

The story of the period from Unification to the aftermath of the First World War is a story of tremendous social and political upheavals in Bologna; dramatic evidence of this transformation is provided by the changes experienced in Casalecchio's local government. Until Unification, Casalecchio's form of government was that mandated by papal rule, with ultimate

Casalecchio di Reno, Villa Tizzano (Marescalchi)

control over the area in the hands of the cardinal based in the city and local jurisdiction for Casalecchio delegated to a cleric. Up to the mid-nineteenth century, local political positions were simply filled by people selected by the central ecclesiastical authorities. However, in the last years of papal rule, a system of local voting was put in place. Manual workers were explicitly excluded from voting, with two-thirds of the eligible voters to be drawn from the local landowners and the remaining third from others of the elite.

Beginning in 1859, Piedmontese laws governing local government were instituted in Emilia-Romagna. Influenced by the earlier Napoleonic period, this system was based on the key role played by the prefect, who represented the central government in the region and who oversaw strict centralization of governmental power. The prefect exercised considerable control over the activities of the local government. All acts of the town council, including minutes of their meetings, had to be reviewed by the prefect, and none of their actions could take force without his approval.

Casalecchio first had a 15-member town council, with the mayor nominated by the central state authorities from among the councillors. The councillors were elected by adult males who paid a specified minimum annual tax, along with certain other professionals who did not have to meet the minimum-tax requirement.

Throughout this period there was a progressive enlargement of the right to vote, leading ultimately to virtually universal male suffrage by 1913. Under the law of 1889 all men who had completed elementary school were permitted to vote, regardless of wealth. The result of these changes was the growth in proportion of the population in Emilia-Romagna having the right to vote. The impact on the Casalecchio electorate was dramatic, with the proportion of the population eligible to vote rising from 4 percent in 1871 to 9 percent in 1889, 15 percent in 1911, and 28 percent in 1914.[38]

Throughout the nineteenth century the Casalecchio town council was in the hands of the conservatives (or "clerical-moderates" as they were often called), representing the large landowners. However, as suffrage was extended, councillors affiliated with a new progressive party began to appear. Socialist successes were scored elsewhere in the area at the end of the nineteenth century, with the city of Imola electing a socialist majority in 1889, and both the city of Bologna and neighboring Borgo Panigale having a substantial representation of socialist workers on their muncipal councils by 1900.

As late as 1904 the Casalecchio town council was dominated by the elite, with seven landowners, two others identified as independently wealthy (*benestanti*), and two landlords' agents among the 20 members. Indeed, nine of the top ten vote-getters were from this restricted group. Just four years later, though, in the election of 1908, the socialists succeeded in electing 14 members to the town council, including two sharecroppers, a *bracciante,* and various small artisans. Yet, three landowning counts were still council members, and the socialist mayor was a physician.[39]

There was no doubt, however, that socialist forces were on the rise and the landowners and other propertied forces on the defensive. This movement intensified in the aftermath of the war when, in a three-way race, the Socialist Party succeeded in garnering 63 percent of the vote in the city of Bologna in national elections, electing a socialist mayor with 58 percent of the vote in the following year (Ballini 1985:212). But the euphoria was not to last long, for the social unrest and political challenge represented by the Left was to be met by a violent reaction on the Right, ushering in two decades of fascism with Mussolini's rise to power in 1922.

4 Life in Casalecchio

This chapter discusses the day-to-day living conditions in Casalecchio during the nineteenth and early twentieth centuries, reviewing household arrangements, diet and health conditions, the extent of poverty, and the decline in mortality during these years.

Households

One of the remarkable features of family life in central Italy, extending north beyond Bologna, was the prevalence of multiple-family households. Indeed, large, complex-family households have a long pedigree in this area, with Ring (1979:17) tracing such a system back to the ninth century. A similar pattern is evident in rural, fifteenth-century Tuscany.[1]

This form of coresidence was intimately associated with the development of the sharecropping system, for maximizing adult family laborers on the farm was one of the aims of the landowners in choosing sharecropping families. Having two or more kin-related conjugal-family units was indeed the norm among sharecroppers in this part of the world. Numerous studies now reveal that a majority of sharecroppers in central and northern Italy typically lived in complex-family (primarily multiple-family) households.[2] Indeed, on the basis of the historical information currently available, these Italian sharecropper communities showed the highest rates of multiple-family arrangements of any part of western Europe.[3]

This is certainly the pattern observed in the Bologna area. For example, in twenty-eight parishes of the rural area surrounding Bologna in the mid-nineteenth century, 46 percent of sharecropper households contained two or more simple-family units, with 17 percent containing three or more such units.[4] In Casalecchio, the proportion of sharecroppers living in multiple-family households was even higher (see table 4.1). In 1871, for example, 76 percent of all those living in sharecropper households lived in house-

Table 4.1. Household Composition of Casalecchio Residents, by Occupation of Household Head: 1871 and 1921 (by percentage)

Household	Sharecropper		Agricultural Wage		Elite		Artisan & Merchant		Nonagricultural Wage	
Composition	1871	1921	1871	1921	1871	1921	1871	1921	1871	1921
Solitary	0	0	0	1	0	1	1	1	1	1
No family	0	0	2	1	8	10	0	0	5	2
Simple family	12	20	74	51	41	55	62	55	58	67
Extended family	11	9	9	12	15	19	16	22	16	13
Multiple family	76	71	14	36	25	14	19	20	20	18
Other	1	0	0	0	11	0	2	1	0	0
N	(994)	(1,197)	(437)	(678)	(215)	(568)	(278)	(773)	(790)	(2,335)

holds containing two or more kin-related simple-family units, with another 11 percent living in households containing kinsmen beyond the simple family (e.g., a widowed mother of the household head).[5]

Wage laborers, on the other hand, typically lived in smaller, simple-family households. In the parishes surrounding Bologna in 1847, for example, 74 percent of the *bracciante*-headed households were of this type, and just 11 percent were multiple-family households. Casalecchio followed this pattern as well, with 74 percent of those living in *braccianti* households in 1871 living in simple-family units, just 14 percent in multiple-family households, and an additional 9 percent in extended-family households containing a single simple-family unit plus an additional relative or relatives. A similar pattern was found among the other wage workers of Casalecchio. Artisans, merchants, and the elite ranged between the two extremes provided by the sharecroppers and *braccianti,* but were much more similar to the wage laborers than to the sharecroppers.[6]

The size and complexity of the sharecropper household entailed the coresidence of a number of married couples, which in turn meant that not all married adults were household heads or wives of heads. Indeed, in neither 1861 nor 1921 were as many as 15 percent of sharecropper men aged 30–39 household heads. This contrasts with the 79 percent of *braccianti* men and 75 percent of other wage laborers in Casalecchio in 1861 who were household heads at this age (65 percent and 71 percent respectively in 1921; see table 4.2). Remarkably, only a minority of sharecroppers were household heads even when they were in their forties.

The household positions of these Casalecchio sharecroppers (table 4.3) reflect a life-course pattern in which the bride is brought into the groom's home, with her father-in-law as household head. Upon his death, headship is often taken up by the groom's older brother. Indeed, even among married men in their fifties, it is not uncommon to have a brother as household head.

The patrilateral preference in household extension runs throughout the population. Rarely did a daughter bring her husband into her parental household, whereas for sons, bringing a bride into their parents' home was a cultural norm. Indeed, at both ends of the period under study, about 90 percent of the people living in households containing two or more simple-family units were in patrilateral households, as were three-quarters of those living in extended-family households.[7]

Considering the historically close association between the multiple-family household system and sharecropping, it is not surprising that Casalecchio had such a high proportion of complex-family households in the early years of the new Italian state. Yet, it is remarkable how stable this household

Table 4.2. Percent of Male Household Heads, by Occupation and Age: 1871 and 1921

	1871		1921	
Occupation and Age	%	*N*	%	*N*
20–29				
Sharecroppers	0	68	3	66
Agric. wage laborers	33	30	20	15
Nonagric. wage laborers	12	81	26	269
30–39				
Sharecroppers	11	56	14	69
Agric. wage laborers	79	19	65	28
Nonagric. wage laborers	75	65	71	213
40–49				
Sharecroppers	47	60	39	46
Agric. wage laborers	94	31	64	25
Nonagric. wage laborers	81	57	89	141
50–59				
Sharecroppers	74	27	71	24
Agric. wage laborers	92	26	96	51
Nonagric. wage laborers	86	28	93	111

system remained well into the twentieth century. Even by 1921, 44 percent of the population were living in complex-family households.

If we are to understand these limited changes in Casalecchio's coresidential patterns during this period of sharp social and economic changes, it is well to distinguish between two factors. On the one hand, complex household organization is specifically identified with the family economy associated with sharecropping. From a purely economic viewpoint, insofar as sharecropping declines and proletarian labor increases, simple-family households should become more prevalent. On the other hand, many scholars of modernization have postulated a more general effect of the rise of literacy, modern secular ideologies, and the liberation of young adults from their parents. From this viewpoint, we should expect a historic decline in complex-family household arrangements within all occupational categories.

In order to disentangle these effects, we look not only at the distribution of household arrangements across the half century running from 1871 to 1921 but also at the extent to which changes in household arrangements may have been produced simply by changes in the occupational structure. We have standardized the coresidence patterns of the 1921 population using the age, sex, and occupational composition found in 1871 (see table 4.4). That is, we ask what the distribution of household arrangements would have been in 1921 if the 1921 population had had the same age, sex, and occupational composition as the 1871 population.[8] The results provide strik-

Table 4.3. Coresidential Situation of Male Sharecroppers, by Age: 1871 and 1921 (by percentage)

Relation to Head and Age	1871	1921
20–29		
Head	0	3
Son	63	67
Brother	13	8
Other kin	22	17
Nonkin	2	6
N	(68)	(66)
30–39		
Head	11	14
Son	57	67
Brother	21	6
Other kin	9	12
Nonkin	2	1
N	(56)	(69)
40–49		
Head	47	39
Son	23	33
Brother	20	20
Other kin	8	9
Nonkin	0	0
N	(60)	(46)
50–59		
Head	74	71
Son	4	4
Brother	22	17
Other kin	0	8
Nonkin	0	0
N	(27)	(24)

ing confirmation of the view that the decline in multiple-family households and the increase in simple-family households are a product of the decline in the proportion of sharecroppers in the population and the increase in the proportion of wage laborers, artisans, merchants, and the elite. There is no support for the view that more general cultural changes accounted for these changes in household arrangements of the various economic groups.

Reinforcement of this point comes from a look back at table 4.1, where we find no consistent pattern within occupational groups of declining proportions of complex-family arrangements. It was as common for an occupational group to increase in complex-family coresidence over this period as it was to show nuclearization.[9]

Table 4.4. Coresidence of Casalecchio Population: 1871 and 1921 (by percentage)

Household Composition	1871	1921	1921 Standardized[a]
Solitary	0.5	1.0	0.6
No family	2.8	2.0	1.4
Simple family	42.7	52.2	45.7
Extended family	12.9	13.7	12.7
Multiple family	39.5	30.7	39.4
Other	1.5	0.3	0.2
N	(2,801)	(5,970)	

[a]Data for 1921 directly standardized for age, sex, and household head's occupation based on the 1871 population composition.

Living Conditions

When a poor person eats a chicken, either he is sick, or the chicken is.[10]

One of the major advantages that the sharecroppers had over both the *braccianti* and the nonagricultural wage laborers was access to better food. Traditionally, sharecropper households grew their own food. Although their diet relied heavily on polenta and bread, they were able to mix these with modest amounts of meat—especially pork—as a condiment. In the summer, when the harvest began to come in, the diet became much more varied, including a variety of vegetables and fruits. The sharecroppers also had access to cheeses, butter, and milk from their cows, as well as chickens and eggs from their chicken coop, although both chickens and eggs were considered precious. The diet, then, was steady but limited. Meat was a luxury, even among sharecroppers, and rarely eaten as a principal part of the meal.[11]

The Agrarian Inquiry of 1881 described the nutritional level of the *braccianti* in the Bologna area as "terrible in every respect." Much of the year the agricultural wage laborers subsisted on polenta and water. When they were working, the *braccianti* were compensated in part by *vinello,* wine diluted with water. Indeed, this was the preferred drink of many, and it was commonly believed to confer great nutritional value. As the Bolognese said, "Good wine makes good blood."[12]

The poor were forced to expend the great majority of their wages on food (largely on wheat and corn), and malnourishment was a constant threat.[13] The diet of the urban workers resembled that of the *braccianti,* consisting largely of corn-based polenta and wheat in the form of bread and pasta. In the summer and fall some fruit—especially watermelons, figs, and grapes—made its way into their diet.[14] Poor nutrition was coupled with sanitation conditions that were bad in Casalecchio and even worse in the city of Bologna. Through the latter part of the nineteenth century various efforts were made to provide drinking water to the Casalecchio population, especially to those living in the more densely populated district, but until the twentieth century many residents had to travel a considerable distance to get to public wells. Indeed, it was only in 1910 that a new water system was in place.[15]

In 1885 Casalecchio had two physicians, a midwife, a pharmacist, and two veterinarians. One of the physicians and one veterinarian were employed by the town. Smallpox vaccinations were being systematically administered to the population. Although malaria was still a problem in the low plains of Bologna, it did not affect Casalecchio. However, various respiratory and eye infections were common, as were rheumatic diseases, and past decades had seen occasional outbreaks of scarlet fever, measles, diphtheria, smallpox, and typhus. Although syphilis was widespread in the city, where there were 135 officially registered prostitutes in twelve houses of prostitution—and many more unregistered prostitutes—the disease was not considered a problem in Casalecchio during this period. Casalecchio had no hospital; those in need of hospitalization were taken to the city.[16]

The effects of poor nutrition and poor sanitation in Italy are visible in the high proportion of young Italian men who failed to pass the physical examination connected with conscription. In the first decade after Unification a total of 39 percent failed the physical in Italy; about half of this number failed due to insufficient height or weight and the other half as a result of various deformities and diseases. Emilia-Romagna actually had the healthiest population in Italy from this perspective, with only 31 percent failing the physical exam (Bellettini 1982:787n). Concern for the poor health conditions in the nation led to a national law in 1888 mandating all communes to provide free medical treatment for the poor. Accordingly, Casalecchio officials drew up a list of those eligible for free medical care which included a good segment of its population. One drawback of the new law, however, was that it did not provide for free pharmaceuticals, with the result that the treatment prescribed by the doctor was often not followed (Della Peruta 1980:758–59).

Despite these continuing health problems, considerable progress was made in the fight against epidemic diseases. Yet, while smallpox was being eradicated, and the last epidemic of cholera took place in the 1880s, diseases such as typhus and diphtheria continued to take their toll into the twentieth century (Del Panta 1984; Brugnoli 1881; Boselli 1904).

Unhygienic and cramped housing conditions were another continuous lament of both rural and urban Bologna in the nineteenth and early twentieth centuries. Sharecroppers again did better, having an entire house, but given the large size of many sharecropper households, they often slept in cramped quarters and, with the proximity of the animals to the living quarters, sanitation continued to be a problem.

The agricultural wage laborers were much worse off. In the words of the 1881 Agrarian Inquiry report on the Bologna area: "For the wage laborer the houses are the most decrepit, the most filthy, the most unhygienic. . . . The space available is always the minimum possible." The report goes on to note that the proprietors showed no interest in repairing or improving the squalid lodgings, since they had no problems finding *braccianti* or nonagricultural wage laborers in need of housing.[17]

Some insight into these squalid conditions in Casalecchio can be gleaned from an 1895 report prepared by the town's sanitation officer on a group of apartments occupied by numerous wage-laborer families. Located in the center of Casalecchio, the complex consisted of 33 units, with 89 tiny rooms, housing 151 individuals. The apartments had been made out of a warehouse originally built as an inexpensive storage area for a salami factory. In 1890, a local nobleman acquired the property and had it converted into housing for the proletariat. It is worth quoting from the sanitation officer's report:

> Humidity and mist plug up the pores of the building materials so that ventilation through the walls is impeded and the air thus enclosed becomes fetid and almost unbreathable. Hence we see rheumatic and respiratory diseases, anemia, etc., etc. . . . In the upper floor under the roof the hygienic conditions are even worse because it is sweltering in the summer and freezing in the winter. . . . It is completely without lavatories or water, so that given the often extremely hot temperature of the dirty water thrown in front of the building, there is a bubbling fermentation of a mass of excrement which gives off a large amount of fetid gas. . . . All around are dung heaps and puddles.

Although the Casalecchio sanitation officer ordered the place closed for reasons of public health in 1895, the proprietor, a marquis, challenged the decision in court and succeeded in nullifying the order by making generic promises for renovations. Nine years later, when a new slum-clearance plan was drawn up for the commune, the building's condition had been little changed.[18]

For taxation purposes, authorities made no distinction between agricultural wage laborers and nonagricultural wage laborers, and, as seen in the case discussed above, the two often lived side by side. Indeed, as other wage-labor opportunities opened up for the *braccianti,* they quickly moved into nonagricultural jobs and, as already noted, many spent their younger years in industrial employment before being forced to return to less secure *bracciante* labor.

Casalecchio, along with all other communes, levied an annual tax (*il focatico*) on each resident household. As part of its collection, each year the local officials compiled a complete list of all households, household heads, and certain household characteristics, including the occupation of the head. These households were then divided into three categories: property owner; a middle category of merchants, artisans, sharecroppers, and others who enjoyed a moderate standard of living; and a third category consisting of all wage laborers, both agricultural and nonagricultural. For the 46-year period (1869–1914) for which these lists survive, the majority of the Casalecchio population was placed in that third category, which was divided into just two "classes," one which was levied a tax of 3 lire per year and the other a tax of just 1.5 lire. In contrast, the property owners were divided into 15 gradations based on income, and paid from 5 to 260 lire per year. The middle category, divided into 20 gradations, paid from 5 to 133 lire per year.[19]

The poverty of Casalecchio's wage laborers is reflected in the fact that 17 percent of the wage-laboring families were judged too poor to pay even the 1.5-lire-per-year *focatico* tax during this period. Most of these were exempted due to old age (defined as having a household head over age 60 and no male aged 18–59 in the household). This points in turn to a major difference between the life course of wage laborers and the life course of sharecroppers and others who had access to property. Living in a multiple-family household, for example, the elderly sharecropper was provided for by his coresident kinsmen. Elderly wage laborers, on the other hand, more often lived in simple-family households: unable to bring wages to the household, they faced poverty, malnutrition, and exposure to the winter cold.

Throughout papal rule, such individuals were the charge of the Church and church charity. With the advent of the secular state, the government attempted to wrest some of these tasks from the Church. Casalecchio had a regular, small budget available for poor relief and, as already mentioned, free medical care for the poor was provided by the state through the town doctor. In 1906 this was supplemented by the provisioning of free pharmaceuticals for the poor, including the elderly. Indeed, the broad scope of this poor relief is indicated by Casalecchio's 1910 listing of 336 families as eligible to receive free medicine due to their poverty, thus including a substantial proportion of all wage laborers. Occasional paternalistic displays of magnanimity toward the poor were also made, as on 22 April 1893, the silver anniversary of King Umberto I and Margherita of Savoy, when the commune compiled a list of the twenty poorest families and disbursed 5 lire to each in honor of the occasion. All but three of the twenty signed for their payments with a cross.[20]

Mortality

In a society in which birth levels remained relatively constant, and quite high, for many centuries, it was the vagaries of the mortality rate that determined increases and decreases in the overall population. The nineteenth century saw not only a sharp lowering of the death rate in Casalecchio—as in Italy more generally—but an end of the sudden spikes in the mortality rate caused by disease and famine. If the population of rural Bologna rose virtually uninterruptedly beginning in the eighteenth century, it was because the bouts with the plague had ended, while the continuing occasional outbreaks of epidemics began to have less of an impact. By the beginning of the nineteenth century, though, epidemics were still regular occurrences. Indeed, a major smallpox epidemic swept through the area. But there is evidence that improved nutrition (linked to the development of such new crops as maize) and rudimentary public-health measures were having a beneficial effect on longevity, even though most of the population remained poor (Del Panta 1985).

Although the emergence of the nonagricultural-wage-based economy in the latter part of the nineteenth century did not in itself solve the problems of rural poverty, improvements in public health helped produce notable declines in mortality in Casalecchio, an elsewhere in the area (fig. 4.1). Despite short-term increases in mortality associated with the continued outbreak of infectious diseases during the twentieth century, the underlying trend following the last cholera epidemic of the 1880s was progressively downward.[21] The crude death rate averaged 30 per 1,000 annually from 1865 to 1879, about 25 per 1,000 from 1880 to 1889, and then declined rapidly to about 15 per 1,000 in the late 1890s. The death rate stabilized at about 10–12 per 1,000 during the early twentieth century.[22]

Casalecchio's mortality decline outpaced that of the nation as a whole: Italy had a crude death rate of 30 in the 1870s, 22 in the first decade of the twentieth century, and 17 by the early 1920s. However, the Casalecchio experience resembles that of the Emilia-Romagna region, which had a crude death rate of 16 per 1,000 in 1922, second lowest of the 16 regions then distinguished in Italy.[23] As elsewhere, a significant proportion of this drop in mortality is accounted for by the sharp decline in infant and child mortality. In Casalecchio, the proportion of all deaths occurring to children

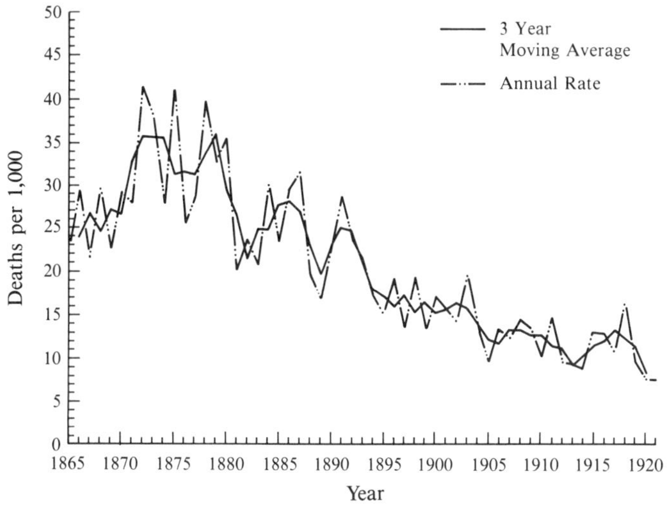

Fig. 4.1. The Age-Standardized Crude Death Rate of Casalecchio, 1865–1921

aged five and under fell from 45 percent in 1869–1883 to 23 percent in 1904–1918.[24]

A total of 5,876 births were recorded in Casalecchio from 1865 to 1921; 753 of these newborns died before reaching their first birthday.[25] The annual infant mortality rate was subject to considerable flux.[26] However, the underlying trend was one of decline (fig. 4.2). The recorded infant mortality rate averaged about 140 per 1,000 between 1865 and 1869. This unusually low rate may have resulted from a short-term trough in infant mortality, or it may be an artifact of incomplete recording of infant deaths in the early years of the birth and death registers. The infant mortality rate of about 200–230 per 1,000 in the early 1870s is more indicative of mortality conditions in Casalecchio in the mid-nineteenth century. The rate declined steadily thereafter to 100 per 1,000 by the turn of the century and to 70–75 per 1,000 by the second decade of the twentieth century.[27]

The infant mortality rate in a small population such as that of Casalecchio is subject to substantial year-to-year variations. The magnitude of these fluctuations was dampened as mortality was brought under social control and the overall infant mortality rate declined. Although the decline in infectious diseases meant greater survival prospects for newborns, such diseases continued to be important, as is shown most graphically by the substantial increase in the infant mortality rate during the 1918–1919 influenza epidemic.[28]

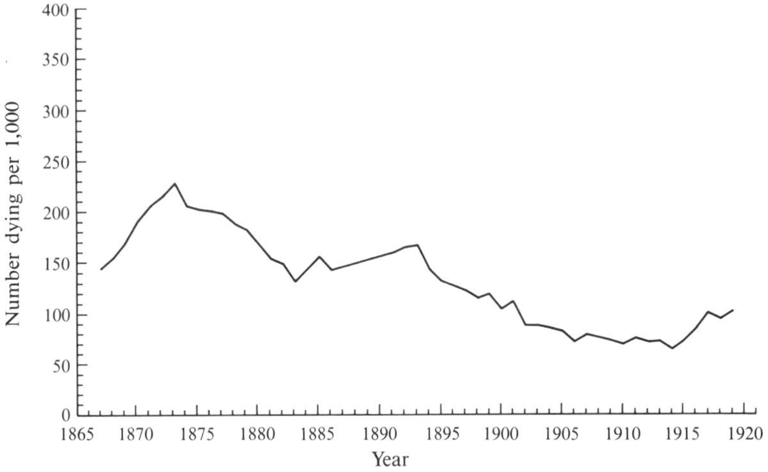

Fig. 4.2. The Infant Mortality Rate in Casalecchio: Five-Year Moving Averages, 1865–1921

Improvements in infectious-disease control (vaccinations, sanitary disposal of sewage, and safe drinking water) were public-health measures that benefited many members of the Casalecchio population. Such public-health activities were of special importance for the wage earners who lived in crowded conditions in the more urban center of the Casalecchio commune. They were probably less important for the sharecropping families, living as they did in dispersed housing throughout the rural areas of the commune.

Substantial differences in the standard of living of the elites, sharecroppers, and wage earners had important consequences for their mortality rates, and for the historical changes in mortality that they experienced (see table 4.5).[29] The poor and wage earners were subject to extreme impoverishment during the 1870s when Casalecchio had not yet developed a full-fledged wage economy. Members of these impoverished families averaged 24 deaths per 1,000 people during this period, much higher than the 15 per 1,000 recorded among sharecropper families. As Casalecchio developed its nonagricultural-wage-based economy the poorest segment of the population became somewhat less impoverished and enjoyed substantial improvements in its mortality rates (which declined to 15 per 1,000 by 1893–1905). Meanwhile, the sharecroppers (who had no noteworthy improvements in their standard of living) and other residents showed more modest improvements in their mortality rates between the 1869–1880 period and the 1893–1905 period. By the beginning of the twentieth century, the death rates of the wage earners and the sharecroppers differed by only

Table 4.5. The Number of Deaths per 1,000 People in Casalecchio, by Family Economic Stratum and Time Period

	Time Period		
Economic Stratum	1869–1880	1881–1892	1893–1905
Elite	13	13	9
Sharecropper	15	13	13
Middle	11	15	11
Poor/Wage	24	18	15

Note: These death rates are directly standardized for age and sex using the average population composition for 1869–1905. As discussed in the text, these rates are biased downward by the systematic exclusion of infant mortality, but accurately represent economic differentials in mortality.

two points (a difference of about 15 percent). An inspection of the age patterns of mortality for the different occupational groups indicates that the biggest improvements occurred in the survival chances of children in wage-laborer households.[30]

Along with the decline in mortality described here, and the decline in fertility examined in chapter 8, the demographic feature most commonly associated with an industrializing and urbanizing area such as Casalecchio is certainly a rise in population mobility. But the Casalecchio case belies these expectations and, in doing so, shows why some of the most common models linking modernization to increased migration may be misconceived. Just why this is so is the subject to which we now turn.

5 On the Move
Changing Population Mobility

In spite of the popular image of the stable rural community in preindustrial Europe, with an agricultural population rooted to the land, the contrary realization of continual population movement now dominates European social history. Although it was once thought that high levels of migration were a product of industrialization and urban expansion, this relationship is no longer so clear. Casalecchio offers an instructive example here both because of its transformation from an agricultural to a nonagricultural economy in this period and because it was becoming increasingly tied to an expanding city. Its value is magnified by the unusual richness of archival material that allows us to trace the movements of individuals into and out of the community.

The case of Casalecchio illustrates some of the pitfalls of associating industrialization and urbanization with increased rates of population mobility, and suggests reasons why migration rates may actually decrease with modernization. It also allows us to examine just which groups within a modernizing population were changing most rapidly in their propensity to migrate and what effects these changes had on the whole population.

Casalecchio experienced a continuous turnover of its population through immigration and emigration during the late nineteenth and early twentieth centuries.[1] People were twice as likely to enter the community through immigration as they were to enter it by birth. Moreover, once there, they were twice as likely to leave through emigration as they were to die there. At the time of the 1861 census less than half (47 percent) of the population was native born, and this percentage changed little over the next 50 years.[2] Most of these native-born residents were young. Among women, for example, about three-quarters of those under age 10 and slightly more than half of those between ages 10 and 19 were natives of Casalecchio, com-

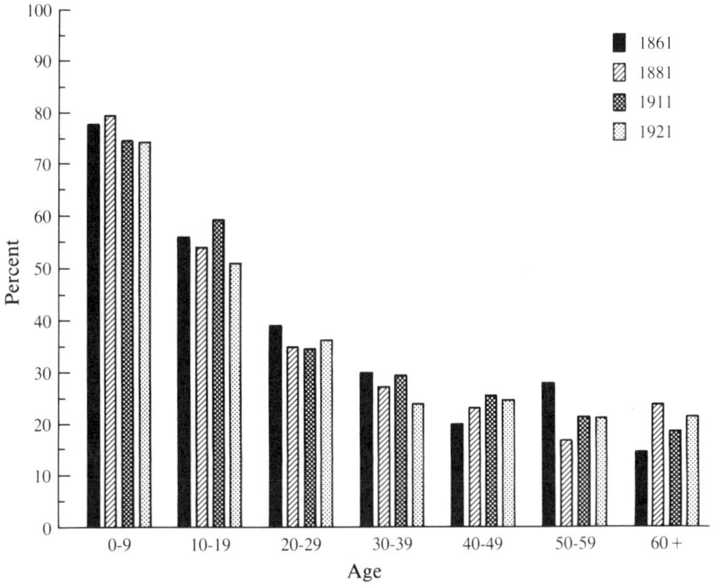

Fig. 5.1. Percent of the Female Population Born in Casalecchio, by Age in Census Year

pared to fewer than one-third of the adult women (fig. 5.1). There was a low proportion of native-born adult men in each of the major occupational groups throughout this period (fig. 5.2). While especially few agricultural wage laborers (*braccianti*) were native born, fewer than half of the men who were sharecroppers, artisans or merchants, or nonagricultural wage laborers were native born.

During this period, the population more than doubled in size, mortality declined dramatically, and fertility began to drop. This demographic modernization was associated with the shift of the mode of economic production from sharecropping to wage labor, entailing dramatic changes in the family economy. While social scientists usually think of such community-level transformations as occurring in a population that has a relatively stable membership over time, such a perception is surely misleading in a population as mobile as this one. To understand the social dimensions of the demographic transformation of Casalecchio, it is necessary to have a fuller understanding of migration—its levels, geographic characteristics, and selectivity. Examining the impact of migration on individual lives involves considering how migration decisions were coordinated with other aspects of the individual life course, viewed in its family context.

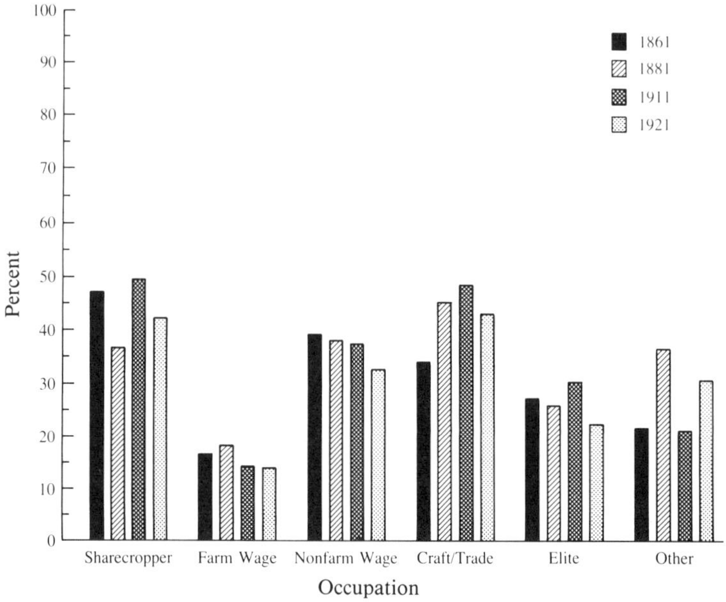

Fig. 5.2. Percent of Men Age 20–59 in the Census Year Who Were Born in Casalecchio, by Occupation

Approaches to Migration in Social History

The Importance of Migration

Our entire concept of community and social life rests on certain assumptions about residential stability. We now know, however, that previously accepted characterizations of the stable peasant community are erroneous, for numerous studies have documented the great population flux that marked much of western Europe in preindustrial times.[3]

Until recently the conventional demographic understanding of population mobility was based on the stage model of migration, in which migration is viewed largely in rural-to-urban terms and linked to the growth of capitalism. Migrants to the city come primarily from the area surrounding the city and their places are taken by migrants coming from more distant points. However, recent evidence indicates that high rates of migration *preceded* industrialization, and that much of this movement involved urban-to-rural and rural-to-rural migration. Far from being a geographically stable population in which peasants lived their lives from birth to death in the same community or even on the same farm, western Europe in the past was characterized by continuous population mobility. Only when the ruling elite could force peasants to remain on their land—as in parts of eastern Europe as late as the nineteenth century—was the traditional view of immobility borne out in fact. Indeed, rates of population mobility declined in many areas with the advance of capital development and urban growth.[4]

What seems to have changed in many areas is not the high rate of population mobility, but rather the extent to which long-distance mobility occurred. For example, the high rates of migration in Casalecchio during the mid-nineteenth century reflected the continual redistribution of populations within limited geographical areas, involving both temporary and circulatory migration. As the improved transportation systems linking Casalecchio to Bologna expanded the economic opportunity structure accessible to Casalecchio residents, the overall rate of population mobility declined, but involved a larger long-distance component.

A major theme of this chapter is that people in this part of Italy in the nineteenth and early twentieth centuries were not divided neatly into agriculturalists and industrial workers. Rather, they were part of a regional network of economic opportunities and constraints, a system of shared knowledge and ramifying kinship networks. Recall from chapter 3, for example, that the small town of Casalecchio had a higher concentration of industrial employment in the second half of the nineteenth century than the great city of Bologna, which was largely a market center. To understand the social order and people's lives in this historical context, our frame of reference must consider the relationships between the village and the city as well as other rural communities in the region.[5]

"The history of European migration," Charles Tilly writes, "is the history of European social life" (Tilly 1978b:68). The study of migration in European history provides not only evidence of the social forces that propelled people to move from community to community but also some insight into just what life in each of those communities must have been like. To understand the massive demographic changes and their relation to the social transformation of north-central Italy, we must recognize that we are studying a society in which people were continually on the move as the age stratification system, the vagaries of the labor market, and the dictates of family demography led to migration from community to community.

Accordingly, we view migration as a complex system which tied together various kinds of communities in a provincial network. Geographical mobility, rather than involving a disruption of ordinary social life for the individual or for the society, was part of the life-course experience of most people. Migration was crucial to the functioning of communities and is key to understanding social changes in those communities over time.

Limitations of Previous Historical Migration Studies

Studies of historical migration behavior in Europe and the United States have largely relied on cross-sectional data that do not capture the dynamic dimension of migration over a lifetime. Most commonly, migration is measured in the historical literature by birthplace information, leading to a division of the population into "natives" and "immigrants" (as done with census data in figs. 5.1 and 5.2). Sometimes, people from a larger area are examined and cross-categorized by their place of residence and their place of birth. Recognizing the limitations of this approach, some scholars have moved toward a longitudinal perspective by comparing successive censuses for a locality, thus dividing the population into "transients" and "persisters" or "movers" and "stayers."[6]

No matter how imaginative the researchers, these procedures severely limit the study of migration. The percentage of the population that is native born is determined by the rates of both immigration and emigration of natives. The persistence of immigrants in their new community also affects the percentage who are not native at any point in time. Some communities may have very high rates of immigration, with relatively short stays, whereas other communities may have lower annual rates of immigration but more successfully retain these new residents. Studies of migration that distinguish transients and persisters will produce accurate accounts of the volume of immigration and emigration if the periods between observations are brief. If such periods are longer (for example, ten years between censuses), many short-term immigrants will not be captured and periods of brief residence elsewhere by persons in the community will be missed.

Besides lacking accurate data on the actual volume of immigration and emigration, historical studies typically lack data on the origins of immigrants (place migrated from rather than birthplace) and the destinations of emigrants. This makes it difficult to assess the larger social and economic context of population mobility. Such data are critical to determine the extent to which migration represents the staged movement of people from rural to urban areas or the circulation of people between economically and socially similar areas. In some cases, migrants move to an area to establish a new, relatively permanent home, whereas in others they come to an area to work as a servant or wage laborer, or to find a bride, and return to their original places of residence afterwards.

To overcome these data limitations, a more direct data source must be employed to see who migrates, the frequency of migration, and its geographic characteristics. While studies of contemporary and recent migration patterns have increasingly employed longitudinal data sources—often based on retrospective residence histories—the necessary data are not so easily obtained for historical populations.[7]

Population Registers

Fortunately, population registers provide such data and exist for significant portions of western Europe, including Italy, in the nineteenth century.[8] Various kinds of population registers were begun in parts of northern Italy as early as 1802, but the population-register system was mandated nationally only with the emergence of the post-Unification government in the 1860s. Each commune was directed to undertake a census of its population and, on the basis of that census, to follow all changes in its population brought about by immigration, emigration, internal population movement, births, marriages, and deaths. Each administratively defined household and each individual were to be continuously followed and their changing characteristics recorded.

In the case of Casalecchio there was both a system of household folders and a system of individual registration cards with cross-reference to the successive household folders in which the individual could be found during his or her time in the commune. Each resident of the commune thus had his or her own data card in the register, as well as appearing as an entry in the household folder for each household in which he or she lived.

As part of the Italian population-register system there were also separate immigration and emigration registers. Each person or family group who entered the commune had to register with the communal authorities, at which time a listing of the individuals was made and transcribed into a new population-register entry. The individual or family group was also listed alphabetically in a year-by-year index of immigrants. When a person emigrated, the commune of immigration was obligated to make a copy of the immigration certificate and send it to the commune from which the individual emigrated. These certificates formed the emigration register of that commune, and the information was used to provide a dated closure for the individual's population-register entry. An alphabetically ordered emigration index was also compiled.

As described in more detail in the Appendix, the data base for this study of Casalecchio relies heavily on the population register of the commune, which is located in the archives of the Casalecchio municipal building. All population-register material for the period 1865–1921 was examined and among the information coded for each individual and entered into the data base were the following: individual's identification number, father's and mother's identification numbers, sex, birth date, birthplace, cause of entry into observation (present at beginning of population-register system in 1865; birth; immigration), place immigrated from and date of entry, marital status at entry, household entered, kin tie to household head at entry, cause of exit from commune (still present at end of observation in 1921; death; emigration), place emigrated to, and date of departure. A variety of other data sources has been used in compiling the data base, including manuscript censuses for the period (conducted in 1861, 1871, 1881, 1911, and 1921), civil and religious marriage records, conscription registers, and annual household tax lists.

Although the population register provides far richer data on migration than are available in most other historical sources, it is far from flawless. Of particular importance is the fact that in about 10 percent of the cases, emigrants from a commune are not immediately recorded as such in the population register.[9] However, using information on a person's enumeration in relevant censuses and on the annual presence or absence of a person's household in the tax list (along with data on changing household membership provided by sex and broad age grouping in this source), we have edited the population-register data to assign dates of exit for the cases missed by the register.[10]

Another limitation of the Italian population register is that it deals only with people who give up one residence and take up a new one. Short-term moves, such as seasonal labor migration, are not captured. This particularly affects our ability to trace the moves of servants who often remained but a few months in a household. However, comparisons of the population of Casalecchio enumerated in the censuses conducted independently of the population register indicate that the censused population missing from the population register was just 1.3 percent in 1871, 1.9 percent in 1881, 3.4 percent in 1911, and 2.5 percent in 1921. Examination of just who these missing individuals were reveals that a substantial proportion (ranging from 50 percent to 74 percent over the four periods) consisted of servants and other individuals (who were not servants) living in households of nonkin. These calculations indicate that the edited population-register data provide almost complete coverage of the population, with the exception of some highly transient young people.

Analyses of the population-register data can provide insights into migration patterns even for these highly transient groups. For example, 82 percent of male servants enumerated in the census of 1871 and 85 percent of those in the census of 1881 were found in the population register. The extent of their mobility is clear, with 41 percent of the male servants and other men unrelated to their household head who immigrated to Casalecchio from 1865 to 1915 departing within one year (Hogan and Kertzer

1985b). Clearly, the population register did record a large number of short-term moves, even among those groups in the population that are most difficult to capture. Nonetheless, it is well to keep in mind that in using the population register we focus on changes of residence that have a certain degree of permanence and that involve the crossing of municipal borders.[11]

Individual economic characteristics are not reliably reported in the population register.[12] By linking the annual household tax records (*focatico*) to the population-register records of individuals, however, we are able to measure the economic activities of the households (as indicated by the occupation of the household head) in which individuals lived for the period from 1869 to 1905.[13]

From 1869 to 1905 the population register recorded over 117,000 person-years of experience; 81 percent of these can be identified as a member of a household registered in the *focatico* in a particular year, and are assigned the economic characteristics of the household. A comparison of the *focatico* and population register indicate that migrants were somewhat underrepresented in the *focatico:* over this period 77 percent of the person-years of experience of persons migrating during that year were represented in the *focatico,* compared to 82 percent of those of the nonmigrants. However, these differences are not large and result in only a minor underestimation of the periods' rates of migration. The average annual emigration rate from 1869 to 1905 was 55 per 1,000 according to the population register, and 52 per 1,000 among persons recorded in the *focatico.* Thus, the *focatico* does not appear to be seriously biased as a data source for the study of economic differentials in migration.[14]

Population Mobility

Aggregate Patterns

We begin by using population-register data to calculate the number of immigrants and emigrants relative to the population of Casalecchio (expressed using the conventional rate of migrants per 1,000 people) each year. We then examine the age and sex composition of the immigrants and emigrants, and their places of origin and destination, in order to characterize the demographic impact of migration on Casalecchio's population structure. Rates of immigration and emigration for men and women classified by age group and according to the economic activities of their households are calculated to show differentials in migration over the life course and its family context. Finally, we characterize the larger geopolitical context of migration by examining the relationship between place of origin and place of destination for those immigrants to Casalecchio who later emigrated.

Magnitude and Rates. Annual rates of immigration and emigration are displayed in figure 5.3.[15] The rates of immigration and emigration increased substantially during the late 1860s and early 1870s, peaking in 1873 at about 125 immigrants and 115 emigrants per 1,000 residents. This is a remarkably high rate of population mobility. The rates of both immigration and emigration display a consistent downward trend for the next 50 years. The immigration rate was between 50 and 60 per 1,000 and the emigration rate was between 30 and 40 per 1,000 by the years immediately prior to World War I.

The immigration and emigration rates exhibit similar trends. Net migration (the difference between the immigration rate and the emigration rate) showed a modest positive balance (a gain of population due to immigration) in 1870–1876, 1882–1891, and 1906–1921. Net migration was negative (emigration exceeded immigration) for brief periods in the late 1870s and early 1900s. Despite the large volume of total migration, however, the magnitude of net migration tended to be quite low, rarely exceeding a gain of 20 per 1,000 or a loss of 10 per 1,000 per year.

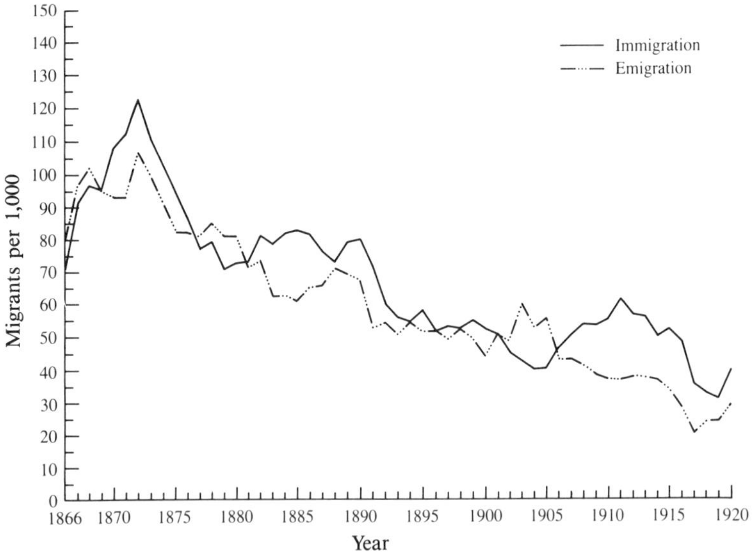

Fig. 5.3. Age-Standardized Three-Year Moving Averages of Annual Immigration and Emigration Rates: 1866–1920

In order to provide a more detailed analysis of the demographic composition and underlying social and economic causes of migration, we have divided the years from 1865 through 1921 into three broad time periods. The first period, 1865–1882, represents a relatively stable agricultural era, and one in which the hemp factory was becoming an established part of social life. A severe economic crisis, due largely to international factors, hit Italian agriculture from 1883 to approximately 1896, and the middle period was therefore a time of impoverishment. In the final period, 1897–1921, the walls of Bologna were torn down, the city spread out, and commercial and industrial activity expanded, leading to increased economic linkages between Bologna and Casalecchio. This period also saw improvements in the transportation system that permitted Casalecchio residents to work in Bologna, commuting on a daily basis rather than migrating to the city.[16]

During these three periods a total of 11,968 people immigrated to Casalecchio and 9,986 residents emigrated. During the period of agricultural stability the numbers of immigrants (3,205) and emigrants (3,116) were virtually equal. The number of immigrants then increased progressively (2,741 in 1883–1896 and 6,022 in 1897–1921), even though the immigration rate was declining. The number of emigrants declined during the agricultural crisis (2,296) and increased afterwards (4,574), even though the emigration rate declined steadily over the three periods due to the larger size of the community.

In the period of agricultural prosperity the average annual total number of immigrants and emigrants was 351, but the average number of net migrants gained annually by Casalecchio was only 5. During the agricultural crisis the average annual volume of migration was about the same (360 persons), but the number of immigrants exceeded emigrants by an average of 32 persons annually. Net migration grew to an average of 58 persons per year by the twentieth century, when the average year witnessed 424 migrants.

As described in chapter 3, the population of Casalecchio grew very slowly from 2,465 in 1865 to 2,870 in 1883. Only 22 percent of this small gain was due to migration. The pace of growth increased thereafter. The population grew to 3,586 by 1897, with 62 percent of this increase due to migration to Casalecchio during the period of agricultural crisis. By 1921 the population of Casalecchio had grown to 5,744 persons, and 67 percent of this population growth was due to net migration. Thus, the increased volume of net migration between the late nineteenth and early twentieth centuries was a major factor in the population growth of Casalecchio, and its impact on population size occurred at the same time as the total volume of migration relative to the population size (rate of immigration and emigration) declined.

Geographic Patterns. While population mobility was intense, migration typically involved short distances. To shed light on this pattern of mobility, we have divided the communities surrounding Casalecchio into three categories: the commune of Bologna, the five neighboring communes of the plains, and the four neighboring communes of the hills. The rest of the province of Bologna has been divided into two categories: the plain, and the hills and mountains. The neighboring province of Modena is distinguished from other remote points of migration.

Just how geographically limited this migration was is evident from the fact that more than 80 percent of the emigrants in each of the three periods went to the nearby plains or hills or to the commune of Bologna (fig. 5.4). Not only did overseas migration have virtually no impact on this part of Italy, but few of the people emigrating from Casalecchio during the nineteenth century (less than 7 percent) even left the province of Bologna, and many of those who did went to the neighboring province of Modena.[17] The geographic pattern of immigration to Casalecchio displayed the same general tendencies as observed for emigration from the community. During the period of major economic expansion, this pattern of intense but short-distance migration began to change—the rates of immigration and emigration declined substantially and the long-distance component

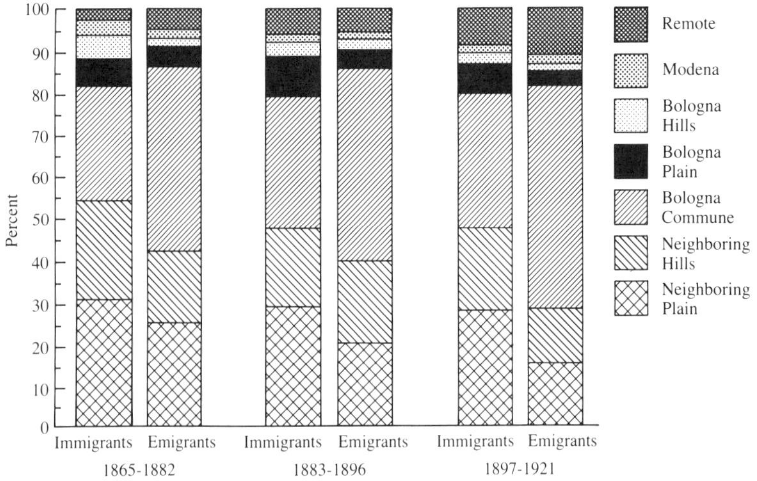

Fig. 5.4. Changing Geographic Patterns of Mobility: Casalecchio Immigrants and Emigrants

increased to 10 percent among immigrants and 12 percent among emigrants.

Population exchanges with Bologna were a major element of migration. During the initial period, 44 percent of the emigrants from Casalecchio went to the commune of Bologna, and this proportion remained about the same (46 percent) during the agricultural crisis. However, the city of Bologna became an increasingly important migration destination (53 percent) during the economic and urban expansion of the twentieth century. Yet, Bologna was not simply an important destination for emigrants from Casalecchio; some 28 percent of the immigrants to Casalecchio came from Bologna in our early period, increasing to one-third by the twentieth century.[18]

Age and Sex Selectivity. For most of this period the sexual composition of the immigrant and emigrant streams was similar. From 1865 to 1882 the sex ratio (number of males per 100 females) of both the immigrants and the emigrants was 113. Over time the immigrant stream began to involve somewhat more females than males (sex ratios of 102 in 1882–1896 and 94 in 1897–1921). During both the agricultural crisis and the period of urban expansion there were 95 males for every 100 female emigrants. These are relatively small differences, however. In general, it may be said that neither sex was predominant among immigrants or emigrants.

The migrants were disproportionately young persons. Throughout the period from 1865 to 1921, about one-quarter of the migrants were under age 12 and another 40 percent were between ages 12 and 29 (fig. 5.5). The

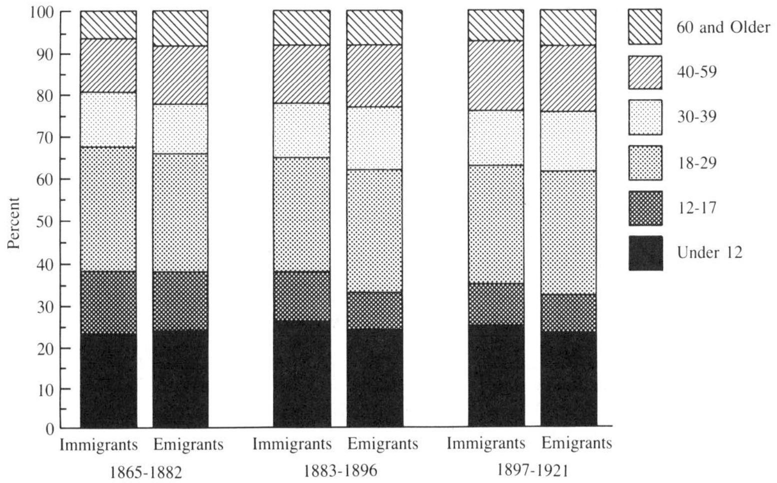

Fig. 5.5. Changing Age Composition of Migrants: Casalecchio Immigrants and Emigrants

age composition of migrants remained stable from 1865 to 1921, and there was virtually no difference in age composition between immigrants and emigrants in any of the three periods. There is little difference in the sex composition of immigrants and emigrants in each age group.

Service and the Family Situations of Emigrants. Sixty percent of men (age 10 and older) who immigrated to Casalecchio in 1865–1882 were single, with little change observed during the agricultural crisis.[19] After this, however, there was a marked decline (to 49 percent) in the percentage of men who were single at the time of migration to Casalecchio. The percentage of migrants who were married increased by a corresponding amount, from 35 percent to 47 percent.[20]

Much of this change is associated with the decline in service as a life-cycle stage among young males.[21] Between 1865 and 1882, 23 percent of immigrants to Casalecchio came as servants, a proportion which declined to 17 percent between 1883 and 1896. By the period of urban expansion (1897–1915), service as a life-cycle stage had essentially disappeared, with only 3 percent of the immigrants entering as servants.

Most other male migrants to Casalecchio either arrived as heads of their own households (40 percent in 1865–1882, increasing to 54 percent in 1897–1915) or as sons of household heads (26 percent, increasing to 33 percent). About 10 percent of the immigrants were tied to the head through other kinship bonds. Fewer than one in twenty immigrants were boarders (unrelated to the household head and not in service).[22]

Differentials in the Rate of Emigration

Demographic Differentials. We next ask how differences in the probability of emigration from Casalecchio are associated with life-course stage (age and marital status), position in the family economy (family economic stratum and relationship to household head), and previous migration experience.[23] We looked at annual migration rates for persons grouped according to these characteristics and examined the effects of these variables on the life-course emigration experiences of individuals.

The historical decline in the overall rate of emigration from 1865 through 1921 characterized males and females of every age (fig. 5.6). Over the three periods the average annual emigration rate (number of emigrants per 1,000) declined among males from 66 to 48 to 41, and among females from 64 to 54 to 44. There were few overall sex differences in the rate of emigration, though it was somewhat higher (6 per 1,000) for females during the agricultural crisis.

Within each time period, the highest rate of emigration is recorded for females between 18 and 29, the ages at which women typically married.

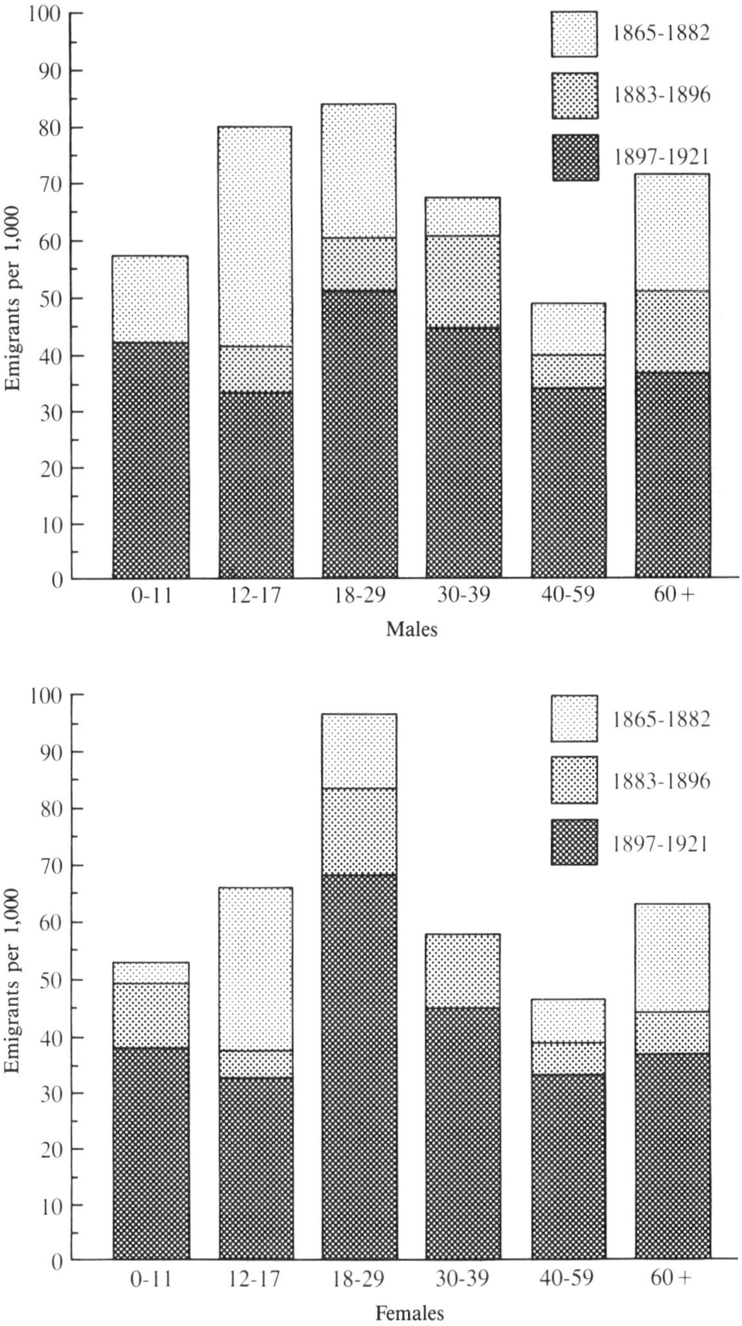

Fig. 5.6. Changing Rates of Emigration from Casalecchio, by Sex and Age

New brides frequently lived with their husbands' family, and emigration from Casalecchio would thus be the common result for a woman marrying a man from another commune. The high rates of emigration of both males and females aged 18–29 reflect the willingness of young persons to migrate in order to establish themselves economically and to begin their own families.

Among both men and women the greatest downward trend in the rate of emigration was recorded for persons aged 12–17. This sharp downward trend in emigration among young persons between the time of agricultural stability and the agrarian crisis was undoubtedly associated with the decline in service as a life-cycle stage, for servants showed high rates of migration. Declines in the rate of emigration were considerably less among adults and among the young children who migrated with them.

As noted above, the greatest sex differential in migration occurred during the years when women married, given the patrilocal norm of postmarital residence. One striking illustration of this difference is provided by a glance at the emigration pattern of people born in Casalecchio (fig. 5.7). As seen in this plotting of the hazard rate of emigration, there is little

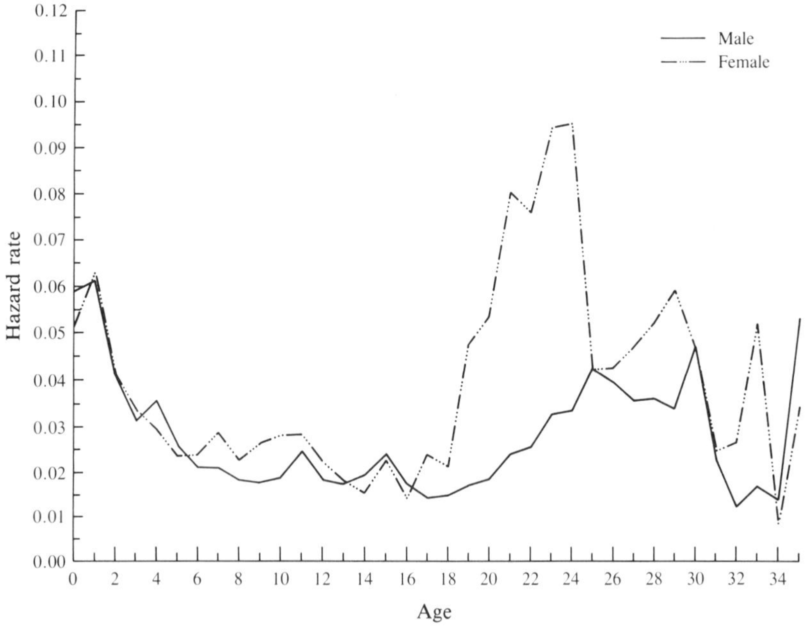

Fig. 5.7. The Hazard Rate of Emigration from Casalecchio for Natives Born 1865–1915, by Sex and Age

difference between males and females from birth through age 17.[24] From age 18 to age 23, though, females are increasingly migration-prone, a differential that declines over the next couple of years as the peak female marriage ages pass.

Economic Differentials. By matching the annual household tax data to the population register, we can identify differences in the rate of emigration (per 1,000 population) for the various economic subgroups of the population, classified according to the economic activity of their household for the years 1869–1905.[25] The elite had the highest annual rates of emigration (61), followed by the sharecroppers (55) and middle stratum (54), while members of the poor and wage-earner families had the lowest rates (45).[26]

During the earlier period (1869–1880) the sharecroppers and the members of the middle stratum were quite mobile (emigration rates of about 70), but this mobility declined sharply (especially among the sharecroppers) during the years of the agricultural crisis (fig. 5.8). The poor and wage-earner families were less mobile than other groups during the earlier period and became even more sedentary during the agricultural crisis. The rates of emigration converged during the early period of urban economic

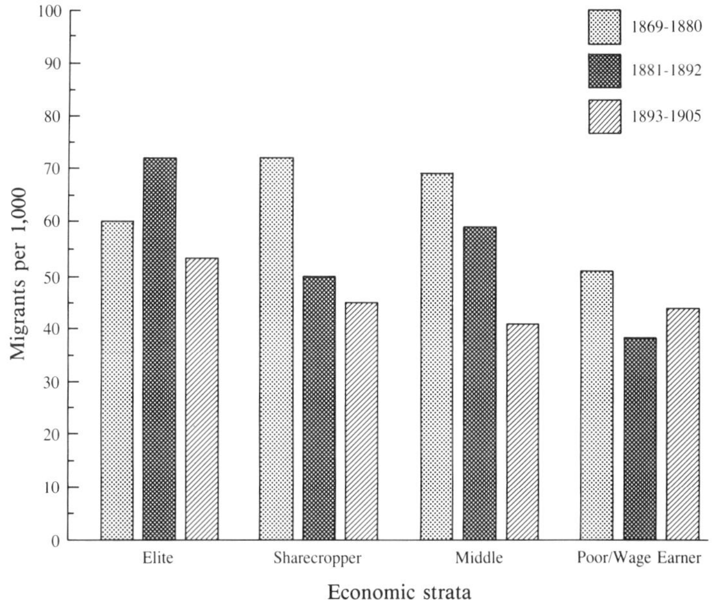

Fig. 5.8. Age-Standardized Changes in the Family Economic Pattern of Emigration

expansion, so that by 1893–1905 economic stratum (excepting the small elite group) had little impact on the probability of emigration.

The differences among family economic groups in propensity to migrate, and their relation to life-course factors, are shown in table 5.1, where male emigrants are examined for the years of the tax register (1869–1905). One is tempted to explain away the surprising mobility of residents of sharecropping households by pointing to the frequent presence of servants there. These servants were highly mobile and their frequent comings and goings could skew our results. But the servants in sharecropper households were largely aged 10–17, and this could not entirely explain greater sharecropper mobility at other ages. Even allowing for the presence of servants, clearly the sharecroppers were not especially stable; in particular, there is no evidence that sharecroppers were any less prone to emigrate than the proletarian workers—both agricultural and nonagricultural—who have commonly been viewed as much more likely to move.

These economic differentials in migration differed by sex as well as by life-course stage.[27] Among males, the rate of emigration was much higher among sharecroppers than among wage earners (60 vs. 42), with the elite and middle classes falling in between (56 and 53). By contrast, among the females rates of emigration were much more similar across the economic strata (54 among sharecroppers, 52 for the middle strata, and 47 for the

Table 5.1. Male Emigration Rate, by Age and Stratum: Selected Periods, 1869–1905

	Emigrants per 1,000 Age Group					
Period and Stratum	Under 10	10–17	18–29	30–39	40–59	60+
1869–1880	*	**	**			
Elite	34	54	58	71	42	33
Sharecropper	64	108	106	62	53	59
Middle	52	73	110	76	63	38
Poor/Wage	43	37	64	56	38	50
1881–1892		**	**	**	*	**
Elite	56	85	105	182	42	53
Sharecropper	32	79	74	55	34	55
Middle	52	52	86	51	53	28
Poor/Wage	38	26	46	52	30	17
1893–1905					**	
Elite	42	28	59	65	29	46
Sharecropper	31	33	56	49	50	41
Middle	45	30	55	42	28	44
Poor/Wage	44	28	58	55	30	29

*$p < .10$. **$p < .05$.

wage earners), with the exception of the small group of elite women for whom rates of emigration were especially high (62). The higher rates of emigration among elite men and women were recorded for the early adult years (18–39). The higher rates of emigration among sharecroppers were especially pronounced in the 10–17 age group during the period of agrarian prosperity, but this differential disappeared with the expansion of urban economic opportunities and the disappearance of servants from sharecropper households.[28]

Migration over the Life Course

The availability of migration histories from population-register data, along with recent innovations in methods for analyzing such data, permit us to go beyond these aggregate descriptions of migration and study emigration as a life-course phenomenon.[29] We used methods for the analysis of survival data to calculate the duration-of-residence-specific rates of emigration on the basis of the total population exposed to the risk of migration, including those individuals who do not migrate. An important feature of this procedure is that those who ultimately leave the population at risk through an event other than migration (such as death) are not ignored, but have their experience in Casalecchio counted as part of the calculation of migration rates.[30] These annual hazard rates can be cumulated to provide unbiased estimates of the percentages of persons who migrated by the end of each year of residence in Casalecchio.[31] More complicated methods permit the simultaneous consideration of the effects of several life-course characteristics on the hazard rate of emigration.[32]

Differences in the annual emigration rates of population groups cumulate year after year to produce major differences in the emigration experiences of individuals over their life course.[33] Of all persons observed in Casalecchio from 1865 to 1915 (including those present in 1865, born in Casalecchio, or migrating to Casalecchio), one-quarter emigrated within three years of initial observation. Only one-half remained for 11 years. Indeed, given the age-specific rates of emigration recorded during these years, a person entering Casalecchio in 1865 and remaining alive for 57 more years had only an 18 percent chance of remaining in Casalecchio through his or her lifetime. Thus, the life course of most persons residing in Casalecchio included a period of residence elsewhere.

Out-migration was fairly heavy even among Casalecchio natives. Thirty percent of the children born in Casalecchio left the commune prior to reaching age 11; another 9 percent left while aged 12–17, and 24 percent more left as young adults (ages 18–29). Although the emigration rates of both sexes were high, there were substantial differences between males and females in the probability of leaving Casalecchio over the lifetime. Of the females who were born in Casalecchio and survived, 63 percent had emigrated by age 25, compared to 48 percent of the males. Fewer than 21 percent of native females and 30 percent of native males who survived remained in Casalecchio from birth until age 45. These gender differences resulted from the patrilocal pattern of postmarital residence, where brides commonly left Casalecchio to move to their husband's hometown. Only one-third (32 percent) of the Casalecchio women who reached reproductive age (15 years) in the community spent their entire reproductive lifetimes (until age 45) in Casalecchio.

The median length of residence in Casalecchio for persons who entered in 1865–1915 was 21.7 years for native-born females and 26.0 years for native-born males.[34] This was substantially longer than the median stay of immigrants to Casalecchio. Even among those immigrants who came to Casalecchio as young children, the average length of stay in Casalecchio was 8.4 years for males and 10.3 years for females. For many of the child migrants (42 percent of the boys and 38 percent of the girls), the length of stay was less than five years.[35]

The rate of emigration declined substantially over time, and the higher male emigration rates converged with those of the females.[36] Although the rate of emigration decreased among Casalecchio immigrants of all ages, the biggest declines were recorded among adolescents and young adults.[37] This relates to the reduced proportion of young immigrants who came to Casalecchio for a period of service. It also suggests that Casalecchio was better able to retain its immigrants as new opportunities for youth employment were offered by the opening of factories and other commercial activities.

The rate of emigration was higher among immigrants to Casalecchio who came from distant locations. About 35–45% of the immigrants from the nearby plains and hills and from the commune of Bologna left Casalecchio within five years. By contrast, 50–60% of the migrants from the more remote hill and mountainous areas of the province of Bologna and from Modena departed within five years, and over 60 percent of the immigrants from other provinces did so.

Casalecchio thus recruited few immigrants from distant areas, and the stays of those who did come were relatively brief. Many of these immigrants from remote places left Casalecchio to return home (24 percent of those from Modena and 46 percent of those from other provinces).[38] However, of those immigrants to Casalecchio who eventually emigrated, about one-third of those who were originally from the remote provinces and almost one-half of those from Modena moved on to the city of Bologna (fig. 5.9).

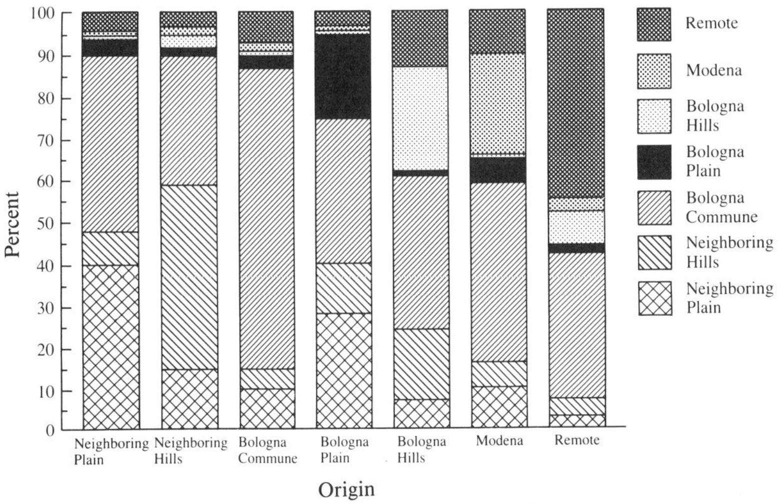

Fig. 5.9. Destination of Immigrants (1865–1915) Who Later Emigrate, by Place of Origin

These data provide substantial evidence of both stage migration (migration from a rural area to Casalecchio and on to Bologna) and return migration. One-third or more of the immigrants who came to Casalecchio from rural areas of Bologna and who subsequently left moved to the city of Bologna. Return migration was especially common among immigrants who had come very short distances (from the nearby plains or hills), and common (although somewhat less so) among immigrants from the more distant rural areas of Bologna. Of the 4,822 immigrants to Casalecchio who subsequently emigrated, 1,599 (33 percent) came from Bologna, and nearly three-quarters of these urban-origin immigrants to Casalecchio subsequently returned to the city.

The results of an analysis of the emigration destinations of men who immigrated to Casalecchio and subsequently left are presented in table 5.2. We have divided the male immigrants into those coming from rural areas in the Bologna/Modena area, those coming from the city of Bologna, and those coming from more distant points. We have concentrated on the first two categories, which account for 93 percent of the total.

We can divide the rural immigrants who later emigrated into those who returned to their area of origin, those who moved to a rural area other than the one they came from, and those who went to the city of Bologna. The immigrants from the city of Bologna are simply divided into those who returned to Bologna and those who went to any other destination. At the aggregate level these men's lives reflect the same two tendencies as

Table 5.2. Destination of Male Emigrants from Casalecchio, by Place of Origin and Characteristics at Entry (by percentage)

	Rural Origin Destination				Bologna Origin Destination			Remote Origin Destination		
Characteristics	Return	Circu-lation	Bologna	*N*	Return	Other	*N*	Bologna	Other	*N*
Total	40	26	34	(1,140)	74	27	(564)	38	62	(137)
Period of Entry										
1865–1882	44	25	31	(363)	70	30	(112)	20	80	(10)
1883–1896	38	31	31	(377)	71	29	(169)	33	67	(30)
1897–1915	38	23	39	(400)	76	24	(283)	41	59	(97)
Age at Entry										
10–17	42	27	32	(306)	71	29	(101)	47	53	(19)
18–29	38	27	35	(426)	73	27	(177)	28	72	(46)
30–39	38	28	35	(181)	73	27	(115)	32	68	(37)
40–59	45	22	34	(184)	73	27	(130)	48	52	(25)
60+	40	28	33	(43)	83	17	(41)	60	40	(10)
Marital Status at Entry										
Single	40	26	33	(751)	70	30	(273)	46	54	(54)
Married	40	26	34	(345)	77	23	(273)	32	68	(78)
Widowed	34	30	36	(44)	67	33	(18)	—	—	(5)
Kin tie at entry										
Household head	36	26	38	(354)	74	26	(266)	33	67	(78)
Son	36	26	38	(264)	73	27	(146)	44	56	(25)
Other kin	51	27	22	(77)	77	23	(39)	—	—	(7)
Nonkin	47	28	25	(276)	65	35	(37)	—	—	(6)
Unknown	39	22	39	(169)	72	28	(76)	48	52	(21)

Note: This table includes only emigrants who had previously immigrated to Casalecchio.

the population as a whole: a tendency to return to their area of origin (return migration) and a tendency to be attracted to the city of Bologna (which, for rural immigrants to Casalecchio, constitutes stage migration). Of course, in the case of immigrants from the city of Bologna, these two vectors (the pull of the city and the tendency to return to place of origin) coincide. The result is that three-quarters (74 percent) of all the male immigrants from Bologna who subsequently left Casalecchio returned to the city.

Over time the city of Bologna became an increasingly powerful magnet, with the expansion of the city in the beginning of the twentieth century. In the earlier period, 44 percent of the rural immigrants who subsequently left Casalecchio returned to their rural area of origin and just 31 percent moved on to the city. Yet by the early twentieth century (among men immigrating to Casalecchio in 1897–1915), as many went on to the city (39 percent) as returned to their previous rural area (40 percent). Likewise, the tendency of immigrants from the city to return to Bologna became even more pronounced, rising from 70 percent to 76 percent of those who left Casalecchio.

For the most part, the paths of migration were similar for men, regardless of age at entry. Among the immigrants from Bologna, however, we do see a somewhat greater tendency for married men to return to the city than is the case for single males (77 percent vs. 70 percent). No similar marital-status effect is found among immigrants from rural areas.

A person's kin relation to the household head is, of course, strongly related to age. Dividing the population by this criterion reveals an interesting pattern. Rural immigrants who entered households of their extended kin (in which neither they nor their parents were household heads) were more likely to return to their area of origin and less likely to move on to the city than were individuals who were either household heads or sons of heads. A similar pattern is found for those who entered a household headed by a nonkinsman, the great majority of these being servants. They too were more likely to return to their rural area of origin and less likely to move on to Bologna. This is undoubtedly related to the fact that young men in service circulated among rural households from year to year, with their skills in demand in the rural area. It is worth noting, in this regard, that only 12 percent of these servants came to Casalecchio from the city of Bologna, as opposed to 33 percent of the immigrants who came as sons of household heads. Thus, part of the decline in return migration in the rural sector over this period is due to the decline in the practice of service.

Alongside the traditional pattern of rural-to-rural migration, the city of Bologna had for many years been exchanging population with its hinterland. Rural-to-rural migration was complemented by a strong current of urban-to-rural migration. It had never been justified to speak in terms of an urban population as opposed to a rural population in the sense of two distinct groups with different subcultures, for in good part the people were the same, oscillating between rural and urban areas. What happened in the period of urban expansion was that this population exchange between the city and its hinterland became even more influential as the circulation of people among rural communities became less intense.

A variety of factors thus affected both the rates at which immigrants subsequently emigrated from Casalecchio and their destinations. These include age and marital status, place of origin, and kin ties in Casalecchio, as well as economic traits. Changes in these characteristics accounted, at least in part, for the declining volume of migration and the increased intensity of population exchange between Bologna and Casalecchio. To measure the relative contributions of these factors to the changing patterns of migration, we estimated a multivariate partial likelihood model of the determinants of the hazard rate of emigration for all male immigrants to Casalecchio who were age 10 and older at entry. We first identified the relative contribution of each factor to the overall rate of emigration. Then, to determine the effects of these factors on the increased population exchange with Bologna, we estimated a separate model that investigates the determinants of migration to the city of Bologna.

The results of these analyses are shown in table 5.3. For each model, a likelihood ratio chi-square statistic and degrees of freedom are calculated to indicate the statistical significance of the overall fit of the model. The independent variables are all categorical, with dummy variables indicating the particular characteristics of each immigrant. Categories with a coefficient of 1.00 were arbitrarily designated as comparison categories, with the dummy variable indicating membership in that category omitted from the model. The coefficients shown in the table are multipliers of the emigration rate associated with persons in the comparison category. A coefficient greater than 1.00 indicates that the rate of emigration for persons with that particular characteristic is higher than the hazard rate of the comparison group, whereas a rate smaller than 1.00 indicates that the rate of emigration is lower. For example, in model 1, which takes age and period of entry into account, the age group 40–59 is taken as the standard of comparison. Boys aged 10–17 have a coefficient of 1.24, meaning that they are 24 percent more likely to emigrate than the immigrants who arrived when they were aged 40–59. The statistical significance of the difference between the hazard rate of emigration of a group and that of the comparison group is indicated in the table by an asterisk.

Young persons have significantly higher emigration rates than men aged

Table 5.3. Effects of Selected Characteristics at Entry on the Rate of Emigration, Male Immigrants to Casalecchio (Partial Likelihood Proportional Hazards Models)

	Models of Emigration to any Destination			Model of Emigration to Bologna Commune
Characteristics	1	2	3	4
Age at entry				
10–17	1.24**	1.10	1.20	.89
18–29	1.32**	1.15*	1.14*	1.06
30–39	1.09	1.08	1.05	1.00
40–59	1.00	1.00	1.00	1.00
60+	1.05	1.08	1.08	1.25
Period of Entry				
1865–1882	1.00	1.00	1.00	1.00
1883–1896	.86**	.90*	.94	1.37**
1897–1915	.63**	.71**	.73**	1.38**
Marital Status at Entry				
Single		1.20**	1.20**	1.20*
Married		1.00	1.00	1.00
Widowed		1.08	1.13	1.06
Kin tie at entry				
Household head		1.00	1.00	1.00
Son		.86**	.90	1.04
Other kin		.71**	.75**	.63**
Nonkin		1.85**	2.00**	1.78**
Unknown		1.14	1.13	1.05
Place of origin				
Neighboring plain			1.00	1.00
Neighboring hills			.99	.76**
Bologna commune			1.37**	2.99**
Bologna plain			1.05	.95
Bologna hills			1.33**	1.82**
Province of Modena			1.09	1.71**
Remote regions			2.12**	2.31**
Unknown			1.69**	3.22**
Fit of Model				
Chi-square likelihood ratio	117.5	332.6	445.8	316.9
Degrees of freedom	6	12	19	19
Probability	.000	.000	.000	.000

Note: A coefficient of 1.00 indicates the omitted category.
$*p < .10$. $**p < .05$.

30–59, but there are no significant differences in the emigration rate of men 30 and over grouped by age (table 5.3, model 1). Over half of the higher emigration rate of young persons is due to the greater proportions who were unmarried and who were servants at the time of entry (table 5.3, model 2). After taking into account these other life-course variables, the emigration rate of persons 10–17 is only 10 percent higher than that of men 40–59, a difference that is not statistically significant. The emigration rate of men 18–29 is only 15 percent higher. These results should not be taken to mean that migration is not highly age-related; rather, they mean that the much higher rate of migration recorded among young persons in Casalecchio is largely accounted for by some of their life-course characteristics (i.e., young persons have not yet married and are more likely to be engaged in service).

The historical decline in propensity to migrate is evident here. The emigration rate of men entering Casalecchio in 1883–1896 is only 86 percent as high as that of men entering from 1865 to 1882, and the rate for men entering in 1897–1915 is even lower (63 percent as high). To some extent these declines in the emigration rate are associated with the changing composition of immigrants to Casalecchio. Taking these into account, there are no statistically significant differences between the emigration rates of people entering during the initial period and those entering in the subsequent period of the agricultural crisis. The decline in the rate of emigration between the first and second periods is associated with the declining proportion of young immigrants who came to Casalecchio as servants. Indeed, if we take into account the decline of service and the somewhat older age distribution and greater headship rates of immigrant men, the emigration rates declined (by one-quarter) only during the third period, as Casalecchio further developed a wage-based economy and the industrial jobs of urban Bologna became more accessible for daily commuters.

Even controlling for the effects of age and kin ties at entry, single persons have rates of emigration that are about one-fifth higher than those of married men. However, the emigration rates of widowed and married men did not differ significantly from each other. This is an indication of the resilience of the household system, in which loss of a wife does not entail demise of a household. When personal characteristics and place of origin are controlled, sons have emigration rates that resemble those of their coresidential fathers.

Intriguingly, immigrants to Casalecchio who lived in a nonparental kin household have emigration rates that are one-quarter lower than those of household heads. We interpret this as in part reflecting particularly low emigration rates of men who joined established households upon their entry to Casalecchio. In contrast, the men who entered as household heads or as the sons of heads typically have no history of household stability in the community. They were likely to have access to fewer sources of social and economic support. More generally, the lesser propensity of brothers, nephews, and grandsons of household heads to emigrate reflects the greater support available to them in such large, complex households. Note, however, that this conflicts with the common notion that such kinsmen would be more likely to migrate as they struggled to found their own households. Complex-family households in Casalecchio were, in fact, quite stable.

It is hardly a surprise that servants and other nonkin have rates of emigration that are twice as high as those of household heads. This reflects the short-term nature of service and the relative unavailability of other local employment opportunities and alternative household arrangements for men who entered this nineteenth-century agricultural community as household servants.

Men who migrated short distances to Casalecchio and those from the Bologna plain have relatively low rates of emigration. Persons from the city of Bologna have higher rates of emigration, as do those from the Bologna hills and mountains. Persons from remote regions have emigration rates more than twice as high as those of immigrants from the neighboring areas. These differentials in emigration rates are not surprising—immigrants to Casalecchio who were from an area that was economically and socially similar, especially one that was geographically proximate, were more likely to become stable members of Casalecchio. This observation remains true when we control for the period of entry and the life-course characteristics of the immigrants.

It might at first glance seem surprising that immigrants from the hills and mountains were more migratory than immigrants from the equally distant plains. Yet, there are reasons for this pattern. Although Casalecchio lies at the beginning of the hills, its social characteristics are more similar to those of the Bologna plain than to those of the mountainous area of the province. Moreover, although distances to the mountains and the plains may have been similar, the time required to travel the same distance could vary dramatically in the nineteenth century, depending on the terrain. The result was that migrants from the mountains were more cut off from their previous residence than migrants from the plains.

Having looked at the propensity of Casalecchio's male immigrants to emigrate, it is worth inquiring into their propensity for moving on to the city of Bologna. In examining the determinants of migration to the city, we have identified the extent to which immigrants with differing characteristics used Casalecchio as an intermediate stopping point in their migration to Bologna (table 5.3, model 4).

At the beginning of the twentieth century, the city of Bologna was becoming an increasingly prosperous commercial center. At the same time as Casalecchio's general emigration rate declined, the emigration rate to Bologna increased in the early years of the twentieth century by one-third over that observed in 1865–1882. Migration to and from Casalecchio came to involve less circulation mobility among rural areas and more of the rural-to-urban migration classically associated with modernization.

This historical shift differed significantly by some of the personal characteristics of the men. Although the overall emigration rate of men 18–29 years of age at entry is higher than that of older men (table 5.3, model 3), there are no significant age differences in the likelihood of a migrant to Casalecchio subsequently leaving for Bologna, if other life-course characteristics are taken into account. Young men were more frequently single, and single persons were somewhat (20 percent) more likely to emigrate to Bologna than married persons. Moreover, servants have substantially higher (78 percent) rates of emigration to Bologna.[39] This suggests that household service in Casalecchio was an important mechanism by which young persons of modest backgrounds and rural origins could migrate to the city.

Return migration to Bologna occurred at three times the rate at which persons from the rural plains emigrated to Bologna. Casalecchio appears to have been used as an intermediate step in migration to the city for persons who had to travel considerable distances to that destination (those from the Bologna hills, Modena, and remote regions). However, Casalecchio was not a stage in the migration process for persons from neighboring plains or hill areas or from the Bologna plains. For these persons direct migration to Bologna was available.

This life-course analysis of emigration provides no direct test of the effects of changes in the family economy on increased migration to Bologna; the population register lacks systematic, longitudinal economic data. To solve this problem, we used the *focatico* files to calculate the annual rate of emigration to Bologna for immigrant men who were age 10 and older when they came to Casalecchio, classified according to the economic activity of the head of their household (see fig. 5.10). The emigration rate of sharecroppers to Bologna remained quite stable (at about 11–14 per 1,000 annually) throughout the period covered by the *focatico* (1865–1905). Immigrant men who came to Casalecchio as part of the middle economic stratum were considerably more likely than sharecroppers to move on to Bologna, and their rate of emigration to Bologna did not change greatly over time. Poor wage earners who migrated to Casalecchio were more likely

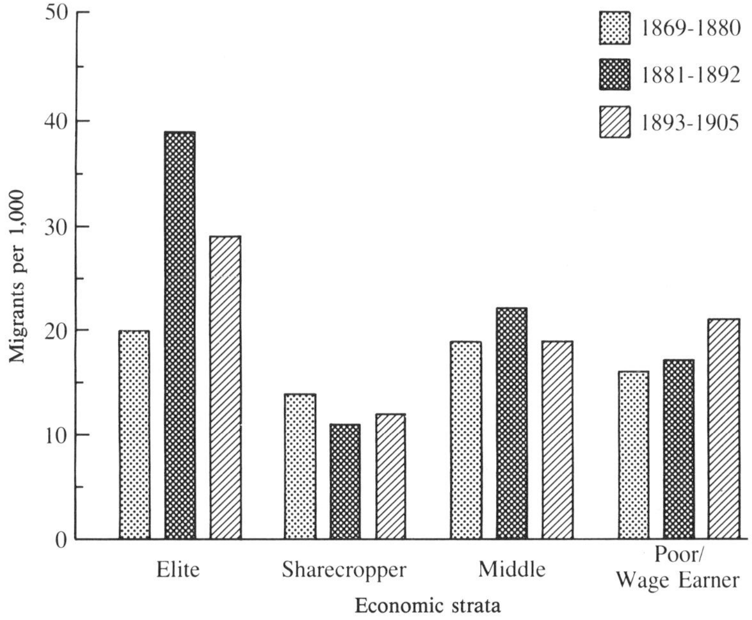

Fig. 5.10. Changing Family Economic Pattern of Emigration from Casalecchio to Bologna: Immigrant Men Age 10 and Older

to migrate to Bologna than sharecroppers, but their rate of emigration to Bologna was lower than that of the middle stratum until the 1893–1905 period. Though their rate of emigration to Bologna fluctuated from one period to the next, the elite had higher rates of emigration to Bologna than any other group.[40]

Thus the wage earners were the only stratum in which the rate of emigration to Bologna increased over time. This is also the stratum that was becoming increasingly dominant among immigrants to Casalecchio. The representation of wage earners among immigrant men increased from 45 percent in 1869–1880 to 53 percent in 1893–1905. Changes in the family economy of Casalecchio (specifically, the deteriorating economic situation of the wage earners and their increasing numbers in the Casalecchio population) provided an economic impetus for increased migration to Bologna during the later part of the nineteenth century. Yet, this migration to Bologna leveled off in the twentieth century as the increased number of wage-earner positions in Casalecchio industry provided more local jobs and the improved transportation system permitted people who might formerly have migrated to commute to their daily jobs in Bologna.

6 Children and the Family Economy

Although vivid popular images of the effects of European industrialization on childhood abound, the actual nature of this impact is still not well documented. Indeed, one scholar charges that the whole historiography of childhood is "dominated by myths" (Pollock 1983: viii). The legacy of industrialization is typically seen against a baseline portrait of the wholesome farm environment, with children pitching in alongside their parents and siblings. This bucolic scene is contrasted with the horrors faced by the small child who, with grease-streaked face, is closed in a sweltering, foul factory for twelve hours or more each day, six days a week. Common, too, is the image of the beleaguered toddler, whose mother, instead of remaining on the family farm to care for her offspring, must go off to the textile factory for seventy or more hours each week, leaving her children to fend for themselves. And these children, rather than romping over the verdant fields of the family farm, remain in a dank, tiny apartment, surrounded by strangers, not kinsmen.

According to one account picked up by numerous historians, the "reign of the machine" entailed the transformation of children's work to conditions of slavery. Radbill (1968) thus writes of "child martyrs to industry," whose living conditions he describes in chilling terms:

> Children from five years of age upward were worked sixteen hours at a time, sometimes with irons riveted around their ankles to keep them from running away. They were starved, beaten, and in many other ways maltreated. Many succumbed to occupational diseases, and some committed suicide; few survived for any length of time. (12)

Nor is it difficult to find contemporary accounts by social reformers telling blood-curdling tales of life in the factories. Typical of this school are the comments of Richard Oastler, a British reformer of the nineteenth century, who spoke of child factory workers as "sacrificed at the shrine of avarice, *without even the solace of the negro slave*."[1]

Historians who have dared to question this view of the role of the advent of factory labor in the history of childhood have been the object of virulent attack. E. P. Thompson (1963), whose work on childhood and industrialization continues to be influential after a quarter century, writes menacingly of a suspected "conspiracy to explain child labour away" (332). He castigates those who downplay the novelty of child-labor exploitation in the factories. While willing to admit that children had always been put to work from a young age, and that aspects of this nonfactory work were often arduous, Thompson claims that there was a major difference in child labor before industrialization, namely, that "the work was within the family economy and under parental care" (334). "The crime of the factory system," Thompson writes, "was to inherit the worst features of the domestic system in a context which had none of the domestic compensations" (335). Admonishing the revisionists who would deny the dramatic worsening of children's lives represented by the coming of factory labor, Thompson states: "We may be allowed to reaffirm a more traditional view: that the exploitation of little children, on this scale and with this intensity, was one of the most shameful events in our history" (349).

Although no one would want to deny the inhumane conditions in which many children worked in European and American factories in the nineteenth century, satisfactory historical understanding of the significance of factory labor and, more generally, of related processes of urban expansion and the movement out of agriculture, requires a different perspective. The danger is that in their zeal to denounce the evils of industrialization for children's lives, scholars promote an overly romantic portrait of childhood in preindustrial times, while failing to grasp some of the positive implications of industrialization for children's lives.

Recent studies, for example, have shown how widespread protoindustrial, home-based manufacture was in earlier centuries in many parts of Europe. In such a system children were often given laborious work to perform for long hours in adverse conditions, albeit alongside other family members. Indeed, Medick (1981) concludes that "infants and children turn out to be the true victims of the proto-industrial system" (88).[2]

Nor was life in the agricultural world necessarily pleasant for children. We do not have to go so far as DeMause (1974), who argues that the "history of childhood is a nightmare from which we have only recently begun to awaken" and that the "further back in history one goes, the lower the level of child care, and the more likely children are to be killed, abandoned, beaten, terrorized, and sexually abused" (1). Yet, we must recognize that in the preindustrial period the wholesome, family-owned farm cannot be assumed to be the norm. Even many of those families who owned some farmland were too poor to provide adequate support for their children, while in many areas of Europe a large portion of the rural population owned no land.

In such settings of rural poverty children were commonly expelled from the parental home at an early age to be taken in as servants in the homes of others, often outside the communities where their parents lived. In earlier centuries in England, but also in France and Italy and elsewhere, it was not uncommon for children to be extruded from their parental families and sent to work elsewhere before reaching their tenth birthday. In any case, after age 10, increasing proportions of children were forced out of their parental home.

The best-known scholarly portrait of the transformation of childhood in the European past is Ariès' (1962) *Centuries of Childhood.* Throughout the medieval period, Ariès argues, children were treated essentially as little adults; they spent little of their time with their parents, for they went out to work as servants or apprentices at an early age. Moreover, the family provided little of the emotional support for which it would later become known. In Ariès' view, the "modern" European family first arose among the wealthier classes in the seventeenth century, with children bound more closely to their parents and the family becoming the focus of emotional life and allegiances. This was a change that, according to Ariès, spread only slowly down to the lower classes in the nineteenth century.

More recently, Stone (1977) and Shorter (1975) have offered somewhat different interpretations of these trends, but they agree in plotting an essentially unidirectional transformation of a patriarchal family system in which parent-child relations were distant to a system in which emotional bonds between parent and child were cultivated and stressed.[3] If this scenario is to be credited, one would expect the situation of children to have improved during the time of industrialization. Rather than undermining the child's position in the family, the period of industrialization would have strengthened it.

The Ariès scenario has the virtue of stressing the importance of changes that took place before the advent of industrialization, and thus gets us away from the traditional view of an unchanging rural peasant society transformed by an industrial "revolution." However, the changes taking place in Bologna in the eighteenth and nineteenth centuries were not entirely in the direction described by Ariès, and important changes in the nature of childhood occurred in the late nineteenth century, long after Ariès' modern-family stage had presumably been reached.

One of the most significant changes for the lives of children in the late 1800s was the substantial fall in infant mortality. Many more infants were surviving the first year of life, a demographic development with far-reaching social implications. Indeed, some scholars relate this change not only to subsequent declines in fertility but also to a strengthening of emotional bonds between parents and children. We therefore turn first to an examination of this drop in infant mortality, concentrating especially on the question of just how this improvement spread through the various segments of the Casalecchio population. We then look at the household context in which children lived, inquiring especially into any changes that occurred in the family context in which children were socialized. Finally, we inquire into the changing economic roles of children in this period, including the decline in service as a life stage and the impact of factory labor on children's lives.

Infant Mortality

For countless centuries in Italy, as elsewhere, death was as much associated with small children as it was with the elderly. Indeed, throughout these centuries at least half of all the people who died were under age five. Thus, giving birth and raising small children commonly entailed facing the sad fate that awaited so many of them. Indeed, over a third of all babies died within their first year in the area around Casalecchio in the seventeenth century, a proportion that declined to one in four by the first half of the nineteenth century. The rapid decline in infant mortality came only in the latter part of the nineteenth century, ushering in, for the first time in history, a society in which infant death would become a rarity.[4]

This pattern is evident in Casalecchio, where the probability that an infant would survive to his or her first birthday improved dramatically between the mid-nineteenth and early twentieth centuries. Indeed, while one of every five infants died within their first year in the 1870s, infant mortality declined to just one of fourteen infants dying by 1910–1914.[5]

Improvements in infant survivorship benefited families from all economic classes (table 6.1), although the greatest improvements were among the elite and the artisan and merchant families.[6] In 1869–1880, about 14 percent of infants born to elite families and 20 percent of infants born to families in all other economic classes died during their first year. By the turn of the century, children born into elite families had a very low probability of dying before reaching age one (none of the 34 babies born to elite families died).[7] By comparison, infant death claimed 10 percent of the children of sharecroppers and 14 percent of those of the wage earners and poor.

These differentials in infant mortality lessened as Casalecchio developed

Table 6.1. Percentage of Infants Born in Casalecchio Dying by Age One and Age Five, by Family Economic Stratum and Time Period

	By Age One			By Age Five		
Economic Stratum	1869–1880	1881–1892	1893–1905	1869–1880	1881–1892	1893–1905
Elite	14	0	0	23	5	3
Sharecropper	19	14	10	28	20	18
Middle	20	15	6	35	26	15
Poor/Wage	22	17	14	40	34	25

a wage-based economy and the lot of wage workers improved. By the second decade of the twentieth century, the infant mortality of all groups declined to around 7 percent.[8]

Even if infants born to wage-earner families survived their first year, their chances of surviving to age five were markedly inferior. In 1869–1880 only 77 percent of the wage-earner children who reached age one survived to their fifth birthday, compared to 88 percent of the sharecropper children. This differential actually grew somewhat during the agricultural crisis, with 80 percent of the wage-earner children and 93 percent of the sharecropper children surviving from age one to age five. Following the agricultural crisis and the development of a full-fledged wage economy, these differences largely disappeared; by 1893–1905, 88 percent of the wage-earner children and 91 percent of the sharecropper children survived from age one to age five.[9]

As described above, the wage earners in Casalecchio in the nineteenth century often lacked adequate food, clothing, and shelter. While their rates of infant mortality were high, these families were somewhat able to insulate their children from their extreme poverty as long as breast milk was a major source of nourishment. Yet, as the children got older and were weaned, they shared more directly in their family's poverty. Adequate food was lacking and housing conditions were unsanitary. Malnourished children were especially susceptible to disease, and often died. Moreover, there was less likely to be an adult at home during the day to provide child care.

Such an interpretation is consistent with the widening of child mortality differentials between sharecroppers and wage earners during the agricultural crisis, which hit wage earners with special force.[10] Only after the agricultural crisis, as the living conditions of wage-earner families improved, did the survival chances of the children of the poor begin to resemble those of the other classes.

Taken together, the rates of infant and child mortality prevalent in Casalecchio during these times are a stark reminder of the uncertain demographic conditions that faced all members of the population, save for the very privileged classes. In 1869–1880, only 66 percent of the children born to sharecropper families survived to age 15. This number increased, but only to 79 percent by the turn of the century. For the children of the wage laborers and poor, the situation was dismal indeed: only 57 percent of the children born to these impoverished families in 1869–1880 survived to age 15. Even by 1893–1905 only 74 percent of the children of wage laborers lived long enough to celebrate their fifteenth birthday.

Where Children Lived

Until the mid-nineteenth century, when sharecropping still dominated Casalecchio and the hills and plains of Bologna, most children grew up in large households with their parents, siblings, grandparents, uncles, aunts, and cousins. If this is the household of Western romantic nostalgia, as Laslett once called it, it is not simply a myth of a past gone by, but an accurate portrait of family life in sharecropping Italy. Prior to this revisionist work, it had been claimed that industrialization meant wrenching children out of a multiple-family environment in which they were surrounded by kin, and leaving them in the more individualistic context of the nuclear family. This older view remains worthy of investigation in this part of western Europe, where children were indeed living in complex households at the time industrialization got under way.[11]

Before looking at the kin contexts in which the children of Casalecchio resided, we set the stage by considering the changing household economic contexts in which they lived during this period. In 1861, almost half of all Casalecchio children lived in sharecropper households, a proportion that gradually declined to just a quarter by 1921. The reverse is seen in the nonagricultural wage sector. Just a quarter of the children of Casalecchio lived in households headed by a nonagricultural laborer at the beginning of the period, but over 40 percent did so by the end of the period. For the most part, there was considerable constancy in the household economic circumstances of the other portions of the population (table 6.2).

It is striking that at both ends of the period over a quarter of the small children (under five years old) lived in households headed by their grandfathers (table 6.3). In other words, at the time of their birth, the children's mothers lived as daughters-in-law of the household head and their fathers did not head their own households. But during this time of great social changes, there was a movement toward being born into a household headed by one's father (the proportion rising from 55 percent in 1861 to 65 percent in 1921). This came at the expense, then, not of living in a three-generation household; rather, it was linked to a decline in the proportion of small

Table 6.2. Children Under Age 18 by Occupation of Household Head, 1861 and 1921 (by percentage)

	Year	
Occupation	1861	1921
Sharecropper	45	24
Agricultural wage	12	10
Nonagricultural wage	24	41
Artisan/Merchant	10	11
Elite	5	8
Other	4	6

children living in households headed by a kinsman other than their parent or grandparent, and a drop in those living with nonkin. The decline in the latter category reflects the end of the practice of shipping Bologna foundlings out to wet nurses in Casalecchio.[12]

As children got beyond the toddler stage they still stood a good chance of living in households headed by their grandfathers, although the majority throughout the period lived in homes headed by their parents. As sharecroppers declined as a proportion of the population, the proportion of children living in households headed by their fathers' brothers and other kin also declined, for this is an arrangement characteristic of the sharecropping household of coresident married brothers.

One of the major changes in childhood to occur in these years involved children over age 10. In the earlier years, many children from poorer households left their parental home at this stage of their lives and found lodging as servants or apprentices in the homes of others. In 1861, for example, 15 percent of all Casalecchio children aged 10–14 lived in households headed by nonkin, but this proportion fell to just 3 percent by 1921. Similarly, 22 percent of the older children (ages 15–18) lived with nonkin in 1861, the proportion declining to 9 percent by 1921. Along with this change, the proportion living in households headed by extended kin declined. The proportion of older children living in households headed by their parents increased substantially as a result. This is seen most dramatically in the 15–18 age group. Just half of these older children had lived in parent-headed households in 1861, while three-quarters of them did so by 1921.

We find a mixture of expected and unexpected results in examining the household context of children in this period of change. The kind of urbanization and industrialization experienced by Casalecchio led to an increase in children remaining in the family home, not to the breaking up of the family that has so often been theorized. Despite the sharp decline

Table 6.3. Relationship of Children to Household Head, by Age of Child: 1861 and 1921 (by percentage)

	Age of Child and Year							
	Ages 0–4		Ages 5–9		Ages 10–14		Ages 15–18	
Relationship to Head	1861	1921	1861	1921	1861	1921	1861	1921
Child	55	65	61	72	61	76	53	77
Grandchild	27	28	24	19	12	14	6	6
Other kin	12	5	12	7	12	7	14	9
Nonkin	6	2	3	2	15	3	22	9

in the agricultural sector of the population, children were as likely to be born into households headed by their grandfathers at the end of the period as at the beginning. However, at the same time, nuclear-family composition increasingly characterized the households in which the people of Casalecchio spent their early years.

A more sensitive view of the changes taking place in the coresidential circumstances of children in this period is provided by dividing the children by the economic characteristics of their households. Here, as seen in table 6.4, a rather different picture emerges. Only a minority of children aged 0–18 in sharecropping households lived in households headed by their parents; a larger proportion of sharecropper children lived in households headed by their grandfathers or uncles. Thus, the changes that took place in Casalecchio during these 60 years had little effect on the principles of household formation and kin organization in the sharecropping sector.

Interestingly, while children of agricultural wage laborers always tended to live in nuclear households, this proportion actually declined somewhat in this period, with the proportion of children living in households headed by their grandfathers increasing substantially, to 23 percent in 1921. This is partly because the occupation of *bracciante* was becoming increasingly an occupation of the older segment of the community. Yet it also reflects the fact that the young children of the *braccianti* were no longer being sent out of the parental household and thus were more likely, at marriage, to be still living with their parents. Hence, they were more likely to be living with one or both parents when their own children were born. Meanwhile, increased longevity made it more likely that the grandparents would still be alive.

A different pattern emerges when we look at the nonagricultural segment of the community. In each of the three occupational categories examined—the elite, artisans and merchants, and nonagricultural wage laborers—the proportion of children living in nuclear-family households

Table 6.4. Children's Relation to Household Head by Occupation of Head: 1861, 1881, and 1921 (by percentage)

	Sharecropper			Agric. Wage			Elite			Artisan/Merchant			Nonagric. Wage		
Relation	1861	1881	1921	1861	1881	1921	1861	1881	1921	1861	1881	1921	1861	1881	1921
Child	38	33	41	79	79	70	57	71	78	74	75	86	74	83	87
Grandchild	29	30	40	9	10	23	8	15	8	10	10	5	11	9	7
Sibling's child	15	21	10	3	0	0	16	3	0	3	4	1	1	1	1
Other	18	17	10	8	11	7	20	12	14	12	11	7	14	8	5
N	(452)	(463)	(539)	(117)	(167)	(223)	(51)	(75)	(170)	(97)	(114)	(252)	(243)	(343)	(895)

increased over the period. In all categories, the proportion of children in households headed by their grandparents or other kin was under 10 percent by 1921. Among the elite, the practice of keeping young domestic servants resulted in a substantial proportion of coresiding children who were not related to the household head. Among artisans, merchants, and nonagricultural wage-worker households, the proportion of children living in households headed by their parents rose from 74 percent in 1861 to about 87 percent by 1921.

To go beyond these aggregate figures to get some idea of what life was like for children from *bracciante,* sharecropping, and nonagricultural wage-laborer families, we look in detail at the experiences of three girls born in Casalecchio within a year of one another in 1869–1870. These brief individual life histories not only show the patterns of extended kin coresidence that marked this area, but also take us beyond the general patterns to see just how important the demographic forces of birth and death were for individuals' experiences.

Growing Up in a *Bracciante* Household

Enrica Benini's parents were still children when they moved to Casalecchio from neighboring communes in the 1840s. At her birth, in 1869, both of Enrica's parents were in their mid-forties, and she had two coresident brothers, aged 20 and 7, as well as a five-year-old sister. Both her father and her eldest brother worked as *braccianti,* farm wage laborers. When she was three, her eldest brother married and brought his wife into the household. Within the year, Enrica's sister-in-law gave birth to a daughter, but the little girl died shortly before her second birthday. Over the next fifteen years, until Enrica left the household at age 18, she was joined by a succession of three other nieces, one of whom died within three days of birth. In the meantime, when Enrica was just four, her 74-year-old grandmother (her father's mother) moved into the household, living there until her death four years later. The grandmother had joined her son's household following her husband's death in a mountain commune in the province of Bologna. Three years before Enrica's departure, her middle brother was married and he, too, brought his wife into the household. The newlyweds had a daughter just before Enrica, at age 18, married a man from the city of Bologna and moved with him to the neighboring rural commune of Castelmaggiore. Throughout her childhood, Enrica's father and eldest brother worked as *braccianti.* Her middle brother, meanwhile, found occasional work as a bricklayer, while her sister worked in the hemp factory. Although direct evidence is lacking, it is likely that Enrica, too, spent part of her childhood working in the factory along with her sister.

Growing Up in a Sharecropping Household

Amalia Ramini, like so many children born into sharecropping households, found herself surrounded by an assortment of young and old kinsmen. She was her parents' first child, born in 1870, just a year after their marriage. A year before her birth, the household had moved from the rural periphery of the commune of Bologna to Casalecchio. Though she did not yet have any siblings, she shared her home with not only her parents but her father's parents and her grandfather's widowed brother, her father's two married brothers and their wives, along with their four children, and her father's unmarried brother. Amalia's grandfather was head of the household, overseeing his three married sons and their children, along with his unmarried son and his widowed brother. In addition, they always had at least one, and often two or three, agricultural servants living with them.

The older generation died off when Amalia was young, her grandfather's brother dying when she was two and both her grandparents dying the following year. During these early years, she was joined by a succession of brothers, Luigi, Mauro, and Cleto, born by the time she was five years old. At age six, her bachelor uncle married and brought his wife into the household, and two daughters were born to them within a two-year period.

Disaster befell the family of her uncle Raffaele, who had had the good fortune of having four sons born between 1866 and 1875. In November of 1875, their six-year-old son died, followed the next month by Raffaele's wife, Angela. Whether this was due to a contagious disease we do not know. Angela left a four-month-old baby when she died and, without his mother to nurse him, the infant Giuseppe succumbed at age eleven months. We do not know if Amalia's mother, who had given birth to one of Amalia's brothers ten weeks before Giuseppe was born, nursed Giuseppe in the interim, though this is likely.

By 1878, when a split in the household occurred, Amalia lived with her parents, her three brothers, three uncles, two aunts, and seven cousins. This was a point when sharecropper households often split, both because the older generation was gone, leaving the married brothers and sisters-in-law to struggle over proper lines of authority, and because there were beginning to be too many mouths to feed on the same farm. Thus, in 1878, at the expiration of their contract year, Amalia's father and his younger brother, Giacomo, left the farm with their wives and children and acquired a contract for another sharecropped farm in Casalecchio, leaving the two other married brothers and their families on the old farm.

In the new household Amalia was joined over the next nine years by two more sisters, though one, born in 1881, died before her second birthday. She was also joined by four cousins, children of her uncle Giacomo, one of whom died in infancy. These were not to be good years for Amalia. Her mother died when Amalia was just 12 years old, and her father died two years later, in 1884. This left Amalia, her three brothers, and one surviving sister as orphans, dependent on their uncle Giacomo, who took over from his deceased brother as household head. In this altered context, Amalia's younger sister left the household at the age of eight, just six months after her father's death, presumably to join other relatives in the neighboring rural commune of Borgo Panigale. Three years later, Amalia followed suit, leaving Casalecchio at age 17.

Growing Up in a Proletarian Family

Ersilia Cuppini was born in 1869, within a year following her parents' marriage. Her father, Vincenzo, had been born in Casalecchio in 1844, while her mother, Giulia, was born in neighboring Zola Predosa and had moved with her parents to Casalecchio in the early 1860s, with her father working as a *bracciante*. At marriage, Giulia had moved into Vincenzo's parental home, where she joined her husband's father, mother, and two unmarried brothers. Vincenzo, his father, and his two brothers all worked at the hemp factory. Over the first nine years of Ersilia's life she was joined by a variety of other relatives. Near her fourth birthday, one of her father's brothers married, bringing both his wife and her 23-year-old unmarried brother into the household. Within the next year two babies, a sister and a cousin, joined the household, followed, when Ersilia was seven years old, by another cousin. Throughout this period the men of the family continued to work at the hemp factory.

Just before her ninth birthday, Ersilia's parents decided to move into their own home, elsewhere in Casalecchio, taking their two daughters with them. Her father continued his hemp factory work, but her parents had no more children. She continued to live with them until, at age 20, she moved by herself to the city of Bologna, where she presumably found work. There she met the man whom she married, returning to Casalecchio, where her husband got a job at the hemp factory, when she was 23. Unlike her own parents, Ersilia and her husband immediately established their own household, where their first child was born. But within days of her child's birth, Ersilia's husband died, leaving her a widow at age 27. Her own mother, a neighbor in Casalecchio, had herself been widowed six years earlier, shortly after Ersilia had gone off to Bologna. Thus, while Ersilia lived alone with her own newborn, her mother and sister lived by themselves nearby. Nine years later, in 1905, when Ersilia's sister married a man from Bologna, all of them moved to the city: Ersilia, her daughter, her mother, and her newly married sister.

The Decline of Service as a Life Stage

One of the hallmarks of childhood in much of preindustrial Europe was the departure of children from their parental home at an early age to join another household as a servant or apprentice. McBride estimates that in the nineteenth century a third of all French girls worked as servants. In 1880, she reckons, one of every six French households employed at least one servant. In France, much of this employment involved bringing girls from rural areas to the city. In England, service was a common experience, antedating the mass migration of rural dwellers to the cities, and characterizing a large portion of the rural population—both male and female—in the preindustrial period. Schofield's study of the English agricultural village of Cardington, in the East Midlands in 1782, gives us a glimpse of this pattern. There, boys began entering service after age 10 and by their late teens four out of five of them no longer lived at home, being out in service. Their sisters, meanwhile, were more likely to spend their childhood at home, for they could be put to work in lace making and textile spinning. Thus, in the 15–19 age range, 71 percent still lived with their parents (McBride 1974:63–64; Schofield 1971).[13]

Service was common in both rural and urban Italy in preindustrial times. It was responsible for the movement of both boys and girls out of their parental homes and meant that a large proportion of children from poorer families spent much of their youth outside their own family context. Service took two major forms. One, associated with sharecropping, involved a circulation of children primarily from *braccianti* or impoverished sharecropping households to work on sharecropped farms where they lived in the household of the host sharecroppers. Such youths were termed *garzoni* and were not domestic servants but, rather, worked primarily in the fields, barns, and chicken coops. Boys were heavily favored for this work. Employment was often short-term, not infrequently under a year, so that the same farm typically had a succession of servants over the years, while a youth might move annually from farm to farm, able to get more compensation as he grew older.

Wealthier households, particularly those of the landowners and other property owners and professionals, typically had domestic servants. These were most often female, particularly by the nineteenth century, and involved a wider age range and more permanency than was found in the agricultural sphere. A much higher proportion of these domestic servants were over age 20, although few were married. The market for such domestic servants was, of course, especially concentrated in the city, where so many of the wealthy lived, and this served as one means whereby girls from the countryside were drawn to the city. For those who did not subsequently marry, a life-long career in domestic service was one of the few possibilities for survival.

Back in the sixteenth century a large proportion of all young people spent a portion of their lives living as servants in their employers' homes. In Parma in 1545, 31 percent of all households had a resident servant, with similar proportions found in Siena and Verona, while in Florence in 1552 40 percent of all households had servants. Conversely, over 14 percent of the entire population in these cities lived as servants in the households of others. However, many of these people might better be described as apprentices, for, especially among the males, their labor involved market-oriented work and not primarily household tasks. Service typified all age groups, although a high point was reached in the age range 16–20. Indeed, in Verona in 1545, nearly a third of all residents aged 16–20 lived as servants in their employers' homes.

With the transformation of the apprenticeship system, fewer individuals lived in the households of their employers, and the huge proportions of urban servants began to decrease.[14] At the same time, domestic service became increasingly feminized.[15] These trends are evident in the situation found in the small central Italian city of Perugia in the mid-nineteenth century. Three-quarters of the domestic servants—who composed 6 percent of the city's entire population—were females over 14 years of age, having a mean age of 33. Yet almost 90 percent of these women were unmarried. About 15 percent of all households had at least one servant.[16]

Thus, by the time of Unification, a substantial number of youths from the rural areas around Bologna were still spending a portion of their lives working as servants and living apart from their own families. Typically, they either found work in the countryside as *garzoni,* living in the homes of sharecroppers, or were hired by wealthier individuals in the city, where they worked as domestic servants.

The servants who lived in Casalecchio were primarily from other rural communities of the province of Bologna. The majority of youths who grew up in Casalecchio families and entered service found work outside the town, either on farms in nearby areas or in the city of Bologna.[17] If we look just at the servants who resided in Casalecchio, though, major changes in the prevalence of service as a life stage are evident. In 1861, 22 percent of all boys aged 10–14 and 9 percent of all girls of that age group lived as servants in the houses of nonkin. Among those aged 15–19, 17 percent of the boys and 14 percent of the girls lived as resident servants. By 1921, just 2 percent of the boys and 3 percent of girls were servants. Although service still existed in 1921, it was no longer an important part of the childhood experience for any significant portion of the community.

To understand these changes, we first need to find out where these servants lived and who they were. At the beginning of the period, almost two-thirds of all servants lived with sharecroppers, and these were overwhelmingly (72 percent) male, as was customary for the *garzoni.* Three-fifths were under age 20, and another 30 percent were in their twenties. The landowners and professionals accounted for another 16 percent of the servants, with 12 percent living with artisans and merchants and the remaining 7 percent elsewhere. These households similarly preferred males: in all, 71 percent of the servants were male in 1861.

Since the overwhelming majority of the servants in Casalecchio entered the commune as servants, and without their families, the only direct information on the occupational characteristics of their families of origin concerns those who reached age 19 as servants in the nineteenth century. In registering for the draft (in the *lista di leva*), the youths listed both their own occupation and that of their father. For those listing a father's occupation, close to two-thirds had fathers who were *braccianti,* with the rest divided between fathers in other agricultural positions and fathers who were nonagricultural wage laborers.[18]

The decline in the practice of service in Casalecchio is linked not only to the declining relative importance of sharecropping to the town economy but also to the erosion of the practice of service among the sharecroppers. Whereas the 95 sharecropper households in 1861 had 64 servants, there were only 4 servants in the same number of sharecropper households by 1921. Now that young males had an opportunity to earn higher wages elsewhere in the developing urban economy, they were not attracted to life as a *garzone.* These other opportunities also must have driven up the wages of *garzoni,* making them less attractive to sharecroppers.

One implication of this development is that children from poorer families were now able to spend their entire childhood in their parental home rather than be forced out at an early age.[19] For sharecroppers, on the other hand, the increased cost of *garzoni* meant that they would have to rely entirely on their own children for child labor.

Child Labor

We have earlier noted the common view that the advent of factories—and especially textile factories of the kind found in Casalecchio—had a major negative impact on the quality of life of children and on family relations. According to this popular image, peasant children who had previously lived in their protective parental home, working alongside their parents and siblings on the family farm, were cast into the forbidding and degrading environment of the factory. There they worked from sunrise to evening in squalid conditions; they were given little education and deprived of the moral socialization traditionally provided by the family.

In Italy, as elsewhere, it is not hard to find sources of support for this viewpoint. For example, at the turn of this century, a decade and a half after the first significant child-labor laws were instituted in Italy, a socialist doctor from Cremona, an industrial city in northern Italy, made the following observations:

> Just think that there are girls of 16 or 20 years old who have their work certificate and yet do not know how to write their name, do not know how to make a bed right, nor do they know the practical matters of how to clean their rooms or their clothes. From the age of 10 they spend 8 or 10 hours a day in the factory, waking up at 5 in the morning and falling down exhausted into their bed, or rather, on a straw mattress. . . . They wash themselves poorly, and comb their hair worse, every eight hours, and so their self-neglect, the filth and uncleanliness enter into their habits and their attitudes. In recent days I have examined in detail the food that the girls bring to the factories; it consists for the most part of a little cabbage poorly seasoned along with a little bread or polenta.[20]

Similarly, Merli (1972), in the best-known work on the social impact of industrialization in Italy, claims that the advent of factory labor brought about an unfortunate revolution in social relations. He argues that the unity of the patriarchal family was destroyed, with women and children able to earn money independently of the patriarch. This, Merli claims, catapulted the youth and the women into "economic and spiritual independence from the family, leaving them freer in their social, human and sexual relations " (254).

There is no question that conditions for children working in factories in this period were poor. Italy in the nineteenth century had no safety or hygiene code covering factories. As a result, space was cramped, ventilation and lighting were poor, and cleanliness was rare. Unification itself, rather than bringing about an improvement in these conditions, undermined what little protective legislation for children existed in the pre-Risorgimento states of the peninsula.[21]

But before we conclude that the introduction of factory labor led to the undermining of the family and the corrupting of the children of the nineteenth century, we should recall what the alternatives were for these children in earlier days. For the most part, the children who went to work in the factories were not those who lived in the traditional peasant households; rather, their parents were already engaged in wage labor. The prospect they faced, then, was not a childhood spent at home working alongside their parents, brothers, and sisters on the farm, but a childhood in which they were likely to be sent off at a young age to work as a servant in someone else's household. Should they have remained in the parental household, moreover, their diet would certainly not have been any better than that described by the good doctor in his lamentation about the young factory workers.

This is a good point to ask from what sorts of families the Casalecchio children who worked in the hemp factory came.[22] We do this by looking at all those under age 20 who worked in the hemp factory in 1871 and 1881, comparing the distribution of the occupation of their household heads with that found for all of Casalecchio's children aged 8–19.[23] The results are striking: while just 17 percent of all children in this age range lived in households headed by hemp workers, 50 percent of the children working in the hemp factory come from such households. By contrast, although 34 percent of Casalecchio's children in this age range came from sharecropper households, none of them were working in the hemp factory. Both *braccianti* and other wage-labor households showed a propensity for sending their children to work in the hemp factory, though this tendency was less pronounced than that found among the households headed by the hemp workers.[24]

Casalecchio's hemp factory was in many ways typical of the kind of child-labor conditions found in the factories of northern Italy in the period of early factory employment. Until the mid-1870s, the preferred child employees were aged just 10–12; after that time there was a tendency to hire children who had already reached age 12 or 13. Girls were preferred over boys, for the girls were seen as especially adept at the kind of needle-threading and other weaving-related tasks for which child labor was favored.

The importance of unregulated child labor to the factory owners is evident from the reaction of the Casalecchio factory management to national attempts to pass legislation protecting child and women workers. The director of the Canonica sent a written protest in 1880 in response to the incipient plans for such social legislation. He maintained that establishing state inspectors of working conditions would undermine the "sentiment of mutually existing love and respect that in general exists in our country between management and workers," leading to strikes and other friction. He protested that limiting the age or hours of child employees was appropriate to children's work only in "mines and quarries and in those factories where there are known to be dangerous conditions." The Canonica director's main fear was that there would be a limitation on the number of hours small children could work. His response is worth quoting at some length for the insight it gives into the importance of child labor as well as the rationalizations provided by management for what seems indefensible by today's standards:

> The majority of girls who are employed in the weaving machines are just in this 11–15 age range. The continuity of the workday is one of the essential conditions for the operation of a factory having mechanical motors, and since we must have a useful workday of at least twelve hours in order to sustain this equipment, the result is that this category of children would be excluded from the factory. One must also take into account that the girls over age 15 would leave the factory barely after they had finished their apprenticeship, given the practice of the girls to abandon the factory as soon as they marry.[25]

As for any concerns about the wisdom of having young children work twelve hours a day, six days a week in the factory, the director gives no ground:

> With the use of machines the bodily fatigue of the work is considerably reduced and we can assure you that our girls are healthy and robust, living in spacious quarters, well ventilated, well lit, and doing light work (reloading the threads), work that by its nature leaves frequent intervals of rest to the girls who are working. But this work requires patience and a delicacy of hand and could not be well substituted by adults, not only because of the greater expense, but rather because of the adults' poorer attitude; moreover, it would be humiliating for them.[26]

It should be noted that at this time the children were being paid just 0.55 lira per day for twelve hours of work. The minimum wage for a man was 1.4 lire daily, while women were paid between 0.55 and 1.6 lire a day. On the other hand, according to an 1883 study of the diet of the hemp factory workers in Casalecchio, children drank only a fifth of a liter of wine (mixed with water) per day, while women drank a third of a liter and men a full liter daily.

Despite the protests of management, a national law regulating children's and women's work was finally passed in 1886. It forbade factory employment to children under age 9 and required that children under age 15 receive a government certificate before they could be hired by a factory. A medical examination was required, certifying their good health. Children under 12 were not permitted to work more than eight hours per day, a stipulation that resulted in the Casalecchio hemp factory moving to a minimum age of 12 for most of its youth work force.[27]

Desite this new law, whose enforcement was apparently erratic, Italy remained, at the end of the nineteenth century, one of the most retrograde countries in western Europe in terms of legislation protecting children working in factories. With its low minimum age of 9, no ban on working on Sundays and holidays, and no regulation of nocturnal factory work by children over age 12, Italy compared poorly to its northern European neighbors.[28]

Improvement of this legislation came with the passage of a new law in 1902. The practice of requiring children under age 15 to receive a government certificate in order to work in a factory continued, and was extended to all females under age 21. In order to get this certificate, children had to prove that they had been vaccinated against smallpox and that they had attended elementary school. The minimum age for factory work was raised to 12, with a three-year period of grace, and children under age 15 could not work more than six days a week, nor more than eleven hours per day, although provision was made for exceptions which were "the result of technical and economic necessity."[29]

Fortunately, a copy of the ledger that recorded the issuing of work certificates by the commune of Casalecchio in accordance with this new law has been preserved for the 1903–1910 period. The ledger lists all children residing in Casalecchio who were going into factory work, whether or not their jobs were located in the commune itself. This gives us some insight into the kinds of industrial occupations children were going into at the beginning of the century, as well as the ages at which they were entering the factories.

Children can be divided into those who went to work in the hemp factory and all others, for 99 of the 267 children under age 16 who received work permits in this period found work at the Canonica. (It should be remembered that this source does not give information on all children who went to work, but only on those who worked in factories or large artisan's shops.) Of these 99 young hemp factory workers, 61 were under age 13 when they began work, and 57 of them were girls. Among the children aged 13–15, there was a similar predominance of females: 31 to 7.

The only other large employer of Casalecchio children in this period was the local Rappini toy factory, which predominantly employed young children: 56 of the 73 Casalecchio children under age 16 hired there were under age 13, and of these 57 percent were boys. Thus it appears that despite the new, more restrictive legislation on child labor, the children who entered factory labor did so at very young ages in the early twentieth century, continuing the nineteenth-century pattern.[30]

The course of children's employment in Casalecchio over the sixty years from 1861 to 1921 shows both change and stability. The most notable change is the steep decline in service as a life stage, particularly for boys. Among girls, too, a decline is evident, though it had been less common for young girls to work as servants in Casalecchio.

Thanks to the preference of textile factories for young female labor, girls had entered the nonagricultural-wage labor force in greater numbers than had boys in the early years of factory labor in Casalecchio. In 1861, in the 10–14 age range, 17 percent of the boys and 16 percent of the girls worked as nonagricultural wage laborers; however, among the older children, aged 15–19, 23 percent of the boys and 35 percent of the girls had such employment. While the proportion of girls in the wage labor force changed little, over the following decades the proportion of boys in wage labor grew markedly in the older years of childhood, so that by 1921 44 percent of the boys aged 15–19 had such employment, compared to 37 percent of the girls. In some respects, then, the changes that took place in this period were greater for boys than for girls, a development related both to the growth of nontextile wage labor and to the decline of service.

Conclusions

Far from tearing children away from a nurturing parental family environment, industrialization often permitted them to grow up in their own family household to an extent that would not have otherwise been possible. In north-central Italy, children of sharecroppers had customarily lived all their childhood with their parents and, indeed, surrounded by a variety of other kinsmen. However, by the time factory labor and modern urbanization affected the people in this area, population growth and the capitalist transformation of agriculture had resulted in an increasingly proletarianized populace. Children growing up in poor families, with no rights to land, were often expelled from the parental household at an early age to live as servants in the homes of others who were better off. Moreover, those who lived at home shared in the poverty of their parents, whose work was sporadic and seasonal. It was just these children who were the first to enter factory labor, which not only provided some sorely needed income to the household but also permitted the children to remain with their parents.

There are indications that this pattern extends far beyond this region of Italy. In a very different context, in the commercial Canadian city of

Hamilton in the mid-nineteenth century, Katz, Doucet, and Stern (1982) find a remarkably similar pattern. There, young people customarily departed from their parental home to find work. Yet, with advancing industrialization, they increasingly remained at home until the age of marriage. Katz, Doucet, and Stern come to the striking conclusion that young people "began to live at home longer than at any previous time in Western history" (282). Their evidence and that from Casalecchio suggest a similar view of the impact of industrialization on children's family lives. Thus, while child factory labor was undoubtedly unpleasant and unhealthful, it must be understood in the context of a society in which many of the previous alternatives had their own grim side.

7 Getting Married
A Mediterranean Marriage Pattern?

Marriage is of central importance to an understanding of household dynamics and family demography, but it also provides a vantage point for examining many other aspects of society. This is nowhere more evident than in the first topic we consider: the ritual of marriage itself. Our period, encompassing the liberation of Bologna from papal rule and the establishment of a secular state, saw fierce battles between Church and state. The struggle over the wedding ceremony was one of the major battle grounds on which this war was fought. In 1866, the new Italian state announced that church marriages would no longer be considered valid. The Church, as part of its larger refusal to recognize the legitimacy of the secular state, likewise branded civil weddings invalid. This left the general Italian population torn between two major sources of authority—God and country—and between producing civil bastards and living as Catholic concubines.

We then turn to the timing of marriage, an issue which is much more familiar to historical demographers. One of the notable features of marriage in Casalecchio, as elsewhere in Europe in this period, was the large proportion of brides who came to the altar already pregnant. We examine how this affected marital timing and also consider the more general issue of just who was most likely to be pregnant at marriage. Related to the question of marital timing, too, is the extent to which definitive celibacy was found; we briefly inquire into how common it was for people to grow old without ever having married.

We also try to shed light on how people selected their spouse, a subject often lost in the historical demographic focus on age at marriage and proportions marrying. Here we ask to what extent people married others like themselves, and whether any changes in patterns of spouse selection occurred in these years. In looking at marriage in Casalecchio, we can scarcely avoid considering the most distinctive feature of marriage in this part of Italy, a feature that makes this area well known to European-family historians: the practice of bringing the bride into the groom's parental home. We examine this patrilocal pattern and the impact that economic change had on it during this period. Finally, we consider the fate of widows and widowers and their prospects for remarriage.

A Mediterranean Marriage Pattern?

Before tackling these individual topics, it is worth pausing to review recent attempts by social historians to identify a general marriage pattern in this part of Europe. Over two decades ago, Hajnal (1965) discerned a distinctive and unique European marriage pattern that, he argued, had existed from at least the eighteenth century up to the Second World War. Its essential features consisted of a high age at marriage and a high proportion of people who never married. Hajnal claimed that this pattern was found throughout Europe, except in the eastern and southeastern portions. His view was subsequently embraced by most demographic historians, who associated this European marriage pattern with nuclear family organization.

As new evidence accumulated, however, reference to a single European marriage pattern, tied to a single European family system, became increasingly untenable. As we have already shown, the family pattern found in sharecropping Italy diverges sharply from the earlier, largely British-based, generalizations. Yet, even though household organization and family relations in this part of Italy differ so dramatically from the pattern previously claimed to be universal in western Europe, it is still not clear how similar or different Italy is from northwestern Europe in its marriage practices.

In response to new evidence from southern Europe, many of the pioneers in the historical study of the European family have been revising their ideas about the nature of marriage on the Continent, and have begun to distinguish between southern Europe—or the Mediterranean—and northwestern Europe. Hajnal (1983) has contributed to this retreat from his earlier generalizations by focusing on "northwest Europe" and specifically excluding Italy from his more recent typology. Although this later work focuses on kinds of preindustrial household-formation systems and not simply on marriage, Hajnal's exclusion of Italy (along with other areas of southern Europe) raises anew the question, How different was the Italian marriage pattern from that found in northwestern Europe?

These revisions are nowhere more evident than in Laslett's recent efforts to limit his earlier generalizations about European family and marriage to northwestern Europe. In his revised overview he now distinguishes four

Mid-Nineteenth-Century View of the Principal Parish Church in Casalecchio

different parts of "traditional Europe," each having its own distinctive family and marriage patterns. One of these is the Mediterranean, which he contrasts with northwestern Europe in a number of respects.

According to Laslett (1983:526), Mediterranean domestic group organization differed from that found in northwestern Europe both in the relationship of marriage to household formation and in the timing of marriage. Whereas in the northwest marriage always meant the formation of a new domestic group, this was seldom the case in the Mediterranean, where new households were formed through the fission or fusion of already existent households. In short, in the northwest people became household heads through marriage, while in the Mediterranean attainment of headship and marriage were largely independent events. As for the timing of marriage itself, Laslett has modified Hajnal's earlier generalizations to suggest that while male age at marriage was high in both the northwest and the Mediterranean, female age at marriage was low in the Mediterranean. Moreover, the age gap between husband and wife, narrow in the northwest, was wide in the Mediterranean. Finally, according to Laslett, the proportion of the population who never married was low in the Mediterranean, unlike the northwestern European pattern.

We take up these questions in our consideration of the timing of marriage and the relationship of marriage to household formation. The evidence from Casalecchio, while supporting some of these new generalizations about a Mediterranean family pattern, casts serious doubt on others.

The Church-State Battle over Marriage

Any study of marriage in Italy in these years confronts the bitter struggle waged between the Catholic Church and the new Italian state for control over the marriage rite. At the beginning of the nineteenth century, when Napoleon's troops swept through the Italian peninsula, the emperor mandated the primacy of civil marriage. In 1806, the bishops of Italy were ordered to ensure that their parish priests observed this rule by refusing to marry any couples who had not already celebrated civil marriage. That the priests resisted this order is clear from the increasingly angry tone of subsequent government directives in 1808 and 1810, commanding the clergy to comply with the civil-marriage ordinance. However, the Napoleonic regime was short-lived, and the identification of marriage with the Church was little affected by this brief period of secularization.[1]

Half a century later, a more enduring struggle began. On 1 January 1866, a law promulgated by the new state went into effect, withdrawing state recognition of religious marriages and insisting that only civilly celebrated weddings could lead to the rights and benefits of legal marriage. Thus, at a legislative stroke, the new government sought to alter customs that had surrounded marriage in Italy for centuries: the church was no longer to be the focal point of the celebration of marriage, and the priest would have no legal right to consecrate bride and groom.

Unlike many of the state's moves against the power of the Church, this one affected the relationship of the masses to the Church directly, and it is not surprising that this state action prompted a virulent response from the clergy. On 2 February 1866, the archbishop of Bologna sent a formal notification to all parish priests stressing the importance of celebrating religious marriage before civil marriage. The priests were instructed to read this notice to their parishioners at mass (Calzi 1866). In no case did priests recognize the validity of civil marriage; they were divided only in the extent to which they tried to discourage parishioners from any subsequent celebration of a civil rite following the holy vows of matrimony celebrated in the church.

Symptomatic of the continued strength of Church opposition to the legal supremacy of civil marriage is a letter sent by a parish priest in the Bologna area in 1906, forty years after the fight had begun and after tensions had cooled down considerably. The letter was addressed to households containing couples who were legally but not religiously married. It was sent in advance of the annual visits made by the parish priest to bless all the homes in the community before Easter:

> Dear Mr. _______,
>
> The time for Easter approaches, the time in which the parish priest goes out to bless the houses. But I am truly sorry to advise you that due to the orders of my superiors I am not able to come to your house, for living there is one of your sons who has been married only civilly. As this is a public scandal, a concubinage, the Lord's benediction cannot enter your home until a religious marriage has been celebrated.[2]

This battle between Church and state left the Italian people in an awkward position. They were accustomed to church weddings, with their grandeur and rich symbolism. Thus, cultural norms defining a proper marriage, together with the influence that parish priests continued to hold in most areas, led the people to turn to the Church when they wanted to marry. But resentment toward the Church for its opposition to a united Italy and its defense of the old order was widespread. The refusal of the Church to recognize the legitimacy of civil marriage was hence seen as part of its larger refusal to recognize the legitimacy of the Italian state. In this context, turning to the Church for marriage was viewed by some as unpatriotic and reactionary.

Most of the Italian rural population in the years following the Risorgimento, however, felt little patriotism toward a united Italy, and traditional norms regarding a proper marriage—in church—continued. By the end of the century this would change in some areas—such as Bologna—with the rise of the socialist movement and the increase in a political anticlericalism among the rural population. Then some hardy souls would refuse a church marriage altogether, but in most areas these remained a small minority.[3]

This dual marital system led to some widely lamented results, as various nineteenth-century examples illustrate. In one case, a couple was married in church. Although realizing that they were legally supposed to go to the mayor to get married civilly, they continued to procrastinate. This oversight made little difference to them, since, according to public opinion, they were married, and they cared little about state bureaucracy. Over the years, however, their marriage became increasingly stormy. Finally, the husband left his wife and children and took up with another woman. Brazenly, he went with his new partner to the mayor and asked to be married. The mayor, whatever his own feelings, had no choice but to marry them, for the law (article 98) stated that the mayor could refuse marriage only for grounds specified in the law. Previous religious marriage could not be an impediment to civil marriage because it was not recognized by the state.[4]

Less dramatic but more common were situations where people took advantage of the state's position to defraud the state rather than to victimize their spouse. For example, in some state pension systems, a widow's payments were sharply cut if she remarried. Such a widow had a strong motive to remarry only religiously. This gave her complete social acceptance as a married woman while allowing her to retain her full pension, since, from the state's point of view, she remained a widow. A similar case is that of an army officer who was forbidden by regulation from marrying until he had attained a certain level of seniority. The state could not prevent him from marrying religiously without recognizing the validity of church weddings.[5]

For most people, the socially significant form of marriage continued to be that celebrated in church. However, many recognized that church celebration of weddings was no longer sufficient, since various civil rights and protections were afforded only to those who had undergone civil marriage. This was particularly true with respect to inheritance of property, for a man who married only religiously did not leave his wife and children as his primary heirs.

The net result of these conflicting forces was that the great majority of people in this period celebrated two weddings: one in church and one at the town hall. However, the two weddings were not necessarily celebrated at the same time. Church weddings, regarded in most areas and by most segments of the population as the real wedding, were generally celebrated first, but the timing of the subsequent civil marriage was variable. Just how variable it was and whether this variability related to other social factors have not previously been studied.

Bologna was among the areas—concentrated in the former papal states—where resistance to civil marriage was greatest in the early years of Unification. In the initial years of the new marriage regime, the total number of state-recognized marriages dropped precipitously, for the custom of going to the town hall to celebrate a wedding had not taken hold. In Emilia-Romagna, the number of marriages per 1,000 population dropped from 8.4 in 1865—the last year in which church weddings were civilly recognized—to 4.1 in 1866. This sharp decline was partially due to the increase in marriages celebrated in November and December of 1865 by people seeking to avoid the strictures of the new law by anticipating the dates of their weddings.[6]

One direct result of the new marriage law was a sharp rise in illegitimate births. Indeed, historians studying levels and trends in bastardy must take great care in using the Italian official data for this period, for they do not describe social bastardy at all, nor children born to unwed mothers. They relate in good part to the birth of children to parents who had been married only in church. At the national level, the proportion of illegitimate births rose from 5 percent in 1865 to 7.5 percent in 1883 before declining as the discrepancy between dates of religious and civil marriages diminished. This effect was even greater in the former regions of the papal states. In Emilia-Romagna, 17 percent of all children born in 1885–1887 were considered illegitimate by the state, compared to just 3 percent in the northern regions of Piedmont and Lombardy, where civil marriage was much more firmly entrenched.[7]

The great majority of people did, in fact, celebrate both a religious and a civil marriage. The extent to which they postponed their civil marriage, after celebrating a church wedding, gives one indication of their attitude toward Church and state. We have examined the behavior of the 929 Casalecchio couples for whom we have information on both their civil and religious marriages in order to judge the changing nature of this Church-state conflict.[8]

The new civil marriage law was only grudgingly accepted in Casalecchio (table 7.1). Of the 470 couples celebrating both religious and civil marriages in the first three decades of the new system, 62 percent had still not celebrated a civil rite by a month after their church wedding. The most common pattern was to observe the civil ceremony between a month and one-half a year after the church marriage, but a full quarter of the couples waited more than one-half a year before going to the town hall to be married.

Cultural change does appear evident over the course of our period, though, for by the early twentieth century increasing numbers of couples

Table 7.1. Relative Timing of Civil and Religious Marriages Recorded in Casalecchio, by Time Period (by cumulative percentage)

	Time Period		
Marriage Timing	1865–1882	1883–1896	1897–1921
Civil Wedding Before Church Wedding			
More than one month	2	5	2
Less than one month	8	14	23
Church Wedding Before Civil Wedding			
Less than one week	18	27	54
One to four weeks	34	41	68
One to five months	74	77	92
Six to eleven months	89	89	96
One year or longer	100	100	100

were celebrating church and civil marriages more or less simultaneously. Indeed, the disaffection of a segment of the population from the Church is seen in the fact that almost a quarter of the couples first celebrated a civil ceremony, a practice condemned by the Church. By a month after the church rite, 69 percent had celebrated a civil wedding in the later period, and by six months afterward 92 percent had.

Were there any differences within the population in the desire to celebrate both church and state marriages at the same time? A number of potentially cross-cutting factors were at work. The Risorgimento was primarily a movement of the bourgeoisie and the educated. Accordingly, we might expect respect for civil marriage to be greater among the literate (in the early years before mass literacy) and the landowners, particularly because those with property would have had the greatest interest in having their marriages civilly recognized as legitimate.[9] In fact, literate women did tend to have less of a time gap between their church and civil marriages than illiterate women (table 7.2). In 1866–1883 the difference was little more than a month, rising to two months over the next fourteen years. By the twentieth century illiterate women were such a small segment of the population that the difference—which became huge—is of less historical interest.

It might be objected that this difference is simply an artifact of the tendency of the wealthier classes (who happened to be more literate) to hasten their celebration of a civil marriage. This view receives support from an examination of the relationship between civil/religious marriage timing and occupation of the groom (table 7.3). The sharecroppers, who were more often illiterate than the nonagricultural wage laborers, nevertheless followed their religious ceremonies with civil marriages much more quickly than their proletarian neighbors did. But the artisans and merchants, who achieved high levels of literacy before either of these other two groups did, also showed consistently short time lapses between religious marriage and civil marriage.

This pattern is not surprising. Not only were many of the artisans and

Table 7.2. Difference in Dates of Civil and Religious Marriages by Bride's Literacy

	Mean Number of Days that Civil Marriage Follows Religious Marriage					
Bride's	1865–1882		1883–1896		1897–1921	
Literacy	No. of days	*N*	No. of days	*N*	No. of days	*N*
Signs name	134	(53)	153	(157)	65	(407)
Does not sign name	170	(183)	219	(76)	429	(23)
Total	162	(236)	174	(233)	84	(430)

Table 7.3. Difference in Dates of Civil and Religious Marriages by Groom's Occupation

Groom's Occupation	Mean Number of Days that Civil Marriage Follows Religious Marriage					
	1865–1882		1883–1896		1897–1921	
	No. of days	*N*	No. of days	*N*	No. of days	*N*
Sharecropper	86	(82)	156	(38)	29	(46)
Agric. wage	214	(52)	196	(42)	194	(30)
Artisan/ Merchant	6	(23)	36	(48)	54	(93)
Nonagric. wage	213	(64)	278	(89)	106	(202)
Other	142	(18)	59	(13)	149	(42)
Total	144	(239)	180	(230)	96	(413)

merchants concerned with the legal aspects of property ownership, but it was among this group that the cultural notions of nationalism and patriotism first took hold and free thinking began to spread. The speed with which sharecroppers celebrated a civil wedding was also, undoubtedly, related to their interest in property, perhaps augmented by the landowners' desire to ensure that the new family unit would be legally bound by the sharecropper contract. The relatively long delay in celebrating a civil wedding among the proletariat points again to the importance of property rights, but with a wrinkle. With the influence of the rural socialist movement sweeping through the province of Bologna in the late nineteenth century and, with it, the rise of a political anticlericalism of the masses, it might be thought that the early proletariat would be least affected by the strictures of the Church. In other words, it might be hypothesized that they would be the least traditional and the most secularized and that all this might be measured by their outright refusal of church marriage or, at least, by their failure to be influenced by the priests' opposition to civil marriage.[10]

That this turns out not to be the case in Casalecchio may tell us more about civil marriage as a measure of secularization than it does about the mentality or political culture of the rural population during this period. Until the twentieth century, the town hall, where the couple went to get married, and the mayor, in charge of the marriage ceremony, represented the propertied interests of Casalecchio. The state, as represented by the local governmental authorities, was resented by the nineteenth-century socialists as much as were the Church and the priests. It was only during the early twentieth century, when sharecroppers and workers acquired the right to vote in large numbers and were elected to, and ultimately controlled, the town council, that local government was viewed differently. It is therefore not surprising that in the late 1800s there was a sharp drop in the time separating civil marriage from religious marriage among both the sharecroppers and the nonagricultural proletariat.

The Timing of Marriage

In the decades since Hajnal identified late marriage as a distinctive trait of family life in European history, much attention has been paid to marital age. The primary impetus to this research has come from the linkage of age of marriage to a society's fertility level. If one assumes lack of birth control within marriage and low levels of nonmarital fertility—as many historical demographers do for the European past—then changes in fertility levels should largely be a function of changes in age at marriage. This is the view taken, for example, in studies that link the long-term fluctuations in fertility in England to changes in age at marriage, which in turn are influenced by macroeconomic fluctuations.[11]

A corollary of the proposition that age of marriage varies over time in response to changing economic conditions is that at any given time, different segments of the population marry at different ages depending on their economic positions. In the traditional view, European peasants, insofar as they were dependent on the family farm, had to wait to marry until they could take over that farm or accumulate the resources to acquire one of their own. This led to a relatively late age at marriage. The proletarianized sector of the population knew no such constraint and tended to marry earlier. This synchronic difference had implications for long-term trends, for as a peasant population became increasingly proletarianized, marriage age would be reduced and total fertility—and with it the rate of population growth—increased. As Anderson argued for Lancashire, this involved not only the urban wage laborers, but also the agricultural wage laborers, with both showing lower ages at marriage than the small farmers or the urban artisans.[12]

This pattern does not merely contrast urban and rural populations or industrial and nonindustrial populations. The kind of industry evidently had a major impact on age at marriage. Wrigley, for example, argued that women in coal-mining communities married earlier than women in textile-manufacturing communities, attributing this not only to the greater independence of women who worked in textiles (only men worked as coal miners), but also to the low proportion of women in coal-mining towns. And, as Anderson suggested, it is not the distinction between urban and rural areas that was most important, but rather the position of the individual in the economy, whether urban or rural. Hence, we would expect rural proletarians to have a lower age of marriage than urban dwellers who depended on their parents to provide the capital necessary for independence.[13]

The uncertainty surrounding these relationships stems from the fact that most studies of age at marriage have not linked individuals' marriages directly to their occupations, relying instead on aggregate data for communities.[14] The overall occupational characteristics of the community are then commonly related to mean age of marriage. In examining these issues of marital timing for Casalecchio, this relationship can be viewed more directly, focusing on individuals, for whom information is available on both age at marriage and occupation.

The history of age at marriage in modern Italy is still not well known, in contrast with the oft-studied English case. Ironically, the Italian peninsula has the best European data on marital age for the centuries before the late medieval period. During the Roman Empire, as in more recent centuries, men apparently did not normally marry until after age 25. Although the issue is still a matter of dispute, it appears that women in the western Roman Empire did not normally marry until their late teens or early twenties.[15] Changes occurred during the early Middle Ages, with some evidence that women's age at marriage first climbed to the middle twenties, with men and women marrying at approximately the same age, before declining again, sometimes to the teens. By the late medieval period, men were typically several years older than their wives in many areas of the Italian peninsula.[16]

Laslett relies on data from Tuscany in the fourteenth and fifteenth centuries to distinguish a Mediterranean pattern of early female and late male age at marriage. This reflects the work done by Herlihy and Klapisch-Zuber, whose studies of the cities of Prato and Florence in the fifteenth century found a mean male marriage age in the later twenties and early thirties, and a mean female marriage age of 18–21. In the surrounding countryside males were somewhat younger at marriage, in their mid-twenties, but female age at marriage was about the same, markedly below the late female age at marriage of Hajnal's original European marriage pattern (Herlihy and Klapisch-Zuber 1985:87).

Yet, though this may have been a common marriage pattern in fifteenth-century Italy, it soon changed, centuries before the first factory appeared or the modern growth of Italian cities began. It is notable in this regard that Hajnal, in his original positing of a European marriage pattern, used Italy as one of his examples, pointing to data in the Parma area to show late age at marriage for both males and females beginning in the seventeenth century.

We still lack enough studies to feel confident about the Italian situation, but it is clear that by the eighteenth century female age at marriage in central and northern Italy was generally over 21 and, by the nineteenth century, closer to 25. By the 1870s, Italy's pattern of female age at marriage differed little from that found in France and England, with 61 percent of Italian women married by age 25, compared to 60 percent of French women and 64 percent of English women.[17] By the turn of the century, the mean female age at first marriage in Italy stabilized at 24, with a male age of 27.

Even in the south, where early marriage was regarded as more common, communities having late female age at marriage were far from unusual. Delille (1977, 1985) has plotted a range of female age at first marriage from 15 to 26 in various southern communities in the sixteenth and seventeenth centuries, and from 17 to 26 in the eighteenth century. He links these differences to differences in the local agricultural economies.[18]

There was no dramatic regional variation within Italy in the nineteenth century, though some southern regions did show lower ages at marriage for women. Emilia-Romagna remained very close to, though slightly higher than, the national mean. In the large cities at the turn of this century, age at marriage was significantly higher, reflecting in part the greater number of women than men.[19]

Age-at-marriage patterns in Casalecchio are typical of those found in Emilia-Romagna and Italy as a whole. Throughout the nineteenth century, age at first marriage for men hovered around 27, with women marrying, on the average, at age 24. What is striking is how little change in this pattern can be seen during a period of considerable social and economic changes.[20]

In looking at what happened to Casalecchio in the latter part of the nineteenth century and into the twentieth, we again employ three time periods: 1865–1882, 1883–1896, and 1897–1915. In this way we distinguish a middle period of agricultural crisis and transition, and a turn-of-the-century period of accelerated ties to the city and increase in wage-labor opportunities. We stop at 1915 because the dislocations of the First World War had a major impact on the marriage market, which obscures the general trend. These disruptions are evident from the sharp changes in marriage rates that occurred in these years. In Emilia-Romagna, the marriage rate fell by more than half from 1914 to the 1915–1918 war years, with compensatory marriage leading to practically a quadrupling of the rate in 1920. Hence it makes more sense to leave the last years of our period to a separate study of the effects of the war on marriage.[21]

At the aggregate level, there was remarkably little change in mean age at first marriage in Casalecchio throughout this period. Indeed, in all three periods, mean age at civil marriage was 27 for men and 24 for women, with mean age at religious marriage a few months earlier.[22] Even if we look at the range of marriage ages, hardly any changes are evident (table 7.4).

Table 7.4. Age at First Civil Marriage, by Sex and Time Period (by percentage)

Age at Marriage	Women			Men		
	1865–1882	1883–1896	1897–1915	1865–1882	1883–1896	1897–1915
Under 20	8	8	9	0	0	2
20–24	49	49	52	20	23	26
25–29	29	29	28	46	46	46
30–34	8	7	6	22	19	16
35–39	2	4	2	8	6	4
40–49	1	2	2	2	3	3
50+	3	2	2	2	2	2
Total	100	100	100	100	100	100

About three-fifths of the women married before reaching age 25, with few marrying before they reached age 20. Around 85 percent of first marriages involved women under age 30 throughout these years. As is reflected in the mean figures, men married somewhat later than women. Marriage before age 20 for men was extremely uncommon; conscription of young men beginning at age 19 would have reinforced a longer-standing aversion to early marriage. The most popular age for a man to marry was in the late twenties, and almost half of all marriages took place in this five-year age range. Moreover, men were twice as likely as women to wait until their early thirties to get married.

Breaking down these general figures by occupations of bride and groom can determine whether any significant differentials in marital age are masked at the commune level and, in particular, whether the Casalecchio data tend to support any of the previously mentioned generalizations relating marriage age to economic position and acquiring the wherewithal to get married. There is some basis in folklore to think that such a relationship would hold. The Bolognese saying "Better to say 'poor me' than 'poor we'" explicitly makes just such a link between economic resources and marriage.[23] Yet, in fact, the Casalecchio case gives at best only weak support to such generalizations (table 7.5). There is little difference among occupational groups in age at marriage, and some of these are not in the predicted direction.

Among the men, the agricultural wage laborers had an age at marriage above that of sharecroppers and that of nonagricultural wage laborers, and this differential increases over time. If, as some scholars have suggested, agricultural wage labor facilitates earlier marriage, it is not evident in Casalecchio. In fact, this represents perhaps the poorest segment of the population and we might hypothesize that not only a wage, but also a wage above a certain level, is needed if marriage is to be encouraged. The artisans and

Table 7.5. Mean Age at First Civil Marriage by Occupation, Sex, and Time Period

Occupation	Time Period					
	1865–1882		1883–1896		1897–1915	
	Men	Women	Men	Women	Men	Women
Sharecropper	27.8 (126)	23.9 (117)	28.0 (99)	24.2 (103)	26.9 (149)	23.8 (168)
Agric. wage and other agric.	29.5 (65)	23.6 (41)	29.4 (76)	25.2 (35)	31.9 (80)	27.6 (30)
Servant	30.9 (7)	25.9 (21)	30.2 (6)	26.4 (25)	31.7 (6)	26.0 (35)
Elite	31.4 (17)	25.3 (9)	28.1 (15)	26.3 (17)	28.7 (48)	30.3 (23)
Artisan/Merchant	28.6 (39)	22.6 (5)	28.2 (67)	22.7 (18)	28.2 (135)	23.0 (62)
Nonagric. wage	27.9 (79)	24.9 (47)	27.8 (120)	24.3 (90)	26.7 (271)	23.8 (193)
Outside labor force and no occupation given	27.3 (15)	25.3 (126)	27.5 (11)	26.0 (122)	27.9 (35)	25.6 (221)
Total	28.5 (348)	24.6 (366)	28.3 (394)	25.0 (410)	27.8 (724)	24.7 (732)

merchants show no tendency toward late marriage, as might be predicted on the basis of earlier studies. However, since many of these individuals had very small-scale enterprises, there was little pressure to delay marriage in anticipation of intergenerational property transmission.

The sharecroppers present an interesting case. As the closest Casalecchio had to peasant farmers, with an interest in property, later age at marriage might be expected for them. Yet, as others have recognized, this expectation is based on a nuclear-family model, which links marriage to the establishment of an independent household. Since there was no such link in the case of sharecroppers, and since it was generally desirable to add an in-marrying woman to the household, a relatively low age at marriage might be expected. This is only partially supported, however, with sharecropper women marrying at just a slightly younger age than other women.

In the nonagricultural wage sector, we find a trend toward slightly lower age at marriage for women, with basically no change in men's age at marriage in the nineteenth century, but a tendency toward somewhat lower age at marriage in the twentieth. With the improving economic conditions for urban wage labor in the twentieth century, nonagricultural wage laborers did become a group that married slightly earlier than the population as a whole. In general, however, the Casalecchio results mirror Knodel's (1986) similar findings for a group of German villages in the nineteenth century. The most striking finding in both populations is, to use Knodel's words, the "similarity in age at first marriage across occupational categories" (351).[24]

Bridal Pregnancy

No study of the nature of marriage in the past would be complete without inquiring into the extent to which women who went to the altar were already pregnant. Indeed, in many parts of Europe such bridal pregnancies were extremely common, and Casalecchio was no exception.[25]

Measures of bridal pregnancy vary, some including only those births taking place within six months of marriage, while others include all births within nine months. Given the speed with which a first child tended to follow marriage in Europe in the past, use of the nine-month criterion is tainted by inclusion of many premature births that were conceived after marriage. However, the measurement of bridal pregnancy is not simply a technical issue: it depends in part on the questions asked. Is bridal pregnancy important because it helps explain the decision to marry and the selection of a spouse, or is it significant as a measure of the social legitimacy of premarital intercourse between already engaged men and women? If we are interested in how bridal pregnancy influences marriage, there is little interest in cases where people get married before they realize that the bride was already pregnant.[26]

It is impossible to disentangle these two effects with demographic data alone. However, we think it is useful to focus on cases where the couple knew of the woman's pregnancy before marriage, and we thus follow other scholars in using a limit of seven months after marriage to first birth as our measure of bridal pregnancy. The figures we provide consequently underestimate the number of women who were in fact pregnant at marriage.[27]

In order to determine if a woman was pregnant at the time of her marriage, we must know the date of her marriage and whether she gave birth within the next seven months. In the Italian case, neither task is simple. The dating of marriage is complicated by the dual civil/religious marriage system. Having only a civil marriage date is clearly insufficient, for civil marriage often followed religious marriage by months and might well have been catalyzed by pregnancy. Any measure of bridal pregnancy based on the civil marriage date would therefore be grossly inflated. Use of the religious marriage date would yield much better results, but in a minority of cases religious marriage occurred after civil marriage. The most prudent solution, and the path we followed, was selecting only cases where records were available for both forms of marriage for the couple and employing the earlier of the two dates as the start of marriage.

Following the bride for seven months after her wedding also raises problems, for there was considerable mobility in the months after marriage, and it was not feasible to track down migratory brides in their new commune of residence. Hence, we had to further limit our study to women who remained in Casalecchio for at least seven months following their marriage. In all, then, we were able to examine the cases of 594 couples.[28]

Little information on bridal pregnancy in southern Europe is available, but scattered studies show that in northern Europe bridal pregnancy was commonplace in the past. The best-studied country is England, where high levels of bridal pregnancy have long prevailed. It is estimated that one in three brides was pregnant in fifteenth- and sixteenth-century England, the number declining to perhaps one in five in the seventeenth century, but then increasing to one in three again by the early nineteenth century. Curiously, premarital pregnancy was considerably less common in France, where fewer than one bride in ten was pregnant until the latter part of the eighteenth century, when bridal pregnancy became increasingly common. Indeed, in a protoindustrial community near Lille, half of all brides were pregnant in the first half of the nineteenth century.[29]

Similarly high proportions of bridal pregnancy have been found elsewhere in western Europe. For example, in a Belgian community in the mid-nineteenth century, nearly half of the first births occurred to women who had been married for under seven months. At about the same time, 30 percent of the brides in a Swedish community were pregnant. A study of a number of parishes in Neuchatel, Switzerland, around the latter half of the eighteenth century yielded bridal pregnancy rates ranging from 30 percent to 50 percent.[30]

Like young women in other parts of Europe, a substantial proportion of Casalecchio's brides knew that they were already pregnant. This proportion rose from 28 percent of all brides in 1865–1869 to over one-half of all brides by the second decade of the twentieth century (fig. 7.1). With bridal pregnancy so pervasive, it seems unlikely that pregnant brides suffered much stigma.[31] Doubtless the high rate of bridal pregnancy reflects both the commonality of sexual intercourse among engaged couples and the strong community pressures on a man to wed the woman he had impregnated, whether they had been engaged to be married or not.

In asking whether certain men and women were more likely to celebrate weddings involving a pregnant bride, we looked at a variety of social characteristics, including the age, literacy, and occupation of the bride and groom. We also looked at birthplace of, and difference in age between, bride and groom, but found no relationship between these latter two characteristics and bridal pregnancy.

Based on modern Western experience, it might be thought that pregnancy speeds up the marriage process by forcing people to marry at an

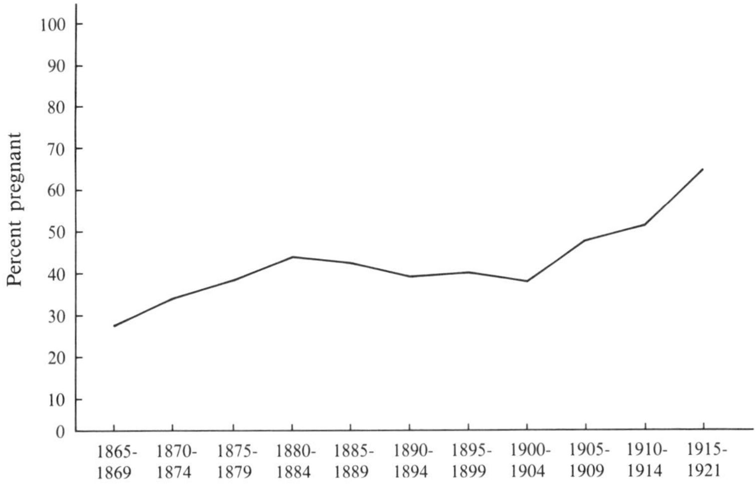

Fig. 7.1. Percentage of Brides Who Were Pregnant, by Time Period

earlier age than they had planned. Casalecchio provides some evidence for this, although the effect is not particularly strong (table 7.6). There was a general tendency during the later nineteenth and early twentieth centuries for the youngest brides to be pregnant. Yet, at the same time, few women married before their twentieth birthday, providing evidence that sexual intercourse before age 20 was less common. Other than this tendency for the youngest brides to be pregnant, there is no clear relationship of the bride's age at marriage to bridal pregnancy. It is worth noting that this finding is in keeping with the picture we have from further north in Europe, where no clear age pattern of premarital pregnancy has been found.[32]

Among men, the youngest were more likely to marry pregnant brides throughout these decades, with this effect being strongest in 1865–1882. A major impetus for a man to marry before he was 25 was having gotten a woman pregnant.[33] Men who married after age 30 were less likely to have a pregnant bride.

Looking at other characteristics, we might be led by contemporary Western evidence to hypothesize that the less educated are more likely to be pregnant at marriage. This is, however, not the case in Casalecchio (table 7.7), where, if anything, couples in which both bride and groom were literate were more likely to experience bridal pregnancy.

What effect did all the changes that accompanied the transformation of north-central Italy from a sharecropping society to one with a burgeoning proletarian population have on the prevalence of bridal pregnancy? One factor of importance here is that women from sharecropping households were considerably less likely to be pregnant at marriage than other women, while women who worked in nonagricultural wage labor—

Table 7.6. Percentage of Brides Pregnant, by Age at Marriage of the Bride and Groom and Time Period

	1865–1882		1883–1896		1897–1921	
Age at Marriage	%	*N*	%	*N*	%	*N*
Bride						
Less than 20	32	(22)	59	(17)	60	(35)
20–24	37	(81)	44	(84)	50	(133)
25–29	38	(24)	23	(44)	47	(77)
30+	38	(16)	44	(18)	47	(30)
All ages	36	(156)	40	(163)	50	(275)
Groom						
Less than 25	50	(44)	54	(56)	59	(85)
25–29	32	(60)	28	(68)	50	(118)
30+	31	(52)	41	(39)	40	(72)
All ages	36	(156)	40	(163)	50	(275)

Table 7.7. Percentage of Brides Pregnant, by Literacy of Bride and Groom and Time Period

	1865–1882		1883–1896		1897–1921	
Literacy	%	*N*	%	*N*	%	*N*
Both literate	50	(30)	50	(88)	54	(211)
Only husband is literate	36	(56)	28	(39)	46	(11)
Only wife is literate	50	(2)	26	(19)	35	(26)
Both illiterate	33	(58)	31	(13)	60	(5)
Total	38	(146)	40	(159)	52	(253)

Note: *N* refers to number of couples.

primarily in textile factories—were generally more likely to be pregnant at marriage (table 7.8).[34] The occupations of the grooms show, for the two earlier periods, a stronger relationship with bridal pregnancy. Here, too, sharecropping men were considerably less likely to celebrate marriage to a pregnant wife, while those men who worked in nonagricultural wage labor were more likely to have a pregnant bride. Interestingly, men in agricultural wage labor were less likely to have a pregnant bride than were the nonagricultural proletarian men.

Given these occupational differences, the historical increase in bridal pregnancy may be a simple product of the shift from a sharecropping to a wage-labor economy. In order to test this hypothesis, we estimated two multiple classification analysis models of differences in the proportion of brides who were pregnant (table 7.9).[35] These models first considered the net differences associated with the wife's characteristics and then those

Table 7.8. Percentage of Brides Pregnant, by Occupation of the Bride and Groom and Time Period

	1865–1882		1883–1896		1897–1921	
Occupation at Marriage	%	*N*	%	*N*	%	*N*
Bride						
Sharecropper	28	(43)	21	(34)	29	(35)
Agricultural wage	44	(23)	29	(17)	29	(7)
Nonagricultural wage	46	(26)	43	(56)	56	(118)
Other	36	(64)	52	(56)	52	(115)
Total	36	(156)	40	(163)	50	(275)
Groom						
Sharecropper	25	(48)	19	(31)	44	(32)
Agricultural Wage	32	(12)	23	(31)	29	(28)
Nonagricultural wage	54	(43)	53	(62)	55	(127)
Other	37	(27)	49	(39)	53	(79)
Total	36	(156)	40	(163)	50	(275)

Table 7.9. Multiple Classification Analysis of Percentage of Brides Pregnant

			Net of Other Variables	
	N	Observed	1	2
Year of Marriage				
1865–1882	153	36.6	44.7	41.7
1883–1896	159	40.3	40.9	40.1
1897–1921	263	51.3	46.2	48.4
Wife's Age at Marriage				
<20	71	52.1	49.6	
20–24	288	45.8	46.7	
25+	216	39.8	39.4	
Husband's Age at Marriage				***
<25	181	56.1		54.3
25+	394	39.0		39.8
Wife's Literacy			**	
Signs name	387	49.6	48.4	
Does not sign name	188	33.5	36.0	
Husband's Literacy				
Signs name	450	47.5		45.1
Does not sign name	125	33.0		41.5
Wife's Occupation			***	
Sharecropper	112	25.9	27.3	
Agricultural wage	45	35.6	39.8	
Elite, artisan, merchant	48	52.1	48.0	
Nonagricultural wage	198	51.5	50.2	
Other	172	48.3	48.9	
Husband's Occupation				***
Sharecropper	111	28.8		30.2
Agricultural wage	94	27.8		30.7
Elite, artisan, merchant	120	48.0		46.8
Nonagricultural wage	225	54.3		53.1
Other	25	51.8		51.9
R^2	–	–	.063	.101

$^*p < .10$. $^{**}p < .05$. $^{***}p < .01$.

associated with her husband's. We do not present a model of the net effects of the husband's and wife's characteristics considered jointly because of the high degree of marital homogamy.[36]

Bridal pregnancy was strongly associated with economic differentiation in Casalecchio. Whether one looks at the occupation of the wife (table 7.9, model 1) or that of the husband (table 7.9, model 2), bridal pregnancy was much less common in marriages that involved a sharecropper. Agricultural wage laborers also had substantially lower rates of bridal pregnancy, relative to other economic classes. Half or more of all brides were pregnant in marriages involving nonagricultural wage laborers.

Casalecchio di Reno, Ronzani Brewery

The transformation of Casalecchio from a primarily agricultural economy to one that was predominantly nonagricultural largely accounts for the upward trend in bridal pregnancy. Overall, the proportion of marriages in which the bride was pregnant rose from 37 percent in 1865–1882 to 51 percent in 1897–1921. Controlling for the changing economic activities of young women and the increased proportion who were literate, there were no significant historical changes in bridal pregnancy.[37] We interpret this as reflecting the greater familial control of young women who lived in agricultural settings, especially those working side by side with their parents and other kin. Young women engaged in nonagricultural wage labor were often removed from parental supervision for major parts of the day. In other cases, such young, unmarried women lived apart from their families in housing provided by their employer.[38]

Literate women were somewhat more likely to be pregnant brides than illiterate women, a differential not accounted for by the wife's economic characteristics. The higher rate of bridal pregnancy among spouses of literate men is associated with the fact that literate men are more likely to be wage laborers.

Regardless of literacy or economic class, persons marrying at young ages were substantially more likely to be bridally pregnant. In this population, marriage was typically delayed to the early or mid-twenties among women and late twenties or older among men, unless an unplanned pregnancy necessitated an earlier marriage.

Definitive Celibacy

One of the defining characteristics of Hajnal's European marriage pattern is the high proportion of individuals who never marry. He cited Italian data, along with data from other countries of western Europe, in support of this thesis, with the 11 percent of Italian men and women never married by their late forties in 1911 comparable to the 11 percent of French men and 12 percent of French women never married by that age at the turn of the century. In England the percentages were only slightly higher (12 percent and 15 percent) (Hajnal 1965:102).

In 1901, in both Emilia-Romagna and Italy as a whole, 11 percent of the women aged 50–54 had never married. However, within Emilia-Romagna, as in the country in general, there were substantial differences between rural areas and the large cities. In the city of Bologna, for example, 18 percent of women aged 50–54 were never married, and forty years later this proportion was unchanged. In the surrounding countryside of the rest of the province of Bologna, just 6 percent of women in this age group were never married in 1871 and 1911.[39] The pattern in Casalecchio followed the unchanging norm in the province of Bologna (excluding the city itself). In 1861, 7 percent of women over age 50 and the same proportion of men of that age had never married. By 1921 this proportion remained virtually the same, at 8 percent.

In general, there was little difference among the major occupational groups in Casalecchio in propensity to marry, as measured by the proportion of men over age 50 who had never married. There is certainly no apparent evidence that poverty acted as a bar to marriage, for the agricultural wage laborers, the poorest segment of the population, showed especially low rates of definitive celibacy.[40] We find no evidence during the 1861–1921 period of any change in the likelihood of remaining a bachelor.[41]

Yet marriage was certainly not universal, especially when the likely movement of unmarried women to the city of Bologna is considered. Roles for the never-married were provided by the kinship system; the never-married lived neither by themselves nor as boarders in these rural areas. Rather, they often lived with their parents or, after their parents' death, with married brothers or other kinsmen. In the absence of marriage a person was likely to remain, in some respects, a dependent of others, either married kinsmen or, in the case of servants, nonkin. That this status was seen as less than ideal is reflected in the Bolognese adage "Better a miserable husband than a wonderful brother."[42]

Choosing a Spouse

In historical studies of marriage in Europe, much attention has been paid to the age at which people married, but very little to the way spouses were chosen. After all, marriage involves at least two people (leaving aside the other family members implicated in the selection process), and understanding how marriages were made involves looking at the joint characteristics of bride and groom. How much of a relative age preference was there in choosing a spouse, and how did this differ as a person grew older without getting married? Did people who were literate have a strong preference for a literate spouse when illiteracy was still common? And how much occupational homogamy was there? Did sharecroppers marry sharecroppers, and proletarians choose other proletarians?

This last question, in fact, brings up another advantage of studying the joint characteristics of newlyweds, for these shed light on the meaning of the social identities assigned to the people in the historical record. We do not otherwise know, for example, how important the social distinction was between agricultural wage laborers and nonagricultural wage laborers, or between artisans and merchants on the one hand and the proletariat on the other. It is fair to assume that the less the tendency for any two of these groups to intermarry, the greater the social barriers between them.

Selection of a spouse was not simply an individual affair in the late nineteenth and early twentieth centuries in Italy, for parents exerted influence on the selection of their sons- and daughters-in-law. Indeed, this role was codified in the first post-Unification Italian civil code in 1866. One section of this code specifies that men under 25 and women under 21 had to have parental consent to marry. In the case of disagreement between father and mother, the father's word was final (Taglioni 1866:175).

Age Differences

"When the woman is born," goes a Bolognese adage, "her husband should already be out hoeing."[43] In Casalecchio, as in Italy as a whole, the norm was for women to marry at a younger age than men. The relative age of husband and wife, however, is not simply a direct outcome of this aggregate difference in marriage age. We do not know, for example, whether women who married relatively late (e.g., after age 30) tended to marry men who were younger or older than themselves, or, if older, whether they were as much older as the men marrying women in their twenties.

Among all Casalecchio women who got married, a fairly distinctive pattern of age assortment is related to the woman's age at marriage. Generally speaking, the younger the woman, the greater the age difference between wife and husband, while among women who married after age 40, it was not at all uncommon for the bride to be older than the groom. The greatest age difference came in cases where the bride was under age 20; in the earliest period, grooms were close to ten years older than their young brides. Even in the twentieth century, when the general age gap between spouses had narrowed, these young brides married men almost seven years older than them on the average. At the other end of the life course another pattern emerges. By the twentieth century, when we have enough cases, women who married for the first time after age 50 were marrying men who, on the average, were three years *younger* than them.

Looking at the age differences between groom and bride according to the groom's age reveals a complementary pattern. Male marriage under age 20 was rare, in part because of the widespread effect of conscription at age 19, along with the legal minimum marital age of 18 for men.[44] However, those few males who married this young did so to women older than themselves, not to younger women. By the early twenties, though, marriage was fairly common, and here there was only minimal difference in age between bride and groom, with many brides older than the groom. It was only by the time of marriage in the later twenties that the characteristic pattern of male seniority asserted itself, a tendency that grew steadily until the men reached their forties. Men who married in their thirties, then, entered a marriage market similar to that of men ten years their junior, competing for the same women. A slight decline in the age gap between spouses is evident over time, and this was evenly distributed among age groups.[45]

One of the defining features of the Mediterranean family system, according to Laslett (1983:526), is the low proportion of wives who are older than their husbands, a corollary of the wide age gap between spouses at first marriage. In both these respects, he maintains, the Mediterranean pattern diverges from that of the rest of Europe. This proposition is difficult to judge, since few have taken up Laslett's call for study of this issue, and the data he presents in support of it are based on tiny samples.[46]

Casalecchio, of course, provides just one case of family organization in Mediterranean Europe, but given its location, the relatively large size of its population, and our ability to distinguish first marriages from others, it is instructive nonetheless. In fact, throughout our fifty-seven-year period, a fifth of all first marriages involved wives who were older than their husbands, about the same percentage noted for northwestern Europe.[47] A recent study of marriage in a number of sharecropping communities of Tuscany in 1820–1859 similarly reveals that one-fifth of first marriages involved a bride who was older than her groom (Rettaroli 1986:260). There is, therefore, some reason to be skeptical about Laslett's claim that the Mediterranean had a relatively low proportion of wives older than their husbands.

Age differences between husband and wife differed little among occupational groups, although it was a bit less common for sharecropping men to marry women older than them.[48] In general, age selectivity was the same throughout the population. One trend that is evident, though, is a decrease in the proportion of husbands who were much older than their wives. In 1865–1882, 40 percent of husbands were five or more years older than their wives, including 13 percent who were ten or more years older. By 1897–1921, only 29 percent of husbands were five or more years older than their wives, with only 7 percent ten or more years older. There is evidence, then, of a historical trend away from marriages of women to men considerably older than them, and this does lend some support to the supposition that marriage was becoming more companionate in nature.[49]

Literacy

The latter part of the nineteenth century saw a tremendous change in Casalecchio, as throughout much of Italy, in the spread of literacy. In looking at the extent to which literate men sought literate women for their wives, and literate women sought literate men for their husbands, we must consider this rapidly changing background. Indeed, as we move from 1865–1882 to 1897–1921, the proportion of all marriages involving two illiterates dropped from 38 percent to just 3 percent, and the proportion involving two literate spouses jumped from 19 percent to 86 percent. Given the near universality of literacy by the twentieth century, then, our focus rests primarily on the earlier years when literacy, especially female literacy, was less common.

In the earlier period, 57 percent of all the men who got married were able to sign their own names, with 43 percent simply marking their marriage certificates with an *X*. In choosing their mate, however, 80 percent of the literate women chose a man who was literate, compared to just half of the illiterate women. Hence, the relatively small group of literate women in the community strongly preferred literate men and were generally able to attract them. In all, just 24 percent of the brides in these years could sign their own names, so that there were simply not enough literate women to go around even if every literate man wanted to marry one. Hence, even if the literate men succeeded in capturing in marriage all the literate women, 58 percent of the literate men would be marrying illiterate women. What actually happened was that one-third of the brides of the literate men were literate, compared to just 12 percent of the brides of the illiterate men. These figures show clear evidence of marital homogamy.

Occupation

In judging the social significance of occupational divisions in a community like Casalecchio, the nature of occupational matching in marriages offers valuable insight.[50] We have used occupational information for bride

Table 7.10. Bride's Occupation by Groom's Occupation and Time Period (by percentage)

	Groom's Occupation											
	Sharecropper		Agriculture Wage		Elite		Artisan/ Merchant		Nonagricultural Wage		Other	
Bride's Occupation	1865–1896	1897–1921	1865–1896	1897–1921	1865–1896	1897–1921	1865–1896	1897–1921	1865–1896	1897–1921	1865–1896	1897–1921
Sharecropper	76	70	11	17	0	0	4	9	11	10	14	33
Agricultural wage	5	6	28	20	0	0	2	0	10	2	0	7
Servant	11	11	6	2	0	1	3	2	3	2	21	7
Elite	1	1	0	0	46	35	6	5	1	1	0	7
Artisan/ Merchant	0	2	1	4	11	10	8	17	3	7	0	7
Nonagricultural wage	2	5	17	31	14	10	24	32	34	42	36	13
Not in the labor force	4	6	37	26	30	44	53	35	38	36	29	27
N	(233)	(197)	(156)	(86)	(37)	(71)	(103)	(179)	(219)	(422)	(14)	(15)

and groom taken from the civil-marriage certificates, looking at two periods: one before the major population growth and urban expansion (1865–1896), and the other covering the years of accelerated economic change (1897–1921).[51]

Turning first to the earlier period, certain patterns quickly emerge (table 7.10). Men from sharecropping families overwhelmingly married women from sharecropping families. In fact, while just 29 percent of the women getting married came from such backgrounds, 76 percent of the women marrying into sharecropper households came from such households. Moreover, of the remaining brides, the great majority came from other portions of the agricultural labor sector: the *braccianti* and the *garzoni,* the agricultural servants who generally lived in the sharecroppers' households. It is remarkable how few sharecropper men married women from nonagricultural backgrounds in a community that not only bordered the city but that also, even in this earlier period, had a sizable nonagricultural labor force of its own. Presumably, expertise in working in a sharecropping household was highly prized by the family of the male sharecropper, strongly influencing the choice of a wife.

The *braccianti* showed less of an agricultural bias, constrained instead by the selection of a wife from among the proletariat, whether agricultural or nonagricultural. Of those marrying women with specified occupations, almost half married other *braccianti,* a number that increases when the servants are included, as they should be, since most of these were probably from *braccianti* families. Of the women married who were not agricultural wage laborers, a goodly proportion came from the nonagricultural wage labor force. It is likely that a substantial proportion of these proletarian brides had originally come from *braccianti* households, since factory labor was a popular alternative for girls from such households.

Men from the elite—here including landowners, professionals, and white-collar workers—tended to marry women from the elite. Since women from elite families often assumed no occupation outside the house, this relationship is not as dramatic as it might otherwise be. It is notable, too, that no man from the elite married any woman from the agricultural sector in these years, despite the fact that some of the sharecroppers were relatively well off.

An unusually high proportion of the brides of artisans and merchants is listed as having no occupation. It seems that women from artisan and merchant families were themselves often not considered artisans or merchants, although they participated in the family business. Here again, however, the tendency of the nonagricultural man to seek his bride from the nonagricultural sector is clear.

Nonagricultural wage laborers included not only factory workers, but also bricklayers, road-construction workers, and workers in a variety of other proletarian occupations. Their preference for women from this same sector of the economy is evident; over half of their brides who had an occupation listed were themselves nonagricultural wage laborers, although only a fifth of the brides of Casalecchio came from this category. Moreover, about half of the rest of their brides came from other segments of the proletariat: the *braccianti* and the servants.

A look at the characteristics of marriages in the later period reveals a basically similar pattern, although the proportions are altered by the changed underlying occupational characteristics of the community. Despite their dwindling as a proportion of the population, sharecroppers still had a strong preference for marrying women from sharecropping households. Agricultural wage laborers largely married women from proletarian backgrounds, whether agricultural or nonagricultural. Elite men heavily favored women from elite backgrounds. Artisans and merchants, while showing a preference for women from this background, also freely married women in the nonagricultural wage labor force. This, in part, reflects the tenuousness of the distinction between these two categories or, put another way, the wide range within the category of artisans and merchants, with a portion little different in social characteristics from nonagricultural wage laborers. The tendency for nonagricultural wage laborers to seek out proletarian brides also continued.

Thus, between 1865 and 1921 there was little change in occupational preferences in the marriage market, although changes in the proportions of people in different occupations—most notably the rise of the nonagricultural wage sector at the expense of the agricultural sector—had an impact on the kinds of occupational pairings brought about by marriage. The social distinctiveness of the sharecroppers, and their continued social isolation throughout this period of rapid change, are especially notable.[52]

Within these broad categories certain social divisions were undoubtedly also important, especially as they sorted young people into different marriage markets. For example, of the 26 brides in the years 1865–1882 who were working at the Casalecchio hemp factory, fully half married men working in the same factory, although just 7 percent of the grooms of that period had such jobs. It was a small world.

Postmarital Residence

Marriage meant a change of residence for at least one of the newlyweds. In the traditional sharecropping system, the bride moved into the household in which the groom already lived, surrounded by his kinsmen. The latter could include his parents, if still alive, and an assortment of married brothers and their families as well as the groom's unmarried siblings.[53]

Given the decline in relative importance of sharecropping and the increasing prominence of wage labor during this period, it is worth asking whether postmarital patterns changed at this time. To what extent did a preexisting Mediterranean pattern, in Laslett's terms, give way to a northwestern European pattern in which marriage was associated with the establishment of a new household?

We began by asking where women went to live at marriage in the early part of the period and what kind of change in this pattern took place between 1861 and 1921. Since marriage was so closely associated with migration, looking only at those women who were both residents of Casalecchio at the time of their marriage and who remained in the community thereafter could lead to biased results. We therefore used census data to look at all married women in Casalecchio, rather than simply follow those who married while resident in the commune (table 7.11).[54]

The remarkable fact is that there was little change, especially in the first fifty years viewed here, in the propensity of brides to move into their husbands' parents' households at marriage. In 1861 and in 1911 a third of all married women in their twenties were living in households headed by their father-in-law. Half of all these women in 1861 were living in households headed by some relative other than their husband, most frequently one of their husband's brothers if the husband's father was no longer alive. This proportion had declined only to 45 percent by 1911.[55]

Some change in this patrilocal residence pattern does become evident by 1921, but the resilience of this form of postmarital residence in the face of such substantial social, political, and economic changes is striking. A residence pattern that evolved in conjunction with the particular exigen-

Table 7.11. Household Headship Situation of Married Women and Men, by Age: 1861, 1911, and 1921 (by percentage)

	Age 20–29			Age 30–39			Age 40–49		
	1861	1911	1921	1861	1911	1921	1861	1911	1921
Women									
Wife of head	51	54	62	68	78	75	83	88	90
Other kin	49	45	38	32	22	25	17	12	10
Men									
Head	58	48	53	55	70	72	75	89	83
Other kin	42	49	47	44	28	28	25	11	16

Note: The small residual category of persons not related to the head of the household is not displayed here.

cies of a sharecropping economy was not altered overnight as a result of the proletarianization of the community. Rather, many of the old cultural norms became adapted to a new social and economic situation.[56]

The transition from sharecropping to proletarian labor thus did not mean that men necessarily founded their own households at marriage. Here, as before, however, we need to distinguish between changes in norms within occupational groups and changes in patterns due simply to the decline in the salience of the sharecropping sector. If we compare young married men (under age 35) across the half century from 1871 to 1921, we note that the proportion not living as household head shrank from 51 percent to 37 percent. Yet, dividing these men by their occupation (table 7.12), we find this decline is due almost entirely to the rise of the nonagricultural proletariat. At both ends of the half century about a third of these proletarian men lived as dependents in households headed by other kin, while at both ends of the period over 90 percent of the young sharecropping married men lived in such households.

What is most striking, then, about postmarital residence behavior is the remarkable stability of the system in this time of great social change. Economic forces certainly had a great impact on these practices, as seen by the sharp differences between the sharecroppers and the rest of the population. Yet, all the other changes—educational, political, the spread of the city—had precious little impact on the old patrilocal norms. The method used here does not capture the initial postmarital residence choice directly; hence, the proportion of Casalecchio's residents following the patrilocal norm was in fact considerably higher than is shown by the figures provided here. When we combine this with the fact that many of the men would not have had living fathers at the time of their marriage, the high proportion of newlyweds continuing to follow the patrilocal norm is indeed dramatic.[57]

Table 7.12. Percentage of Married Men, under Age 35, Not Household Head, 1871 and 1921

Occupation	1871		1921	
Sharecropper	92	(36)	91	(32)
Agricultural wage	31	(16)	42	(26)
Elite	25	(8)	12	(25)
Artisan/Merchant	35	(20)	27	(45)
Nonagricultural wage	35	(40)	32	(205)
Total[a]	51	(121)	37	(341)

[a]Includes men having occupations other than those listed above.

Widowhood and Remarriage

Every marriage in Italy, in the absence of any law permitting divorce, ultimately led to widowhood for one individual. Given the age difference between spouses, wives generally survived their husbands. As in any system where widows outnumber widowers, especially where cultural norms prescribe the husband's seniority, widows were more likely to remain widows than widowers were to remain widowers.

The frequency of becoming a widow or widower can be compared with the frequency of widow and widower remarriage in Casalecchio. Between 1865 and 1921 there were 361 men whose wives died and 539 women whose husbands died. Of course, the older the couple, the more likely one of them was to die. However, 16 percent of the widowers and 20 percent of the widows were under age 40 when their spouse died, with a total of 33 percent of the widowers and 39 percent of the widows under age 50. Thus, it was thus not uncommon for a person to lose his or her spouse while still caring for dependent children.

Remarriage was not common in Casalecchio, and it became even less common over the years. In the earlier period (1865–1882), 12 percent of all marriages involved at least one widow or widower, but by the latter period (1897–1921) this number had sunk to 5 percent. Widowers were more likely to remarry than widows; in fact, remarrying widowers outnumbered remarrying widows by three to one in the nineteenth century and by two to one in the twentieth. This Casalecchio trend reflects the Italian national pattern during this period. In the late 1860s, 19 percent of all civil marriages involved at least one person who had been previously married, a proportion that was almost halved by the 1920s. The preponderance of widower remarriage over widow remarriage is also evident at the national level.[58]

A corollary of the tendency of widowers to marry women who had not themselves been previously wed was that there was often a considerable age gap between widower and new bride. Half of all remarrying widowers in the years 1865–1882 in Casalecchio were ten or more years older than their brides, a proportion that remained at over a third in the early twentieth century. In the late nineteenth century only 16 percent of the widowers' brides were less than five years younger than they, a proportion that rose to a third by the twentieth century.[59] That younger, never-married women may have had some mixed feelings about these marriages with older widowers may be garnered from the Bolognese proverb "An old husband, better than none."[60]

Not only were Italian men more likely to remarry than women, they also waited less time before remarrying. In the mid-1880s, for example, almost a fifth of all Italian widowers who married did so within six months of the death of their wives, and another fifth did so within the next six months. By contrast, widows were considerably more restrained, with widow remarriage within six months of husband's death extremely rare (0.5 percent). Such rapid widower remarriage, however, was not as common in the Bologna area, including Casalecchio, perhaps because the household system allowed adult men to survive without wives, with the aid of kinsmen.[61]

Of the 110 men who remarried in Casalecchio from 1865 to 1921, almost half (46 percent) were still in their twenties or thirties. Yet only 16 percent of the men who lost a wife in Casalecchio did so while they were under age 40. This provides strong, though only indirect, evidence of the relationship between age and propensity to remarry. Put differently, only 58 men in this age category became widowers in this period, while 51 widowers in this age category remarried. By contrast, while 303 men over age 40 lost their wives in these years, just 59 men over age 40 remarried.

Although widows were much more likely to remarry if they were in their twenties or thirties (indeed, 52 percent of all widows remarrying were in this age range), even young widows had only limited remarriage possibilities. Though 539 women became widows in Casalecchio during these years, just 44 of them remarried.[62]

For the great majority of women who lost their husbands, widowhood would be their lot for the rest of their lives. Even those who lost a husband at an early age, although much more likely to remarry than were older widows, seldom remarried. This reflects a cultural bias against widow remarriage, together with a social system that provided, through kin coresidence, a means for widows and widowers to survive without remarrying. Nevertheless, there did seem to be the general expectation that men who were widowed early should remarry, and such remarriages were not hard to arrange.

It is likely that the propensity for remarriage among older widowers was linked to their economic and household positions, but the relationship here is complex. The well-off sharecropper, for example, might have been a good bet for attracting a spouse, despite his age and widowed status. But, since he had a multiple-family household, there was considerably less pressure on him to remarry, even if he had young children, for he was surrounded by female kinsmen. Indeed, the other women of the household might not have looked favorably on the prospect of a new female authority figure among them. By contrast, the poor proletarian widower might have had a difficult time surviving without a wife, especially if he had small children; yet he was much less desirable as a spouse.

Although few of the widowed remarried, widowhood did not mean social or family isolation in Casalecchio. The widowed—both male and female—typically lived with other kinsmen. The proportion living alone did not rise above 10 percent in these years, while those living in extended- and multiple-family households ranged from 71 percent of the widowers in 1861 to 63 percent in 1921, hovering around 60 percent for the widows (table 7.13).

Table 7.13. Living Situation of Widows and Widowers: 1861 and 1921 (by percentage)

Household Composition	Widows		Widowers	
	1861	1921	1861	1921
Solitary	7	6	8	9
No family	3	4	2	3
Simple family	30	29	19	25
Extended family	23	35	26	33
Multiple family	38	25	45	30
N	74	252	53	130

8 Falling Fertility and Social Change

Previous chapters traced many of the ramifications of the form of the family economy for the lives of the people of Casalecchio. The migration histories of individuals were affected by their family's position in the economy, as was the composition of the household in which they lived. The transition of young people to adulthood and their selection of a spouse were also structured by family economic needs and resources. Turning now to one of the most historically significant changes to take place in this period, the beginning of the decline in fertility, we find again that family economy played a central role.

Indeed, the number of children born to couples from different strata in Casalecchio depended on the value of children in the family economy. Sharecropping families continued to benefit from large households throughout the nineteenth and early twentieth centuries, and their fertility remained high, despite all the social, political, and cultural changes taking place around them. By contrast, changes in economic opportunities for families that depended on wage work, linked in part to government intervention in regulating child labor, increased the costs of having many children and led to fertility decline.

Casalecchio's elite reduced their fertility first, followed by the middle stratum of artisans and merchants and by the wage earners. These fertility reductions were not related to the literacy of wives, nor were they limited to those women who had themselves worked as wage laborers. Although the evidence is somewhat mixed, couples who had lived previously in Bologna may well have been leaders in initiating family-size reduction among the nonelite population.

Theory and Method in Explaining the European Fertility Decline

The classic formulation of the demographic transition explained European population growth during the past two centuries by declines in mortality which were followed by reductions in fertility. This demographic transition consisted of a number of stages: an initial premodern stage of high fertility and variable but high mortality was ultimately replaced by a modern stage of low mortality and controlled, usually low, fertility.[1] In its simplest form, this was described as a three-stage process in which a population that had high levels of fertility and mortality (stage 1) experienced declines in mortality which increased the rate of population growth (stage 2), and after a period of adjustment reduced its fertility to match the low levels of mortality (stage 3).

Although details differed, the general thesis held that improved nutrition, the widespread adoption of measures of public health that reduced the risk of infection, and improved preventive and curative medical procedures reduced mortality. Fertility control came about as part of a multifaceted response to the pressures of population growth in a situation where urbanization and industrialization increased the real and opportunity costs of children, and provided better access to the idea and methods of fertility control. This description of the demographic transition largely grew out of the prevailing view of England's demographic history, but it was extended to describe the way demographic modernization occurred in most European populations.

This picture of demographic change closely paralleled the stage theory of modernization then popular in the social sciences.[2] This classic account of the demographic transition reached its apex with the formal linkage of the stages of the demographic transition to social modernization, especially urbanization and industrialization (Davis 1963). Changes in marriage and coresidence, as well as the migration of populations, were seen as societal responses to the pressures of population growth, the constraints and opportunities of an industrial economy set in urban areas, and individuals' aspirations to share in the rewards of modern prosperity.[3]

While this account of the demographic transition took longer to die than the stage theory of modernization, demographers ultimately cast it aside in the face of mounting counterfactual evidence. Research showed that the mortality and fertility declines in many parts of Europe did not resemble the schematic outline of the demographic transition. Mortality reductions could be attributed as much to government public-health efforts that bettered living conditions and improved medical care as they could to the higher standard of living purchased with the higher earnings of modern-sector workers.[4] Using census and vital-register data, Princeton University's European Fertility Project assembled and analyzed time-series data on the fertility rates of more than seven hundred European districts.[5] The evidence they assembled indicated that fertility declines sometimes preceded mortality reductions. In some nations the declines in fertility were quite gradual, and in others they were much more rapid. Furthermore, the initial timing or pace of the fertility declines failed to correspond to such features of the modernization model as literacy levels or the urban and agricultural percentages of the population.

Demographers therefore began to search for another explanation of the demographic changes that, regardless of their timing, distinguish pretransition and posttransition societies. The most significant clue was provided by researchers from the European Fertility Project, through their ingenious use of formal demographic models of the age patterns of fertility in so-called natural-fertility populations (Coale and Treadway 1986). They were able to show that the marital fertility declines that were the principal component of the European fertility decline occurred when older women limited their fertility. Once women had borne the desired number of children, they took deliberate steps to limit subsequent childbearing (i.e., the decision to prevent another birth was dependent on the number of children already born). It was these individual decisions that produced the European fertility decline.[6]

Declines in marital fertility were first observed in a substantial number of populations beginning about 1870; by 1940 nearly all European populations were engaged in limiting family size.[7] Marital fertility declines occurred first, and were most extensive among, women in the later reproductive ages, women who had presumably already achieved their desired family size and were actively preventing the birth of additional children.[8] Once such family-limitation behavior began to spread in an area, it rapidly diffused to most segments of the population. There is no recorded instance of a population returning to unregulated fertility once people began to limit their completed family sizes.[9]

Despite these regularities in the form of fertility reduction, there were substantial differences among European districts in the date at which family limitation was first observed and in the subsequent pace of its local diffusion.[10] Attempts to explain the timing of these changes in fertility are typically based on ecological models that use the population districts within a nation, or the individual nations themselves, as the units of analysis. These studies have failed to find any consistent relationship between the timing of initial family limitation or the pace of its diffusion and urbanization, industrial development, literacy, education, or the rate of infant mortality.[11]

A number of scholars have, instead, hypothesized that family limitation diffused through each nation along cultural (ethnic, religious, linguistic) lines. Indeed, they show that geographically contiguous areas having similar levels of social and economic development often differed remarkably in the date of onset of family size limitation if the populations were culturally distinct.[12]

Whereas the classic explanation of the demographic transition interpreted European fertility declines as resulting from a reduction in the demand for children, during the past decade an alternative explanation has been advanced that is based on the idea of contraceptive innovation. This theory attributes the reduction to the sudden articulation of a desire for a particular, limited family size, along with reductions in the cost of fertility regulation. Prior to this rationalization of reproduction, according to these theorists, family size was not "within the calculus of conscious choice" (Coale 1973:65).[13]

Unfortunately, researchers have not been especially successful in identifying the mechanisms that lead to a rationalization of fertility. Formal schooling has been regarded as a prime candidate.[14] However, the effects of schooling are multifaceted, and may operate by rationalizing reproduction, by reducing the demand for children, or by increasing contraceptive effectiveness.[15] As a whole, though, research strongly suggests that the effects of education on fertility decline may have as much to do with the increased opportunity costs associated with childbearing by more educated women and with the increased costs of educating children as with any liberating or rationalizing influences. Contrary to the picture presented by the contraceptive-innovation theorists, the evidence suggests that even uneducated couples were rational in their high pretransition fertility regimes, and continued to behave rationally to reduce their family sizes when large numbers of children were no longer beneficial.[16]

The way of life associated with urban residence is another factor sometimes credited with encouraging rationality in fertility decisions. Cities tended to be the leading areas in fertility declines within regions, and the evidence generally supports the finding that the larger the city, the lower the fertility rate. Despite the consistency of this evidence, however, other differentials (notably, regional variations among different cultural groupings) are larger. Moreover, the distinction between rural and urban life can be misleading; rural and urban areas are rarely entirely distinct, and the rural family economy was certainly affected by dramatic economic changes taking place in nearby cities. Also, rural manufacturing, which employed many women and children in wage labor, may well have changed the reproductive calculus outside urban areas, so that couples there began to limit their fertility.[17]

Though a major finding of the European Fertility Project was the discovery that areas with a common cultural heritage tended to be leaders or laggards together in the diffusion of birth limitation, most analysts have been remarkably vague in suggesting just which cultural elements matter most.[18] More boldly, some researchers have explicitly adopted a modernization approach to the cultural-change argument, going so far as to attribute fertility regulation to the personality characteristics thought typical of "modern man."[19] While most demographers have never explicitly acknowledged the obvious connections to the work of Alex Inkeles and other modernization theorists, the general theme of the rationalization of reproductive behaviors clearly owes much to the modernization model.[20] Such an unsophisticated interpretation of demographic change has proven to be as unappealing to social historians as the modernization theory on which it is based. Evidence has accumulated suggesting that peasants in European society sometimes regulated their fertility in response to economic conditions.[21]

Livi-Bacci (1977), in evaluating his Italian research that formed part of the European Fertility Project, has succinctly described the shortcomings faced by analysts of aggregate population data:

> The independent variables that demographers are forced to correlate with fertility are the social, economic, and educational characteristics of the population of each area, which have to be measured through the use of percentages, ratios, or rates. It is tempting, though not logically justifiable, to extend to individuals the relationships found between the "average" characteristics of each area and the corresponding level of fertility. (189)

The basic difficulty with aggregate-level cultural explanations is that they have failed to consider the situations in which the individual behaviors that constitute these demographic processes occur.[22] Comparative studies of the effects of socioeconomic factors within different cultures have been rare. The diverse ways in which people can live out their lives in a single culture have typically been ignored.[23] Levine (1986) makes this same point:

> Individuals must be assumed to make strategic decisions for their own reasons, in order to optimize their perceived circumstances. Such strategic decisions are not wholly determined by the cultural milieu as "modernization theorists" would have it; they are themselves part of a continuously evolving definition and redefinition of the individual's

> relationship to his or her cultural inheritance. Men and women must, therefore, be understood to interpret cultural norms in terms of their own experience. (335)[24]

Besides inattention to variations in individual behaviors across social settings, the failure of aggregate studies to find relationships between economic and social variables and fertility decline may be a product of the crude measures of modernization. While the use of aggregate data offers an impressive geographical scope to historical demographic study, it unfortunately entails significant limitations in pinpointing the process of innovation.

Another practical difficulty with the reliance on population aggregates is the common assumption that the population of each district was relatively closed to migration. Both the geographical descriptions of the diffusion of family-limitation behavior and the ecological analyses that link various indicators of social and economic development to the pace of diffusion of family limitation implicitly assume that migration between the geographical units being analyzed is minor. That is, it is assumed that the population of an area that is not practicing family limitation at one point in time, but later begins to limit births, is largely composed of the same persons. This is not a realistic assumption for historical research in Europe. Migration tends to follow cultural boundaries. If migrants were at the forefront of birth limitation, the migratory behaviors of the population could provide the mechanism for diffusing family-limitation behaviors between culturally similar areas.[25]

Studies based on aggregate population data are inadequate to test a variety of other explanations of the social, economic, and cultural factors underlying the demographic transition. The most critical issue in explaining fertility declines is to identify those groups in the population that initiated family limitation and to trace its diffusion through the rest of the population.[26] These questions are best addressed with individual-level data. As Livi-Bacci (1977) concluded in his Italian component of the European Fertility Project:

> It is our opinion that further research at the aggregate level is not likely to add to the general picture of fertility decline given in this book. . . . At the micro-level, the characteristics of fertility decline could be followed for selected groups of the population. For instance, the comparative evolution of fertility and nuptiality in the agricultural classes, according to the type of land-ownership system and in connection with the analysis of the structure of the family and of response to changing economic conditions, could prove extremely productive. (289)

Hypotheses about Casalecchio's Fertility Decline

Just this sort of fertility analysis is the goal of this chapter. We believe that the spread of agricultural wage labor in Casalecchio, as throughout much of rural Bologna, during the nineteenth century preadapted the agrarian population to fertility reduction prior to industrialization. In this context, we sought to test our hypotheses that changing patterns of female employment, the growth of public education and the spread of literacy, and shifting patterns of coresidence between parents and their adult children during this period provided the social bases for fertility reduction. We also wanted to test the thesis that migration itself may have provided a mechanism for the diffusion of the idea of family limitation from urban Bologna to the more rural surrounding areas, such as Casalecchio.

Family Economy and the Economic Value of Children

Sharecropper (*mezzadri*) families lived in large households in which children contributed to agricultural activities. This pattern did not basically change between 1861 and 1921 and, from the point of view of household economics, there is little reason to suppose that fertility should decline. In the mid-nineteenth century children were of economic value to the agricultural wage laborers (*braccianti*) and nonagricultural wage earners, but not for any contribution they made to a household work force. Rather, these children either left home early to work as agricultural or domestic servants, or sought wage work in the textile factories or in the fields. The economic value of younger children to wage-earner families declined during the remainder of the nineteenth and early twentieth centuries as the institution of service was abandoned and governmental restrictions on child labor in the factories raised the age at which these children could find employment. We therefore expected to find a greater decline in fertility among the wage laborers than among the sharecroppers.

What was crucial in determining the net value of children, then, was not whether the family was engaged in agriculture but the role of the children in the family economy. We hypothesize that the wage earners—both agricultural and nonagricultural—reduced their fertility as the net value of children declined.[27] Increases in formal education and the decline of apprenticeships also reduced the net value of children for many of the artisans and merchants of Casalecchio.[28] Thus, we hypothesize that the fertility of this middle stratum declined at about the same time as that of the wage-earners. Other differences between the classes probably modified these expected patterns. The higher educational attainment of the middle-stratum parents and the prolonged school enrollments of their children may have hastened their fertility decline. But high fertility might have persisted somewhat longer among these artisans and merchants, for their greater incomes could enable them to continue to have large families even as the net cost of children increased. Moreover, for some middle-stratum families, children could be put to work in the family enterprise, and the fact that the wives of these families were less likely to be engaged in wage work meant reduced opportunity costs for child care.

Female Wage Labor

Except among the elite and some artisan and merchant families, adult women in Casalecchio were engaged in production. But the mode of these productive activities differed significantly between sharecropper and wage-earner families. Women contributed to the sharecropper household economy by working in the ongoing activities of peasant agriculture in the fields and in the house. The large sharecropper households provided numerous sources of child care (by young girls and old women) so that the labor loss associated with motherhood was minimized. Moreover, the reproductive capacity of young women was important for sharecroppers, since they depended on a continual supply of children to maintain the pool of household labor contractually obligated to the *padrone*.

Wage-earner households did not have access to the physical resources needed for home production. Women contributed to the household economy by working for wages in jobs outside the household. Alternatively, women might remain at home and bear and raise children who would soon work for wages in the textile mills or whose labor would be contracted out as a servant or apprentice.[29] But as child labor became restricted during the late nineteenth and early twentieth centuries, the benefits of the second option diminished. Moreover, most wage-earner households lacked ready sources of child care. Thus, the opportunity costs of childbearing were greater among the wage-earner households than among those of the sharecroppers. This situation would have further reduced the net economic value of children for the wage earners over the period.[30]

Literacy and School Enrollment

Throughout the latter part of the nineteenth century, children of sharecroppers were less likely to attend school than were the children of wage laborers. Sharecropper families were reluctant to send their children to school since they made significant contributions to the household work force; the young children of wage laborers did not. Moreover, travel time to school was substantially greater for sharecropper children who lived in isolated farmsteads. The result was that, despite their higher standard of living, sharecroppers were less literate than wage laborers.

Literacy and increased levels of education of adults have conventionally been linked to smaller completed family sizes. The new home economics has associated increases in maternal education with increases in women's economic opportunities.[31] The presumed effect of this movement is to increase the opportunity cost of children, and thus lead to parental preferences for fewer children, with a greater investment made in each one. Likewise, modernization theory has viewed education as a modernizing influence that provides access to information and teaches secular attitudes, values, and behaviors consistent with rational fertility decision making.[32] In either model, greater education means greater likelihood of family limitation.

While the new home economics and the modernization approaches to literacy and fertility reach similar practical conclusions, the economic approach does not embrace the modernization thesis that often equates illiteracy with irrationality. Indeed, this equation has been increasingly undermined in the face of extensive evidence of the economic rationality of family, household, and forms of social organization in preindustrial and preliterate populations. In this light, it is significant that recent empirical research has found no linkage between literacy or education and the timing of the European fertility decline. Evidence for developing nations suggests, instead, that additional education may reduce fertility only for those with more than a primary school education and that the effects of education may differ between rural and urban communities.[33] In this chapter we measure the linkage between literacy and fertility in Casalecchio to test our supposition that there is no simple relationship between the two.

Birth Limitation Leaders

Research suggests that elite groups and urban dwellers often led the rest of the population in reducing fertility (Livi-Bacci 1986; Sharlin 1986). These were the groups for whom children were most costly, and who were the most "modern" in their socioeconomic and cultural characteristics. Given the continuing interchange between urban and nearby rural populations, it seems likely that ideas about birth limitation often diffuse from the one to the other.[34] We hypothesize that the elite of Casalecchio, following the elite throughout much of Italy, reduced their fertility earlier than any other group.[35] However, the great social distance between the elite and the rest of the Casalecchio population makes it unlikely that attitudes tov ard birth limitation diffused directly from the former to the latter.

It is worth asking, though, whether it was the large number of artisans, merchants, and wage earners who had previously lived in Bologna who were the initial limiters of fertility among this sector of the Casalecchio population. Sharecroppers had no motivation to reduce their fertility and migrant sharecroppers seldom had experience of urban Bologna, limiting the exposure of sharecroppers to these ideas.

Household Composition and Fertility

The sharecroppers had larger, more complex households than did other Casalecchio residents. We believe that these differences in household composition were associated with fertility in three ways, two of which we have already discussed. First, sharecropper households needed labor, and labor was primarily recruited through reproduction. This economic imperative produced large, complex households and involved a high demand for children. Second, the sharecropper households included many young girls and older women who could assist in child care, limiting the opportunity costs of children. Third, we hypothesize that coresidence of the wife with her husband's family maintained high fertility. Research has associated greater autonomy of the wife in family decision making with the adoption of fertility regulation. Neolocal residence is likely to promote greater husband-wife communication and greater equality in family decision making, both of which increase the influence of the wife on reproductive decisions.[36]

The Fertility Decline in Italy, Bologna, and Casalecchio

Prior to the fertility transition, Italy had an annual crude birth rate (number of births per 1,000 people) of about 37. The birth rate of Bologna province was 37.5 in 1810–1812.[37] The national Italian birth rate did not begin to decline until the 1880s, dropping from 36.3 in 1880–1882 to 34.8 in 1890–1892. The birth rate continued to decline very slowly, reaching 32.4 in 1910–1912. The index of marital fertility recorded a 10 percent decrease from natural fertility levels in 1913, and the fertility of Italian women declined rapidly thereafter. The crude birth rate was 28.9 by 1921–1926. The birth rate of the Emilia-Romagna region displays a similar history, declining from 37.9 in 1862–1866 to 28.2 in 1921–1926.[38]

There were significant preexisting differences between urban and rural fertility levels, and the fertility decline appears to have begun somewhat earlier in the cities. In northern Italy as a whole in the 1870s, localities having under 20,000 inhabitants showed a birth rate of 37.1, while in cities of over 100,000, like Bologna, the rate was 31.5. By the last two decades of the nineteenth century, rural and urban birth rates were 34.3 and 26.7, and, in the first decade of the twentieth century, 34.9 and 23.1 (Natale 1982:221). These rural-urban differences may be a bit misleading, due to the higher concentration of unmarried adults in the cities (and, indeed, to the tendency of unmarried adults to move from rural areas to big cities).

However, the fact that the urban rate dropped from 85 percent to just 66 percent of the rural rate during this period provides clear evidence that the fertility decline gathered force earlier in the cities than in the countryside of northern Italy.[39]

The existence of this underlying difference in fertility rates between the city and the countryside is clear in the Bologna area as well. In 1847, the number of births per 1,000 women aged 15–50 in the city of Bologna stood at just 108, as opposed to 139 in the plains, 125 in the hills, and 152 in the mountains.[40]

In that same year, the crude birth rate for the whole province of Bologna stood at 33. The birth rate of Casalecchio prior to its fertility decline hovered around the same figure: 33 in 1865–1874, 36 in 1875–1884, and 34 in 1885–1894. It was only in the latter part of the nineteenth century that Casalecchio began to depart from this stable level of high fertility, dropping to 27 in 1895–1904, 29 in 1905–1914, and 21 by 1915–1921.

As discussed in chapter 7, there was little variation in age at marriage during the period of our study. Births to unmarried women were few because premaritally conceived births were ordinarily legitimated by marriage.[41] The crude birth rate of Casalecchio declined because the fertility of married women decreased. We look at the timing of this decline and try to tease out the social and economic differentials in the fertility decline that remain hidden at the aggregate level.[42]

In 1811–1812, the number of births per 1,000 married women of reproductive age (called the *marital general fertility rate*) of the province of Bologna was 271.[43] The marital general fertility rate of Casalecchio from 1867 to 1877 was just slightly lower, averaging 258 and fluctuating between 244 and 275. From 1878 to 1888 the marital fertility rate declined by 6 percent to an average of 243 (fluctuating between 233 and 257). The marital fertility rate declined continuously thereafter until it reached the 170s at the beginning of the twentieth century, a 34 percent drop from pretransition marital fertility (fig. 8.1).

The European Fertility Project defined the beginning of the fertility transition as that date by which marital fertility first declined by at least 10 percent from its pretransition fertility level. Employing this definition, we can date the beginning of Casalecchio's fertility decline as 1890 (when the marital fertility rate dropped below 232). After dropping down to 174 in the first years of the twentieth century (1901–1906), the marital fertility rate showed a short-term modest increase—to 190—in 1907–1915.[44] It then plummeted to 142 in 1916–1919 as hundreds of Casalecchio men were mobilized into the Italian armed forces during the First World War.[45]

The fertility history of Casalecchio thus shows many similarities to the

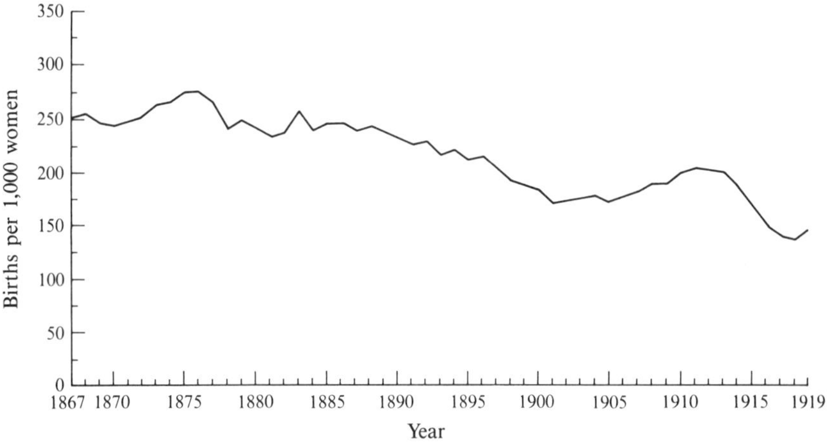

Fig. 8.1. Five-Year Moving Average of the Annual Number of Births per 1,000 Married Women: Casalecchio, 1867–1919

general Italian experience, but displays certain differences. The pretransition birth rate of married women in Casalecchio was very similar to that found in other parts of Italy. The crude birth rate of Casalecchio likewise resembled that of the rest of the province of Bologna at the beginning of our period of study. However, the fertility decline in Casalecchio began earlier than in much of the rest of the province of Bologna, reflecting its ever closer social and economic ties with the city of Bologna, which had lower fertility than its rural hinterland. In common with the pattern found throughout Europe, once Casalecchio's marital fertility fell by 10 percent, it never again returned to its former high levels. The period we study here thus encompasses the onset of the fertility decline, providing the setting for a microlevel inquiry into the fertility transition.

Fertility Differentials in Casalecchio

Data and Methods

We used several sources of data and a variety of methods to shed light on marital fertility differentials and decline in Casalecchio. The birth data for all of these analyses were ultimately drawn from the civil birth register files. We matched these births with data from three different sources to relate fertility to maternal and family characteristics. The first file matches births to households in the annual household tax list (the *focatico*), the second uses manuscript census data; and the third employs marriage record data.

Using the *focatico,* we divided all women of reproductive age into four categories based on occupation of their household head: (1) members of the property-owning elite, (2) artisans and merchants (middle), (3) sharecroppers, and (4) wage earners and the poor.[46] We were thus able to classify the Casalecchio population for each year from 1869 to 1905. This allowed us to calculate, for each year, the marital general fertility rate for each category, and to identify trends in each rate over time. We also calculated the age-specific fertility rates of married women separately by their economic category. Social-strata differentials are identified and we investigate their association with mother's age and time period by using log linear modified multiple regression models.[47]

The *focatico*-based models document fertility differences among the four major social strata during a crucial period in the fertility history of Casalecchio. They provide direct insight into the role of the household economy in the fertility transition. However, the *focatico* data do not go beyond 1905, when fertility reached a temporary nadir, and they do not provide any direct information on the characteristics of either the women or their husbands.

Moreover, the *focatico* does not provide information on all women who were resident in Casalecchio during the years 1869–1905, as we can see by comparing the women found in the *focatico* households with the complete list of women found in the population register. A total of 15,976 person-years of experience was recorded in the population register for married women of reproductive age during this period. The *focatico* includes only 12,826 person-years (80 percent) of this reproductive exposure. A total of 2,432 births (68 percent) were matched to women who were covered in the *focatico* from 1869 to 1905, out of a total of 3,577 births recorded in Casalecchio during this period. Moreover, the representation of Casalecchio women in the *focatico* decreased over time (from 85 percent in 1869–1880 to 78 percent in 1881–1892 and 79 percent in 1893–1905). In 1869–1880, 68 percent of all births were recorded to *focatico* mothers, compared to 66 percent in 1881–1892 and 70 percent in 1893–1905. Thus, the marital general fertility rate recorded in the *focatico* is too low, especially in the early years. (According to the *focatico* data, the general marital fertility rate during these periods declined from 206 to 200 to 181. The population register records the declines during the same period as 251 to 244 to 191.)[48] The *focatico* does accurately track the timing of the fertility decline, although the magnitude of the decline recorded is too low because of the biased coverage of the early period. The *focatico* therefore provides valuable, but potentially biased, insights into the fertility transition in Casalecchio.

For more direct data on the social and economic characteristics of women of reproductive age and their husbands, we used the censuses of 1871 and 1911.[49] We selected women who were married and aged 15–49 at the time of each census. The birthplace and literacy of the wife, the occupation of her husband, and the relationship of the wife to the head of the household were ascertained as of the census date. The number of months these women were both present and married during the sixty-month period centered on the census was calculated from the population register (to measure the period of exposure to the risk of a birth), and the number of births each of these women experienced in Casalecchio during this period was determined by reference to the birth register.[50]

The census data provide a rich source of information on the women and their spouses, but they, too, have several weaknesses. They provide a view of fertility behaviors before and after declines in marital fertility, but do not give continuous coverage of the critical period when the fertility decline began. The number of women observed in the censuses is small (334 in 1871 and 587 in 1911) and their fertility rates are thus subject to considerable random variations.[51] As with the *focatico,* the recorded birth rates using the censuses are also too low, although the bias does not appear to change over time. (The marital fertility rates for the censused women compared to the population-register-based rates were 227 vs. 254 in 1870–1874 and 174 vs. 198 in 1910–1913.) The census data do, however, show that a fertility decline did occur, and can shed light on the differential participation of women in that decline.

The *focatico-* and census-based analyses of the fertility decline in Casalecchio refer to the behavior of women during specific time periods and permit tests for changes in the age pattern of fertility. However, making use of microlevel, longitudinal data, we can go beyond this. The final step in our analysis of the fertility decline is the examination of differentials in the life course of fertility. Here we used the birth histories (based on the birth registers) of Casalecchio women, following individual women through their reproductive lifetime. However, here too we faced a limitation, for the population register did not record the number of children previously born to women who moved to Casalecchio as adults; nor did any of the censuses during this period collect data on lifetime fertility. Thus, we can construct birth histories only for those women who were married in Casalecchio or who moved to Casalecchio immediately after marriage.[52]

Each parity progression, beginning with the interval between the first and the second birth and ending with the seventh to the eighth birth, is a fertility episode in this analysis.[53] The experience of all women who began a given parity interval is investigated, with that interval ending either with the birth of the next child or by being censored (at the date of migration from Casalecchio, the fiftieth birthday, death, or the end of observation in 1921). A total of 939 women fulfilled the conditions for inclusion in this study. They contributed a total of 3,201 episodes of second- to eighth-parity progression intervals.

Independent variables in this analysis include the occupation of the husband and the wage-labor work experience of the wife, the literacy of the wife, and migration experiences of the husband and wife. These data are obtained from the marriage registers. The effects of these variables, controlling for parity interval, time period, and mother's age, are estimated by means of proportional hazards models fitted with partial likelihood procedures.[54]

The major advantage of this marriage-registry-based analysis is the view it provides of the life course of fertility. It enables us to model differentials in the pace of childbearing directly. The major disadvantage of the marriage-registry-based analysis is our inability to consider the experience of women who moved to Casalecchio more than ninety days after marriage. Another problem is that many women moved out of Casalecchio during the course of their childbearing years, for, as seen in chapter 5, this was a highly migratory population. The result is that the higher the parity level under examination, the more the population represented by the study is biased toward women who were less migratory.

We now turn to our analysis, beginning with differences among the economic strata in their period rates of fertility, and their age patterns, for the years 1869–1905.

Fertility and the Household Economy

Wives from the middle economic stratum—the artisans and merchants—had an average fertility rate of 207 births per 1,000 women from 1871 to 1887, with only modest year-to-year variations during this period. After 1888, the fertility rate of middle-stratum wives increased for a period of five years, before beginning its substantial decline in 1892. By the later years of the nineteenth century the marital fertility rate of middle stratum wives was 111, 46 percent below the fertility level recorded in the mid-nineteenth century. The fertility rate of the middle-stratum wives increased modestly from 1901 to 1903 but remained far below its pretransition level (fig. 8.2).

The fertility of the wage-earner households remained fairly constant from 1871 until 1895, averaging 195 births per 1,000 married women. After this long period of stability, the marital fertility of the wage earners began to decline in 1896, leveling off at 138 in 1900–1903, a decline of 29 percent.

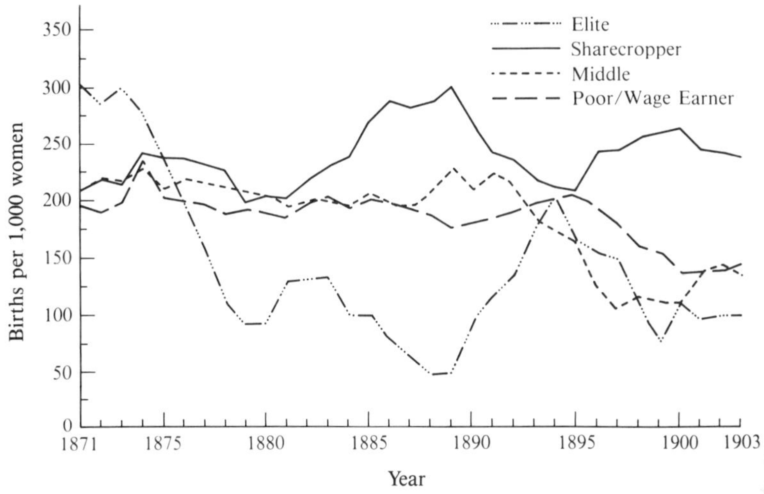

Fig. 8.2. Five-Year Moving Average of the Annual Number of Births per 1,000 Married Women by Strata: Casalecchio, 1871–1903

Thus, the fertility decline of the wage earners began at roughly the same time as that of the middle stratum, but the pace of the decline was somewhat slower. By the turn of the century, though, the two groups once again had similar, but greatly reduced, fertility rates.

Throughout the period of study the sharecroppers had higher marital general fertility rates than the other strata (fig. 8.2). This differential was relatively small during the 1870s, a period of high, stable fertility rates among the sharecroppers, the middle stratum, and the wage laborers. The marital fertility of sharecroppers increased substantially during the agricultural crisis of the 1880s, climbing from recorded rates in the 199–244 range to rates of 269–299 by the late 1880s. Their fertility returned to earlier levels immediately after the agricultural crisis, but then increased again in the late 1890s, staying at a level of about 247 births per 1,000 women into the twentieth century. By 1900–1903, the sharecroppers had a fertility rate that was three-quarters higher than that of either the wage earners or the middle stratum.[55]

The decline in marital fertility in Casalecchio thus did not involve all economic groups. The small Casalecchio elite were the first to reduce their fertility.[56] Other groups in the population did not limit their fertility until two decades later, when women in the middle stratum, as well as the wage earners and poor, began to reduce their fertility. Sharecroppers, for whom large families remained an economic necessity, showed no sign of a fertility decline, despite the changed fertility behavior of all the other groups surrounding them.[57]

We wanted to make sure that these intergroup fertility differences and trends were significant, and to determine whether these fertility declines were due solely to lower fertility on the part of older women or whether younger women were lowering their fertility as well. To do this, we estimated log linear modified multiple regression models of fertility using the *focatico* data. Each woman-year of experience is a unit of observation in these models. The dependent variable is simply whether a woman had a birth during the year.[58] Independent variables include the woman's age (divided into five-year age groups), time period, and household economy (table 8.1).

Each of the log linear models takes as a given the associations found among the independent variables (that is, each allows for the changing age composition of the social strata). The model-fitting strategy we use starts with the most complicated model and tests whether successively simpler specifications of the relationships between the independent variables (age, time period, and strata) and the dependent variable (whether a birth occurred during the year) can provide an adequate account of the associations between them.

The first model estimated (table 8.2, model 1) says that the probability of a birth changed over time, with these changes being concentrated more in some age groups than in others, and with these trends in fertility differing by economic stratum. This model is called a *saturated model* since it includes every possible interaction and has a chi-square value of 0.0 with 0 degrees of freedom. We next estimated a model (table 8.2, model 2) that includes every lower-order interaction but excludes the four-way association between age, birth rate, stratum, and time period. The comparison of this model and the saturated model indicates the statistical significance of the four-way interaction term (NAYS). The claim that the age pattern and level of fertility changed over time in a strata-specific fashion (i.e., that NAYS is statistically significant) is rejected, since the chi-square statistic associated with the contrast (table 8.2, model 3) is not statistically significant ($\chi^2_{LR} = 37.4$, $df = 36$).

Further investigations indicated that the average age pattern of fertility during this period did not differ by stratum (see table 8.2, model 7, which compares models with and without the ANS term).[59] In fact, combining persons from all strata, the age pattern of fertility did not change despite the substantial declines recorded in the fertility level (see table 8.2, model 11, which compares models with and without the YAN term).[60] These results provide evidence that the fertility decline in Casalecchio was not simply

Table 8.1. Woman-Years of Exposure to the Risk of a Birth by Birth Status, Age, Period, and Social Strata, 1869–1905

	Time Period					
	1869–1880		1881–1892		1893–1905	
	Birth	No Birth	Birth	No Birth	Birth	No Birth
Elite						
15–19	0	5	0	1	0	1
20–24	2	8	1	11	5	6
25–29	9	11	7	16	6	17
30–34	13	28	3	17	2	26
35–39	5	25	3	17	2	31
40–44	6	23	2	36	1	38
45–49	0	24	0	32	0	28
Middle						
15–19	2	14	3	7	0	2
20–24	24	41	31	39	24	44
25–29	37	62	46	89	33	91
30–34	33	110	33	123	22	130
35–39	20	91	36	157	26	147
40–44	9	93	6	138	10	155
45–49	1	61	1	99	0	171
Sharecropper						
15–19	3	9	1	6	3	14
20–24	59	92	65	75	37	74
25–29	82	179	82	154	94	148
30–34	57	158	59	155	74	159
35–39	39	164	44	153	58	175
40–44	20	183	10	127	12	184
45–49	1	159	1	110	0	174
Wage Workers and Poor						
15–19	7	14	5	31	7	23
20–24	56	90	84	161	89	152
25–29	83	208	118	307	119	401
30–34	81	246	98	272	121	496
35–39	69	301	54	252	90	507
40–44	23	273	27	280	31	458
45–49	3	279	0	324	2	402

produced by changes in the behavior of older women and that the declines in the fertility rates of particular strata were not concentrated among older women.[61]

Nevertheless, these models do indicate that, net of the age pattern of fertility and the changing age composition of the four strata, trends in the probability of a birth differed significantly across strata (see table 8.2, model 13, which compares models with and without the YNS term). The

Table 8.2. Log Linear Models of Trends in Age-Specific Nuptial Fertility by Social Strata, 1869-1905

Model	χ^2_{LR}	*df*	*p*
1. (YANS)	0.0	0	–
2. (YAS) (YNS) (YAN) (ANS): constant age pattern by strata	37.4	36	.404
3. 2 vs. 1 (YANS): strata differences in changes in the rate and age pattern of births	37.4	36	.404
4. (YAS) (YAN) (ANS)	57.2	42	.059
5. 4 vs. 2 (YNS): changing birth rate by strata	19.8	6	.004
6. (YAS) (YNS) (YAN)	58.7	54	.309
7. 6 vs. 2 (ANS): different age pattern by strata	21.3	18	.268
8. (YAS) (YAN) (NS)	77.8	60	.061
9. 8 vs. 6 (YNS): changing birth rate by strata	19.1	6	.004
10. (YAS) (YNS) (AN)	64.2	66	.541
11. 10 vs. 6 (YAN): changing age pattern	5.5	12	.904
12. (YAS) (AN) (YN) (SN)	83.8	72	.162
13. 12 vs. 10 (YNS): changing birth rate by strata	19.6	6	.004

Note: N = birth during year (0/1 or more); Y = time period (1869-1880/1881-1892/1893-1905); A = age (15-19/20-24/25-29/30-34/35-39/40-44/45-49); S = strata (elite/middle/sharecropper/wage workers and poor).

model that fits the *focatico* fertility data best—the model that includes all statistically significant terms and deletes those terms that are not significant—is one that takes into account the changing age compositions of the strata (YAS), the average age pattern of fertility (AN), and the changing marital fertility levels of women in the different strata (YNS) (table 8.2, model 10).[62]

Thus, the model that best fits the data is equivalent to a set of age-standardized marital fertility rates arrayed by strata and time period. To simplify the presentation of the size and magnitude of these statistically significant fertility differentials, table 8.3 provides the annual nuptial fertility rates for each of the strata in each period, directly standardizing for differences and changes in the age compositions of the strata. The marital fertility rates of the elite declined by 45 percent between 1869-1880 and 1881-1892. The marital fertility rates of the middle stratum and wage workers declined only slightly between the first and second periods, with larger declines observed between 1881-1892 and 1893-1905. By contrast, the marital fertility rates of the sharecroppers actually increased between 1869-1880 and 1893-1905.

Were the declines in fertility observed among the wage workers linked to declines in the net economic value of children for households whose economic basis was wage labor, or were the declines observed first among

Table 8.3. Births per 1,000 Married Women by Period and Social Strata, 1869–1905

	Time Period		
Social Strata	1869–1880	1881–1892	1893–1905
Elite	239	132	139
Middle	207	200	154
Sharecropper	212	228	236
Wage workers and poor	201	190	164

Note: Rates for each strata are directly standardized on the age distribution of all married women observed in the *focatico* from 1869 to 1905.

those in this category who were poorest and who were driven by abject poverty to limit fertility? To address this question we reanalyzed the *focatico* data, distinguishing between women whose households were in the lower and higher tax categories within this stratum.[63] The results were negative: distinguishing income level within the stratum did not improve the explanation of changing birth rates.[64]

A second possibility that we investigated is that immigrants, particularly those with urban experience, might have led the fertility decline. This question is most pertinent for those in the middle stratum and for wage-earner households, since sharecroppers who immigrated to Casalecchio typically came from other rural areas. The population registers permit us to compare the marital fertility of women who migrated to Casalecchio from Bologna with the marital fertility of those who came from rural areas. Among married women living in artisan and merchant households for the years 1869–1905, the age-standardized number of births per 1,000 was 151 for those who had immigrated from Bologna, compared to 253 for those who had immigrated from other rural communities. Among wage earners the differences were in a similar direction, but their magnitude was considerably less (173 for those from Bologna and 212 for other immigrants). The evidence suggests that women who had lived in Bologna prior to coming to Casalecchio may have been at the forefront in introducing family limitation behavior to the artisans and merchants and among the proletariat of Casalecchio.

Analysis of the *focatico* data clearly shows that the decline in marital fertility differed by the kind of household economy in which women participated. The marital fertility of the elite declined first, as was the case in much of Europe. The fertility of artisans, merchants, and wage earners declined later in the nineteenth century, while the fertility of sharecroppers remained high well into the twentieth century. This evidence is consistent with the thesis that families began to reduce their fertility as histori-

Casalecchio di Reno, Panoramic View

cal changes in the bases of the household economy reduced the value of children.

However, the same groups that began to limit their births were also more "modern" (being more literate and more involved in the emergence of modern political organizations) and more often had previous urban experience. Were the changes in the family economy of central importance in the fertility decline or can the spread of family limitation be accounted for by these other modern characteristics? An analysis of the census-based fertility data can permit us to measure the effects of women's characteristics, such as literacy, more directly.[65] The inclusion of a measure of the husband's occupation, moreover, provides us with another test of the effects of family economy on marital fertility.[66]

Economic Activity and Modernity in the Fertility Decline

The census data confirm the importance of the family economy in the marital fertility of Casalecchio couples, especially by highlighting the sharp difference between the sharecroppers and the rest of the population (table 8.4). In both periods the fertility of the sharecroppers was high (239–251), with no evidence of any decline. By contrast, the elite (who are few in number), artisans and merchants, and wage earners all show clear evidence of decline between 1870–1874 and 1909–1913. A multiple classification analysis indicates that the magnitude of the differences among the four strata changes somewhat when the woman's age at the beginning of the

Table 8.4. Multiple Classification Analysis of Number of Births Per 1,000 Married Women by Social Characteristics, 1870–1874 and 1909–1913

	1870–1874			1909–1913		
Social Characteristics	Observed	Net	*N*	Observed	Net	*N*
Woman's Age		***			***	
15–24	–	415	(46)	–	347	(124)
25–34	–	282	(144)	–	198	(234)
35–49	–	112	(144)	–	55	(229)
Woman's Birthplace		*				
Casalecchio	293	288	(86)[a]	181	175	(148)
Plains	205	201	(100)	169	167	(192)
Hills	212	222	(62)	204	200	(126)
Bologna	186	175	(61)	177	172	(78)
Woman's Literacy					–	
Literate	274	269	(63)	–[b]	–	–
Illiterate	221	218	(270)	–	–	–
Relationship to Household Head		*				
Wife	201	199	(227)	156	168	(430)
Other kin	285	286	(103)	226	186	(152)
Husband's Occupation		*			***	
Elite	329	318	(17)	132	146	(50)
Artisan/Merchant	224	184	(35)	168	164	(80)
Sharecropper	251	226	(105)	239	224	(123)
Wage worker	216	238	(169)	170	172	(295)
Total Population	227	227	(334)	174	174	(587)

[a]Total number of cases may vary because of missing data, for which a category was included but results are not shown.

[b]Literacy information not available in 1911 census.

*$p < .10$. **$p < .05$. ***$p < .001$.

interval, commune of birth, literacy, and coresidential pattern are taken into account. However, even controlling for these other variables, the basic contrast between the sharecroppers and the rest of the population remains prominent.

As discussed in chapter 4, men often became household heads relatively late in life, a pattern particularly pronounced among sharecroppers. The wife's relationship to the household head is commonly seen by demographers as an indicator of the couple's autonomy in making decisions about family limitation. Presumably, when a young married woman is living in a household with her husband's parents, she is more likely to be influenced by their attitudes toward fertility than she would be if she were living in a household of her own. Indeed, this relationship is reflected in Casalecchio, for women living in households headed by their in-laws had higher fertility in both periods. Even by 1909–1913, women living as daughters-in-law of the household head had substantially higher fertility than women who were wives of the household head.

These cross-sectional differences are in the expected direction, but they do not mean that women whose husbands were household heads necessarily led the fertility decline. Although the fertility of women living in households headed by their parents-in-law was higher than that of other women in both periods, their fertility declined from one period to the next at virtually the same rate as did that of women living in their own households. The more fertile daughters-in-law reduced their fertility by about 21 percent, no different from the 22 percent reduction recorded among women whose husbands were household heads.

Before we reach any hasty conclusions about the role of place in the household in determining fertility behavior, we need to recall that the likelihood of a married woman living in an in-law-headed household was directly related to whether she was a sharecropper and whether she was relatively young. Women who were daughters-in-law or other kin of the household head were more likely to be from sharecropper households and were on average younger than women who were wives of the household head. If we take these factors into account, controlling for occupation and age, we find that although wives of the household head had lower fertility than other women in 1870–1874, this difference had disappeared by 1909–1913. Thus, controlling for confounding factors, the greatest fertility declines seem to have occurred among women who had the least autonomy in household decisions. This suggests that rather than greater autonomy in decision making enabling women to act on their desire to limit fertility, changing exigencies of the household economy affected the fertility decisions of women whether or not their husbands headed their own household.

In both the traditional demographic transition and the modernization models, it is presumed that fertility reduction is led by women with more education, a variable commonly measured by literacy. Casalecchio, however, offers no support for this notion. Indeed, literate women had higher recorded birth rates than illiterate women in 1870–1874, although this difference is not statistically significant. There is no evidence that literate women were pioneers in the reduction of fertility. Even when controls are introduced for other variables, this pattern remains unchanged.

Fertility over the Life Course

As described earlier, we reconstructed the fertility histories of women who lived in Casalecchio from the time of their marriage until their fiftieth birthday or through the date of their emigration from Casalecchio, their death, or the end of our period of observation (1921), if any of these came before the woman had reached age fifty. In order to exclude women whose fertility was biologically impaired, we restricted consideration to the second and later parity intervals, that is, to wives who had had at least one child.

We consider the effects of the independent variables on overall parity progression rates, pooling the different parity intervals across all time periods. By distinguishing between lower and higher parity of the woman at the beginning of the postbirth interval, we can determine whether birth limitation begins at higher parities. The age of the wife is measured as a spline function in which one variable codes for ages between 15 and 35 and a second variable indicates additional years of age beyond 35.[67]

Our independent variables encompass both demographic and social characteristics, and are drawn from data provided by the husbands and wives at the time of marriage. The husband's occupation serves as an indicator of the nature of the family economy. Most women worked prior to marriage, although certain kinds of labor—especially factory labor—declined sharply with years after marriage. Our analysis includes an indicator of whether the woman's work involved wage labor. This employs the woman's premarital labor experience to provide a crude measure of the opportunity costs of childbearing. The wife's literacy at the time of marriage is determined by whether or not she signed the civil marriage register.[68]

Finally, we employ a measure of the couple's residential history to determine whether migrants, especially those from Bologna, had lower fertility rates. The couple's residential history uses information on commune of birth and commune of residence at the time of marriage. Couples classified as "Casalecchio natives" were both born in Casalecchio and lived there at the time of marriage. "Bologna migrants" are couples in which either the husband or the wife was born in Bologna or the marriage ceremony occurred in Bologna. "Rural migrants" are people who were either born in another rural commune or married there. A fourth value is used for couples for whom some residential information is missing.

Considering all parity progression intervals in combination, the downward trend in fertility between 1865 and 1921 is clear (table 8.5). Between 1865–1882 and 1883–1896 the rate of parity progression declined by about 21 percent. The rate of parity progression declined by an additional 20 percent between 1883–1896 and 1897–1915, and 19 percent more by 1916–1921. The rate of parity progression in 1865–1882 was 95 percent higher than the rate observed in 1916–1921.[69]

There is no evidence that this decline was parity-specific, once age differences between high- and low-parity women are taken into account. The fertility of these women declined rapidly in the later reproductive years, with the rate at each additional year of age beyond 35 being only 76 per-

Table 8.5. Partial Likelihood Proportional Hazards Analysis of Differentials in the Rate of Parity Progression: Women Resident in Casalecchio Since Marriage

Independent Variables	Number of Cases	Multiplier of Rate
Parity Interval	3,177	1.034*
Period		
1865–1882	562	1.952***
1883–1896	862	1.546***
1897–1915	1,323	1.239**
1916–1921	370	1.000
Age of Wife 15–35	3,177	0.954***
Years Wife Beyond 35	3,177	.760***
Literacy of Wife at Marriage		
Literate	1,816	0.982
Illiterate	202	1.000
No civil marriage	1,099	0.993
Wife's Work at Marriage		
Wage earner	485	1.005
Not wage earner	2,632	1.000
Husband's Job at Marriage		
Elite, artisan, merchant	211	0.831**
Sharecropper	916	1.243***
Wage earner	1,990	1.000
Residential History at Marriage		
Casalecchio natives	432	0.951
Rural migrants	1,457	1.000
Bologna migrants	726	0.920
Information missing	502	1.037
Fit of Model		
χ^2_{LR}		339.9
Degrees of freedom		14
p		0.000

$^*p < .10$. $^{**}p < .05$. $^{***}p < .01$.

cent as high as that found in the immediately preceding age.[70] This represents a combination of biological impairments and other factors affecting natural fertility, as well as any deliberate age-related actions taken by these women to reduce their fertility. A more modest reduction in the birth rate (4.6 percent) was associated with each additional year of age up to the thirty-fifth birthday. The parity progression rates of women aged 35 at the beginning of the interval were only 60 percent as high as those of women aged 25. Thus, the fertility behavior of Casalecchio women depended upon their age but was largely unaffected by the number of children already born.

Literate and illiterate wives had identical rates of parity progression during this period. There is no evidence that literacy provided special access to modern ideas that promoted birth control. Women who were engaged in wage work when they married had parity progression rates during their marriage that were identical to those of women who were not working for wages. At least as measured by this crude indicator, it does not appear that wage work before marriage caused fertility reduction by providing human capital experience that raised the opportunity cost of childbearing or by providing women with an alternative role to motherhood. It should bc kcpt in mind, though, that factory owners generally preferred younger women workers. Moreover, the low level of training required for most wage labor and its low pay and unpleasant working conditions do not make it especially suitable for an opportunity-cost explanation of lowered fertility.[71]

There were no statistically significant differences in the family-building behaviors of Casalecchio natives and couples with migrant experiences. Nor did exposure to Bologna produce any overall decline in the rate of parity progression. It is well, however, to keep in mind that our variable—composed of birthplace and place of residence at time of marriage—is not as good an indicator of urban influence as was provided in our *focatico*-based analysis, which used actual place of origin of immigrants to Casalecchio to show a lower fertility rate among urban-origin migrants to Casalecchio.

Consistent with the occupational differences in period fertility rates, the wives of sharecroppers have the highest life-course fertility, with rates of parity progression one-quarter higher than those of the wives of wage earners. The rate of parity progression among wives of members of the elite, artisans, and merchants was about 17 percent lower than that of women married to wage earners. Once again, then, the economic situation of the family emerges as the social factor that differentiates high- and low-fertility couples.

9 European Social History and Demographic Theory

As scholars have sought to come to grips with the great social changes that transformed Western societies over the past two centuries, they have tried to piece together just how it was that people's behavior changed so dramatically. The illiterate have become literate, women today typically bear one or two children rather than seven or eight, the large complex families once flourishing in parts of Europe exist today only in attenuated form, and children are expected to spend their childhood living with their parents rather than as servants or apprentices in the homes of others as they commonly did in the past.

Given the apparent contemporaneity of these massive social changes with historical economic changes—especially the rise of modern industrialization—it is not surprising that economic explanations have been so central to the scholarly debate. Insofar as social relations and cultural values and views represent ways of adapting to economic circumstances, the social and cultural transformations of Western society in the nineteenth and early twentieth centuries can be seen as products of fundamental changes in the economic structure. In this perspective, for example, if people begin having fewer children, it must be because changes in the economy make having many children no longer economically beneficial. People are seen as fundamentally rational creatures, ever seeking to maximize their security and their well-being.

An alternative, noneconomic perspective on these historic social and cultural changes also has a long pedigree, linked to a branch of modernization theory. In this view, the radical change that took place in the West over the past two centuries involved a switch to the use of economic rationality as people's customary mode of assessing what constitutes desirable behavior. This perspective holds that human behavior was long dominated by irrational principles, such as religion, superstition, and family and local chauvinism. The fact that fertility was so high in the past was not due to any advantage people derived from having many, as opposed to few, children, but merely to the dominant cultural ideas regarding marriage, sexuality, and control over one's fate.

In recent years, increasing numbers of scholars have voiced reservations about both of these positions. A simple economic determinist position fails to fit the evidence in many cases—such as in accounting for the decline of fertility in the West. Moreover, in its classic form it is murky about the mechanisms whereby economic change brings about social and cultural change. A key issue here is the level at which principles of rationality work. For example, it may be beneficial for a society to have a high birth rate without it being beneficial for individual women or couples to bear many children. In such cases, there is a conflict between adaptation at the societal level and adaptation at the individual level. Since individuals, not societies, bear children, presumably some social mechanism must operate if people's behavior is to be brought in line with societal requirements. This in turn raises the central issue of the role of culture and social organization in influencing people's behavior, apart from any direct economic calculation of the benefits of that behavior on the part of the individual.

Yet, scholars who today reject economic determinist models in accounting for social and demographic change are not clamoring aboard the once-popular alternative described above. The notion that we modern Westerners are guided by rational principles and by clear notions of means-ends relationships, while people in the past and, presumably in other parts of the world today, act irrationally, has been increasingly rejected as a product of Western ethnocentrism. The alternative to viewing people everywhere as guided in their behavior by rational economic considerations, then, is not that of seeing rational calculation as a recent innovation explaining social and cultural change. Rather, the alternative is seeing humans everywhere and at all times as living in worlds that are both economic and symbolic, both composed of material relations and culturally-influenced ways of viewing life.

In asking what lessons the Casalecchio case has to teach us about the modern social and demographic transformation of Western society, we face these classic issues of the basis of human behavior. This is not to deny, of course, the particularity of Casalecchio or the pitfalls of generalizing from a single town to an entire continent. Yet, in some respects, intensive study of a particular community, which enables us to actually examine the course of individual lives over time, offers as valuable a vantage point for considering these general questions as do the aggregate-level statistical studies that compare whole regions or countries. This is especially true when we move from general questions of correlation between economic characteristics of regions and the social or demographic behavior found there and inquire into the actual path by which these changes spread through populations.

Yet it is well to recall Casalecchio's distinctive traits, some of which make the community of special historical and theoretical interest. Although long dominated by farmland and sharecropping agriculture, Casalecchio had become notable by the mid-nineteenth century for its large textile factory. Moreover, even in its more purely peasant past, Casalecchio's proximity to the large city of Bologna was significant. This was no isolated rural zone; it had had close relations with the city for centuries.

With its centuries-old sharecropping economy, Casalecchio shared in the same complex-family system that operated throughout a large portion of central and northern Italy. It was a family system that differed dramatically from that found in many other parts of western (and especially northwestern) Europe. Here the household containing three generations and two or more married couples, related through the male line, was indeed the norm and not simply the myth of Western nostalgia that some scholars have claimed it to be. What we have in Casalecchio, then, is not so much a typical case of the impact of industrialization, the spread of modern capitalism, and the growth of city life on family life, as a classic case. Casalecchio embodies in dramatic form both a traditional way of life in a kin-enveloped European family context and the impact of industrialization and urbanization on family and demographic behavior.

The Transformation of Family Life

Rapid changes in the economy brought about significant changes in family life in Casalecchio, but not all aspects of family relations were equally affected. Indeed, in some respects, family organization and norms remained surprisingly constant in the face of the economic and political transformation of the community, the province, and the country.

The sharecroppers, the segment of the community with the most traditional system of family organization, proved to be the most resistant to change. Even after six eventful decades of dizzying historical changes around them, amazingly little change was evident in their family lives. Just as about one hundred sharecropper households dotted the agricultural land of Casalecchio in the mid-nineteenth century, so were the same number of households found on the eve of the Fascist era. These households continued to be occupied by multiple-family groupings, with sons bringing their brides into their parental household and children growing up surrounded by their paternal grandparents, paternal uncles, and their patrilateral parallel cousins, as well as by their own parents and siblings. Sharecropper daughters continued to leave their parental household at marriage, commonly moving into the complex-family household of their sharecropper husband. Indeed, sharecroppers were not only traditional in their family organization but also socially isolated from other parts of the community, despite their ongoing relations with the agricultural wage laborers who helped on their farms and who often spent cold winter nights with them in their barns. A boy or girl from one sharecropping family was encouraged to find his or her spouse from another sharecropping family, and the great majority did so in the early twentieth century as they had in past centuries.

Insofar as household-formation processes changed over these years, the changes appear to have little to do with the major cultural, political, and social developments occurring during this period. Those who argue in favor of a cultural-modernization view of family change can find little comfort in the Casalecchio case. Political changes could hardly be more dramatic, as the masses moved from a position of total subordination to the landed elite and the Church to a new empowerment via the socialist and union movements. With this came the spread of new ideas about emancipation, about taking one's life in one's hands and questioning centuries-old sources of authority. Yet, in themselves, these changes had no dramatic effect on family life. In particular, the sharecroppers, who must have learned of these new ideas, showed no sign of altering their family behavior as a result. Under pressure from the landowners, they were in no position to give up on multiple-family household living and all that went with it.

Among the rest of the population, many of the most significant changes in family life predated the major social, political, and cultural developments of the late nineteenth century. It was not literacy, political organization, or spreading socialist ideas that led much of the rest of the population to spend the majority of their lives in simpler family households, more closely approximating our ideas of modern family organization. Economic forces had long operated to encourage such simpler forms of coresidence, with the household no longer serving as a primary productive unit and with the task of providing housing—most often consisting of small, dank apartments—the responsibility of the family rather than of the landowner.

Indeed, the changes in household composition that occurred in the half century from 1871 to 1921—as the proportion of the Casalecchio population living in complex-family households declined from 52 percent to 44 percent—can be accounted for largely in terms of the expansion of the proletarian sector and the decline in the proportion of the population involved in sharecropping. Within individual occupational categories, we find no clear pattern of decline of complex-family arrangements, despite the cultural changes sweeping the area. While only the sharecroppers showed a clear predominance of multiple-family household organization, it is also worth recalling that other parts of the population typically lived in complex-family households for portions of their lives. Among the non-sharecropping population, it was not uncommon for newlyweds to live, if only for a relatively brief period, in the parental home of the groom before setting off on their own. Moreover, at the end of our period, as at the beginning, the elderly were not left on their own but were cared for in the homes of their married children.

One of the aspects of family formation that has often been regarded as especially susceptible to changes in macroeconomic forces is age at marriage. Indeed, the sensitivity of age at marriage to economic change is central to the efforts of many historical demographers to find the homeostatic mechanism that brought population and resources into balance in the centuries before modern birth control (Wrigley and Schofield 1981). A decline in age of marriage has also been linked to changes in cultural norms that move marriage increasingly under individual, rather than parental, control. These cultural changes are themselves reinforced by economic changes that undermine the sources of parental control over children's marriages.[1] Yet, we are again struck by the tenacity of family norms and behavior in Casalecchio despite the changes taking place in so many other aspects of life. Women's age at first civil marriage remained unchanged (24.6 in 1865–1882 and 24.7 in 1897–1915), while men's age declined minimally (from 28.5 to 27.8).[2] These results cast some doubt on any simple link between economic change and marriage age. Cultural norms regarding the appropriate age for marriage are remarkably tenacious and tend to spread throughout the population across economic groups.

Reflections on Demographic Change

Other aspects of marriage and fertility reflected cultural and economic considerations as well as family control of sexual behavior. Bridal pregnancy was common during these years, especially among the proletariat. Research has typically emphasized the economic need that forces women and children to work in factories, or, alternatively, stressed the economic autonomy that paid factory labor provides. We find little support for the second interpretation. Women's work among the Casalecchio proletariat was not an option but a necessity—these poor, often destitute, families were in desperate need of the meager income women and children could bring to the household.

While women's economic autonomy proved unimportant in Casalecchio, the social and economic realities of wage labor are critical in understanding changes in reproduction during these years. The disappearance of service as an early life stage, coupled with the needs of newly built factories and service industries for child labor, made it increasingly likely that a child of the proletariat would live at home until marriage. This transformed the nature of family life for older children and young adults.

Yet such coresidence did not imply the successful imposition of family authority in all aspects of life. Although factory work was regimented, it provided young men, and, especially, women, with considerable autonomy from their families in day-to-day life. By their early twenties many of these women became pregnant, and legitimated the birth by marriage. Their husbands typically came from the proletariat, and often were fellow factory employees. Daughters of the more conservative sharecroppers, by contrast, were subject to continuous family supervision and were far less likely to be pregnant at marriage.

While the extended family has commonly been viewed in demographic research as a major factor in the persistence of high fertility, we find little evidence for such a claim. The number of children born to a couple in Casalecchio reflected the economic value of children to the household; these same economic considerations had led to the formation and persistence of extended families in the first place.

Proletarian families continued to have large numbers of children as long as it was economically rational to do so. During the second half of the nineteenth century, compulsory school-attendance laws began to raise the costs of children for the proletariat. The disappearance of service further increased the costs of children by extending their stay in the parental household. The incomes that could be earned by these children declined with the disappearance of service and the passage of increasingly restrictive labor laws regulating children's factory work. Faced with these declines in the economic value of children, proletarian families substantially reduced their fertility. In short, the proletariat responded to changes in the economic structure by opting for smaller, less expensive families in which their meager household incomes could be maximized by having both wives and husbands employed.

There was little change in marriage age during this period. Instead, fertility declines were accomplished by the limitation of childbearing within marriage. It is unlikely that fertility control by the proletariat was accomplished by increases in postpartum sterility due to changes in breast-feeding practices. The medical literature of the time suggests, if anything, a decline in breast-feeding. Factory labor, even after the introduction of regulations to enable mothers to breast-feed their children, was not conducive to the type of continuous, long-term suckling commonly associated with longer interbirth intervals. It is likely, then, that traditional methods of contraception (withdrawal, abstinence, folk contraceptives, and abortion) were used by these couples to limit their fertility.

It appears that such contraception was practiced among women of all childbearing ages and was not limited to older women who had already had the desired number of children. This pattern makes economic sense in several ways. Factory employment was more readily available for young women, raising the opportunity costs of childbearing early in the life course. Few proletarian families had the kind of economic surplus (from dowry or savings) that would have permitted young wives to remain out of the labor force and bear children during the early years of marriage. Finally, given the economic costs of children and the cramped living quarters of the proletariat, the costs of children could be more easily shouldered if they were spaced over a number of years.

Family economic interpretations of demographic change have typically been contrasted with the idea of contraceptive innovation, a situation in which couples come to recognize that fertility is subject to intervention and control, freeing them to limit family size (which, it is presumed, would have been beneficial all along). Casalecchio certainly exhibits the ingredients necessary to advance a modernization argument for the observed demographic changes. As we have seen, this was a time of dramatic social change in Casalecchio. The expansion of schooling led to widespread literacy. There were increased population exchanges between this rural town and the city of Bologna, and these accelerated with improved transportation for daily commuting between the two. It was a time in which a nation-state replaced ecclesiastical political rule, and common people became politically radicalized, successfully demanding participation in the political process. Unions were formed to demand improved working conditions.

Surprisingly, our evidence suggests that a modernization argument can be most successfully made for two demographic processes in which such factors have seldom been considered: population mobility and mortality. The evidence for such an explanation of the fertility decline is decidedly less persuasive.

Population mobility in Casalecchio had traditionally been high, involving population circulation between Casalecchio and neighboring rural communities as well as movement to and from Bologna. Until the late nineteenth-century resurgence of Bologna as an economically prominent urban center, the city was not an especially powerful population magnet, although its sheer size made it an important source of population exchange for Casalecchio. Indeed, for a time, the presence of the largest textile factory in this part of Italy made the small town of Casalecchio an important industrial (albeit still rural) outpost.

The Casalecchio case illustrates that urbanization and industrialization need not entail any increase in migration rates. Indeed, just the opposite was the case, as rural industrialization provided relatively stable jobs in rural areas, and improved transportation systems enabled individuals in the twentieth century to select among a broader range of jobs without having to move to a city. These changes were particularly pronounced among the young, with the disappearance of service (which typically had involved short-distance migration) as a life stage.

While urbanization and industrialization did not lead to greater mobility in the area under study in this period, they were associated with the increased importance of long-distance movements, a type of migration that had previously been quite rare. The growth of a sense of national consciousness and the conscription of young men from Casalecchio seem to have facilitated this change.

Improvements in public health in the late nineteenth century (inoculation programs, improved disposal of sewage, and the provision of safe drinking water) were among the most important sources of change in life chances. These government programs led to sharp declines in mortality during these years as the epidemics of prior centuries were increasingly brought under control. But infant and child mortality among the proletariat remained high until the turn of the century. The employment of women in factories, associated with bottle-feeding of infants, substantially increased the likelihood of infant death. The government intervened with the passage of legislation requiring factories to provide breast-feeding rooms or schedule breast-feeding periods during the workday. Other measures provided free medical care and pharmaceuticals to the poor. These government interventions, rather than marked improvements in the economic standard of living, appear to have been the key factors leading to substantial mortality declines in the population, improving, in particular, the life chances of the children of the proletariat.

It is noteworthy that these changes did not occur automatically as a feature of modernization. Rather, they were the results of the demands of an increasingly vocal and radicalized proletariat, a proletariat that was also seeking improved wages for its labor. It is important, then, to view the declining fertility of the proletariat as but one part of the response of that class to its harsh economic circumstances. At the same time that individual proletarian couples were acting to improve their personal economic chances by limiting fertility, they were demanding government actions to advance their life chances and those of their children, and they were organizing to demand better wages and working conditions from their employers.

Certainly, these behaviors reflect the advent of a new epoch in this part of the world. But these new ideas represent rational human responses to changes in the class organization of the society, not the sudden emergence of rational thinking coupled with individual self-interest. The story of demographic change in Casalecchio thus cannot be understood as the simple result of culture, the forces of modernization, or changes in the family economy: it involved all of these. The story of the demographic transition must be understood in its larger context – it represents an interplay of forces of demographic, social, economic, and political change. With the passage of time the growth of the proletariat changed the nature of the Casalecchio population as a whole.

Further evidence for this argument is provided by the persistence of traditional marriage, fertility, and family patterns among the sharecroppers. The sharecroppers did not decline in numbers but did decline as a proportion of the population. Socially isolated, and economically shackled by their contracts with the landowners, their demographic behavior and family situation remained remarkably unchanged well into the twentieth century. While their declining share of the population meant that their behavior became increasingly unimportant for the character of Casalecchio as a whole, only the demise of sharecropper contracts ultimately led to the disappearance of their traditional demographic regime.

Contrary to popular image, those sharecroppers forced off the land did not become industrial proletarians directly. More often, they became agricultural wage earners. After a time, they and their children sometimes joined the ranks of factory laborers. Nonetheless, this study demonstrates that the key distinction for Casalecchio families was not agricultural versus nonagricultural work, but source of income (share of product as opposed to a wage) and who was contractually obligated (the entire household or a single worker). On these dimensions, agricultural wage laborers resembled factory workers rather than sharecroppers. Changes in economic opportunities over time meant that an increased share of the proletariat were nonagricultural workers. But agricultural wage labor and factory labor coexisted as work options for the proletariat during much of this period. Individual workers moved between factory work and agricultural work at different stages in the life course; sons of wage earners became wage earners themselves, with little importance attaching to the agricultural vs. nonagricultural distinction; and agricultural and nonagricultural laborers intermarried with each other, but rarely did they marry outside the proletariat. Thus, agricultural wage laborers and nonagricultural wage earners were both part of a single proletarian class.

Artisans and merchants shared in many of the same changes in economic value of children and in migration behavior. They benefited from the public-health measures that reduced the diseases ravaging the poor population that surrounded them. Some members of this class differed little from the proletariat in terms of their social origins and economic resources. While the fertility declines among the elite preceded those in the rest of the population, artisans and merchants were the first to follow this example. Our evidence suggests that artisans and merchants who had been residents in Bologna were leaders in the adoption of birth limitation; the proletariat followed shortly after.

Over time, this artisan and merchant class became larger. More cohesive class interests emerged. While some artisans and merchants sided with the socialists, the political and economic interests of most members of this class differed considerably from those of the proletariat. These political interests gradually became organized, leading ultimately to the political confrontation of fascism and socialism that marks the end of our period of study.

Thus, the growing percentage of the population in the proletariat and artisan and merchant classes increasingly meant that the behaviors of these groups, rather than those of the traditional elite and sharecropper classes, came to define life in Casalecchio. The changes we have recorded in the patterns of birth, marriage, death, and household formation and dissolution among the proletariat and artisans and merchants were an integral part of the changes that marked the emergence of the modern Italian population. By the end of our period of study, we can see in place the elements that continued to characterize social and economic life, demographic behavior, and political interests in this part of Italy throughout much of the twentieth century. Only in more recent decades have dramatically changed demographic patterns begun to emerge, with the aging of the population, the decrease in proportions marrying and increases in marriage age, and declines in fertility to only one child per woman.

Implications for Demographic and Family Research

We hope that this study will encourage researchers to seek out data archives and reconstitute other key populations of the past. The pitfalls inherent in generalizing from a single such study—be it based on Casalecchio or Colyton—to entire regions and continents are apparent. Yet the temptation to do so will always be present, given the richness of the data such studies provide and the limited number of such studies that have been undertaken. Evidence from other communities undergoing the demographic transition is the only realistic approach to assembling the kinds of evidence needed for continued improvements in our knowledge of social history.

Aggregate-level studies of populations remain the common strategy of demographers studying the history of the demographic transition as well as current fertility declines in developing nations. These will continue to be valuable for the description of changes that have occurred. But such studies are typically inappropriate for a comprehensive explanation of multifaceted demographic behaviors. There are substantial, theoretically relevant variations in demographic behaviors among groups within a single population. Population studies that rely on geographic units (be they districts, provinces, regions, or nations) lack the individual-level data needed to identify such variations and may therefore fundamentally misconstrue the nature of the demographic changes that are occuring. This is compounded by the related problem of ecological fallacy, to which aggregate demographic studies too often fall prey. The analysis of trends is subject to even greater problems if the population being studied was subject to considerable mobility and if migrants were leaders in demographic change.

Other problems in typical demographic analyses (both microlevel and macrolevel studies) arise from the mechanical nature of models of change and the fundamental misspecification of critical concepts. Too often, culture is treated as a black box that accounts for residual changes not associated with economic or social factors. Studies must attempt to identify what it is about an ethnic, religious, or linguistic group that conditions their demographic behavior. It is important to understand the social context of these changes as well. Level of industrial development and a rural/urban distinction—two measures frequently used as proxies for "modernization" in these studies—may be fundamentally incorrect for analyses of changing demographic behavior. The Casalecchio study supports the conclusion reached by other social historians that the type of industrial development is important because of its implications for female and child labor and that class position, which determines the form of the family economy, is more important than an agrarian/nonagrarian or rural/urban distinction.

Finally, political change and state intervention may be key ingredients in demographic modernization. The forces of secularization may weaken religious authority; education in state-run schools and conscription of young men can widen world horizons; improvements in transportation systems can expand economic opportunities and alter the costs and benefits of migration; state laws regarding the education and employment of children may change the economic calculus of reproduction; and public-health measures and the provision of adequate medical care can significantly reduce mortality. While the demographic debate has tended to focus on the effectiveness of overt attempts by government to intervene in reproductive processes (to lower fertility by means of family planning programs or to raise fertility with various pronatalist measures), such indirect, but quite powerful, governmental influences have been neglected. We must attend to the importance of the state if we are to further our understanding of demographic processes and provide better-grounded recommendations about demographically desirable public policies.

We believe that the groundwork has been laid for improvements in demographic research. The continued strength of the field of social history and the renewed social scientific interest in combining quantitative and qualitative research methods facilitate truly interdisciplinary demographic research. The life-course perspective encourages research that considers the household and family context of individual behaviors and the relation of societal changes to demographic behavior over the life course. New computer technologies assist in the task of reconstituting populations and manipulating the complex data files that result, and new statistical methods ease the analysis of these data. A much more ambitious and intellectually challenging research agenda than has been the norm for demographic studies is emerging. We believe it will be well worth the effort.

Appendix

Notes

References

Index

Appendix
Archival Sources and the Casalecchio Data Base

Many archival sources were used to breathe life into the Casalecchio of times past. In this appendix we limit ourselves to describing those that were employed in constructing the individual-level data base used for our demographic studies. (Other archival sources are described in the endnotes.) We also provide an overview of the record system employed in translating the data gleaned from our sources into computer-readable form, consider problems of data quality and completeness and how these were addressed, and give a sketch of the data-base management system designed for this project.[1]

Archival Sources

The Casalecchio data file is the product of many different archival sources, encompassing both civil and religious records. Of course, before Unification there was no distinction between civil and church records, for the two were one under the papal state system. However, by 1860 Church and state were not only separate but mutually antagonistic and their records were totally distinct. Most civil records regarding residents of Casalecchio were kept by the municipal government, following instructions from higher levels of the state bureaucracy. Most church records, on the other hand, were kept by the priests of Casalecchio, separately for each of the four parishes. Indeed, Casalecchio no longer had any ecclesiastical unity. All civil records employed in constructing the demographic data base came from the communal archives of Casalecchio, with the exception of the conscription registers, which were found in the state archives in the city of Bologna. Religious records are not only scattered among the four parishes of Casalecchio but also found in the city of Bologna, in the archives of the central baptismal church. We had full access to all civil records, but more restricted access to religious records, particularly to those pertaining to the twentieth century.

A. The population register (l'anagrafe). This is the fundamental source for the construction of the Casalecchio data file, for it follows the population of the commune continuously through time (though not without a number of imperfections, as noted below), describing demographic events and changes in coresidence throughout the period of study (1865–1921). The population register consists of the following four parts:

1. The initial population listing of 1865. In order to initiate the population register in 1865, the commune undertook a complete census. This served as the base point for the register.

2. The household forms. For administrative purposes, the population of the commune was divided into households, and each such administratively defined household was provided with a folder (documents 1 and 2). The folder was designed to give the date of entry and exit of the household and the initial address and dated subsequent changes of address; it identifies successive household heads; and it provides a list of all individuals who ever lived in the household (though a num-

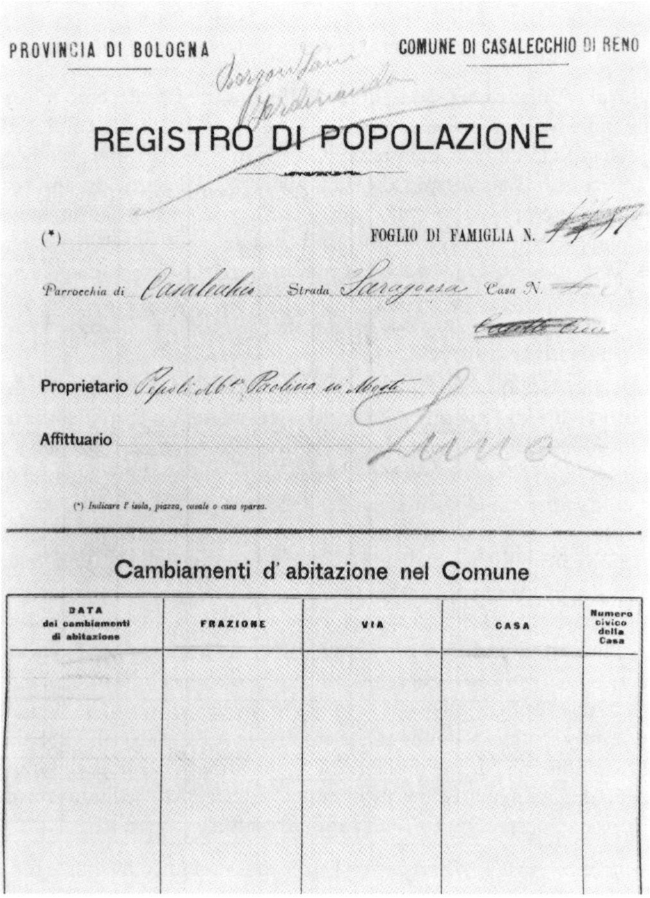

PROVINCIA DI BOLOGNA — COMUNE DI CASALECCHIO DI RENO

REGISTRO DI POPOLAZIONE

(*) FOGLIO DI FAMIGLIA N.

Parrocchia di Casalecchio Strada Saragozza Casa N.

Proprietario

Affittuario

(*) Indicare l'isola, piazza, casale o casa sparsa.

Cambiamenti d'abitazione nel Comune

DATA dei cambiamenti di abitazione	FRAZIONE	VIA	CASA	Numero civico della Casa

Document 1

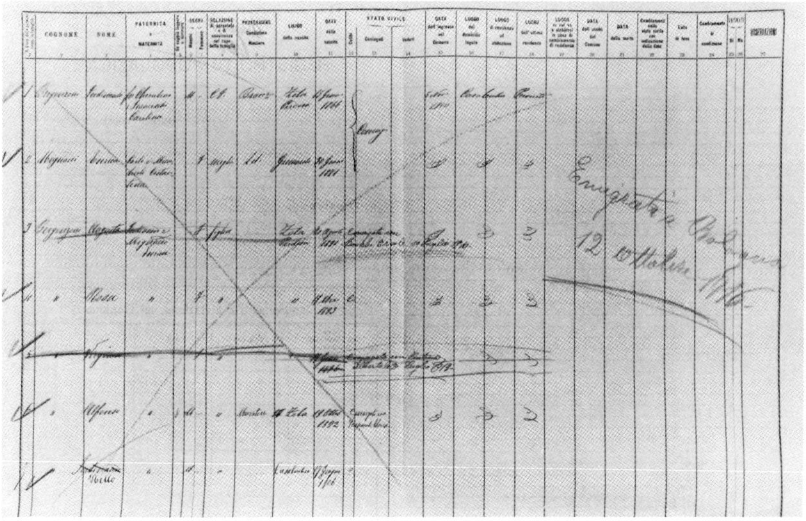

Document 2

ber of gaps are found, especially with respect of the highly transient household members, such as servants). For each individual it provides the date of entry to, and exit from, the household; relationship to successive household heads; and, in cases of migration, the commune immigrated from and the commune emigrated to. Information for each individual also includes names of father and mother (including maiden name), sex, date and place of birth, marital data, and occupation. However, as the occupational entry is undated, and there was no legal compulsion to register changes in occupation, this information was not used for the data base. A few hundred of the over three thousand household forms were missing. Fortunately, it proved possible to reconstruct these using information contained in the individual forms described below.

3. The individual forms. Each individual is provided with a record card (documents 3 and 4). These cards are kept in alphabetical order, containing all demographic and coresidential data pertaining to the individual for the time he or she lived in Casalecchio. Dated cross-references to the household register are also provided, giving the number of the household form in which the individual is listed. All information pertaining to the individual that is found in the household folder is also found on the individual form.

4. The migration forms. The population-register system includes both immigration and emigration registers. These provide data on all individuals who ever moved into or out of Casalecchio during the period of study. The entries are arranged in chronological order and ordinarily give a cross-reference to the number of the household form in which the individual is found (document 5). Information is provided on individuals who moved together, including both date of migration

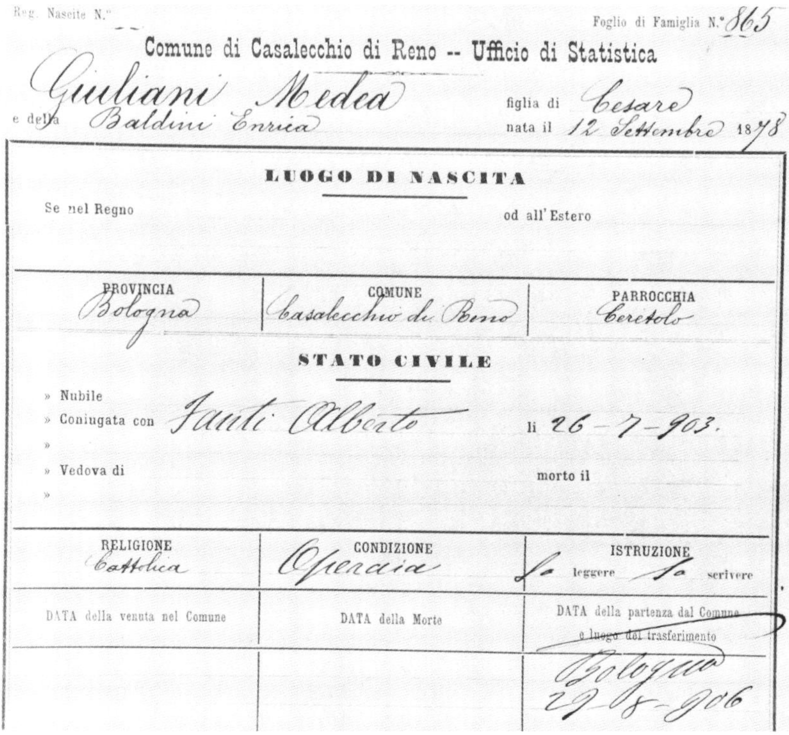

Reg. Nascite N.°

Foglio di Famiglia N.° 865

Comune di Casalecchio di Reno -- Ufficio di Statistica

Giuliani Medea figlia di Cesare

e della Baldini Enrica nata il 12 Settembre 1878

LUOGO DI NASCITA

Se nel Regno od all'Estero

PROVINCIA	COMUNE	PARROCCHIA
Bologna	Casalecchio di Reno	Ceretolo

STATO CIVILE

» Nubile

» Coniugata con Fanti Alberto li 26-7-903.

»

» Vedova di morto il

»

RELIGIONE	CONDIZIONE	ISTRUZIONE
Cattolica	Operaia	sa leggere sa scrivere

DATA della venuta nel Comune	DATA della Morte	DATA della partenza dal Comune e luogo del trasferimento
		Bologna 29-8-906

Document 3

and commune of origin/destination. When Casalecchio residents moved to another commune they had to register with the officials of their new commune. These officials were required to send a copy of that immigration record back to Casalecchio, where it was entered into the emigration record (document 6). Both immigration and emigration records are provided with an alphabetical index covering ten-year periods.

B. Civil registers. These are of three kinds: the birth register, the civil marriage register, and the death register. Each of these registers has an annual alphabetical index, as well as an index covering each decade. Not only do they contain information on all births, marriages, and deaths that took place in Casalecchio, but they also contain this information for all such events involving Casalecchio residents which took place outside the commune.

C. Manuscript censuses. The available manuscript censuses for this study encompassed 1861, 1871, 1881, 1911, and 1921 (document 7). No census was conducted in Italy in 1891, and copies of the 1901 census were not generally retained. Casalecchio had long ago disposed of its 1901 manuscript census sheets.

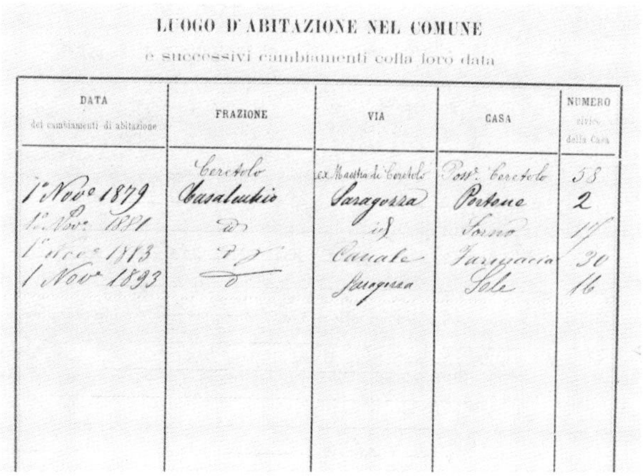

LUOGO D'ABITAZIONE NEL COMUNE

e successivi cambiamenti colla loro data

DATA dei cambiamenti di abitazione	FRAZIONE	VIA	CASA	NUMERO civico della Casa
	Ceretolo	ex Maestra di Ceretolo	Poss. Ceretolo	58
1° Nov° 1879	Casalecchio	Saragozza	Portone	2
1° Nov° 1881	do	id	Forno	17
1° Nov° 1883	do	Canale	Farmacia	30
1 Nov° 1893	do	Saragozza	Sole	16

Document 4

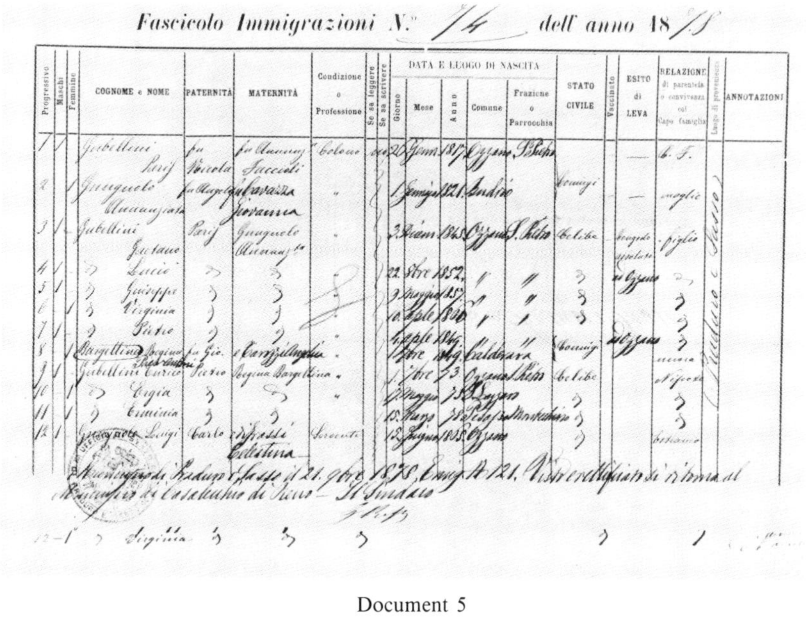

Fascicolo Immigrazioni N.° 14 dell'anno 1878

Progressivo	Maschi	Femmine	COGNOME e NOME	PATERNITÀ	MATERNITÀ	Condizione o Professione	Se sa leggere	Se sa scrivere	Giorno	Mese	Anno	Comune	Frazione o Parrocchia	STATO CIVILE	Vaccinato	ESITO di LEVA	RELAZIONE di parentela o convivenza col Capo famiglia	Luogo di provenienza	ANNOTAZIONI
1	1		Gubellini Paris	fu Nicola	fu Annunziata Facciòli	colono			20	Genn	1817	Ozzano	S. Pietro			—	C. F.	Budrio e Sasso	
2		1	Gnugnolo Annunziata	fu Angelo	Albavazza Giovanna	"			1	Giugno	1821	Budrio		Coniugi		—	moglie		
3	1		Gubellini Gaetano	Paris	Gnugnolo Annunz.ta	"			3	Dicem	1848	Ozzano	S. Pietro	Celibe		Congedo assoluto	figlio		
4	1		do Lucio	do	do				22	8bre	1852	"	"	do		in Ozzano	do		
5	1		do Giuseppe	do	do				9	Maggio	185[illegible]	"	"	do			do		
6		1	do Virginia	do	do				10	Aprile	1860	"	"	do			do		
7	1		do Pietro	do	do	"			4	Aprile	1864		"			in Ozzano	do		
8		1	Bargellini Regina	fu Gio.	Carrozzi Angelica	"			1	9bre	1846	[illegible]		Coniugi			nuora		
9	1		Gubellini Enrico	Pietro	Regina Bargellini	"			1	7bre	73	Ozzano	S. Pietro	Celibe			Nipote		
10		1	do [illegible]	do	do	"			[illegible]	Maggio	75	Ozzano					do		
11		1	do Erminia	do	do				15	Marzo	78	[illegible]	[illegible]	do			do		
12	1		Gnugnolo Luigi	Carlo	Rifrassi Celestina	Servente			15	Giugno	1858	Ozzano		do			[illegible]		

Municipio di Budrio e Sasso il 21. 9bre 1878. Emig. N. 121. Visti e rettificati di ritorno al Municipio di Casalecchio di Reno – Il Sindaco

12-1 do Virginia do do do do 1

Document 5

Fascicolo Emigrazioni N. 29 dell'anno 189/ 22 …

Progressivo	Maschi	Femmine	COGNOME E NOME	PATERNITÀ	MATERNITÀ	Condizione o Professione	Se sa leggere	Se sa scrivere	DATA E LUOGO DI NASCITA: Giorno	Mese	Anno	Comune	Frazione o Parrocchia	STATO CIVILE	Vaccinato	ESITO di LEVA	RELAZIONE di parentela o convivenza col Capo famiglia	Luogo di trasferimento	ANNOTAZIONI
1	1		Pascuiti Enrico	Serafino	Vidotto Teresa	Muratore			25	Nov	1859	S. Pangolo		Coniugi			C. F.	Bologna	
2		1	Salarmoni Enrica	[illegible]	[illegible]	Id.			13	Xbre	1863	Casalecchio					moglie		
3	1		Pascuiti Socrate	Enrico	Salarmoni Enrica	—			5	Xbre	1886	Bologna		—			figlio		
4	1		Id. Fernando	"	"	—			12	Maggio	1888	Id.		—			Id.		

Comune di Casalecchio di Reno
Il 23 Giugno 189[illegible]
Visto regolare per il rilascio
Il Sindaco

Document 6

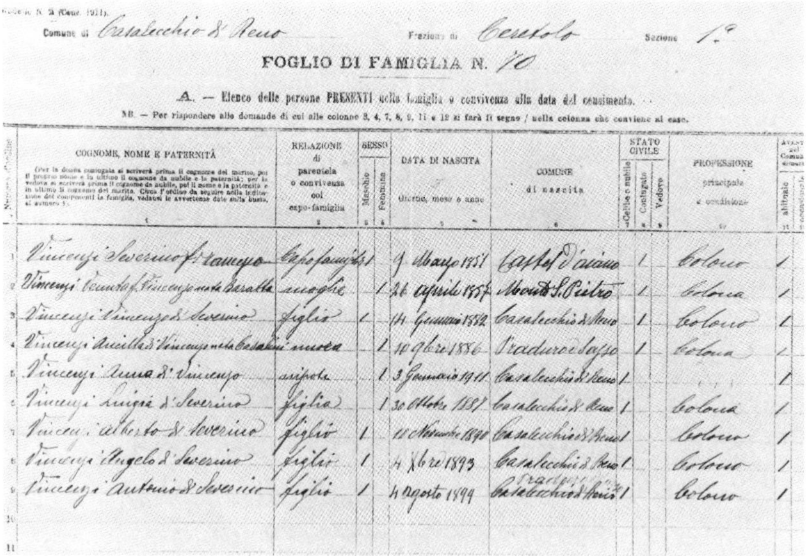

Modello N. 2 (Cens. 1911).

Comune di Casalecchio d'Reno Frazione di Ceretolo Sezione 1ª

FOGLIO DI FAMIGLIA N. 70

A. — Elenco delle persone PRESENTI nella famiglia o convivenza alla data del censimento.

NB. — Per rispondere alle domande di cui alle colonne 3, 4, 7, 8, 9, 11 e 12 si farà il segno / nella colonna che conviene al caso.

Numero d'ordine	COGNOME, NOME E PATERNITÀ (Per la donna coniugata si scriverà prima il cognome del marito, poi il proprio nome e in ultimo il cognome da nubile e la paternità; per la vedova si scriverà prima il cognome da nubile, poi il nome e la paternità e in ultimo il cognome del marito. Circa l'ordine da seguire nella indicazione dei componenti la famiglia, vedansi le avvertenze date sulla busta, al numero 1.) 1	RELAZIONE di parentela o convivenza col capo-famiglia 2	SESSO: Maschio 3	Femmina 4	DATA DI NASCITA Giorno, mese e anno 5	COMUNE di nascita 6	STATO CIVILE: Celibe o nubile 7	Coniugato 8	Vedovo 9	PROFESSIONE principale e condizione 10	Avente nel Comune: abituale 11	occasionale 12
1	Vincenzi Severino fu Francesco	Capofamiglia	1		9 Marzo 1851	Castel d'Aiano		1		Colono	1	
2	Vincenzi Teresa fu Vincenzo nata Baratta	moglie		1	26 Aprile 1857	Monte S. Pietro		1		Colona	1	
3	Vincenzi Vincenzo di Severino	figlio	1		14 Gennaio 1882	Casalecchio di Reno		1		Colono	1	
4	Vincenzi Ancilla di Vincenzo nata Casalini	nuora		1	10 9bre 1886	Praduro e Sasso		1		Colona	1	
5	Vincenzi Anna di Vincenzo	nipote		1	3 Gennaio 1911	Casalecchio di Reno	1				1	
6	Vincenzi Luigia di Severino	figlia		1	30 Ottobre 1887	Casalecchio di Reno	1			Colona	1	
7	Vincenzi Alberto di Severino	figlio	1		11 Novembre 1890	Casalecchio di Reno	1			Colono	1	
8	Vincenzi Angelo di Severino	figlio	1		4 Xbre 1893	Casalecchio di Reno	1			Colono	1	
9	Vincenzi Antonio di Severino	figlio	1		4 Agosto 1899	Casalecchio di Reno (Praduro e Sasso)	1			Colono	1	
10												
11												

Document 7

D. Communal tax records. A variety of annual taxes were levied by the commune on the citizenry of Casalecchio. Corresponding to each is an annual register. The most important such register is the *focatico,* or household tax based on income (document 8). The available registers continuously cover the period 1869–1914, lacking only 1908. However, from 1906 to 1914 only a minority of households (from 129 to 206 per year out of over 800) were enumerated. Each household head is listed each year, regardless of whether any taxes were levied on the household. When a household was exempted from payment, the reason for the exemption was noted. This listing also provides, for each household in each year, a count of the number of males present by age group, and the total number of females present. The household's tax status (elite, middle, proletarian) and a measure of income within that status category are given, as well as the actual amount of tax levied.

E. The conscription register (lista di leva). Each year all males at age 19 were required to register for conscription. The series of such registers compiled for residents of Casalecchio is available in the Archivio di Stato of Bologna. All registers covering birth dates from 1843 to 1903 were photocopied and later entered into the data base. Information provided includes whether father and mother were alive at the date of registration, occupation of registrant, and occupation of registrant's father.

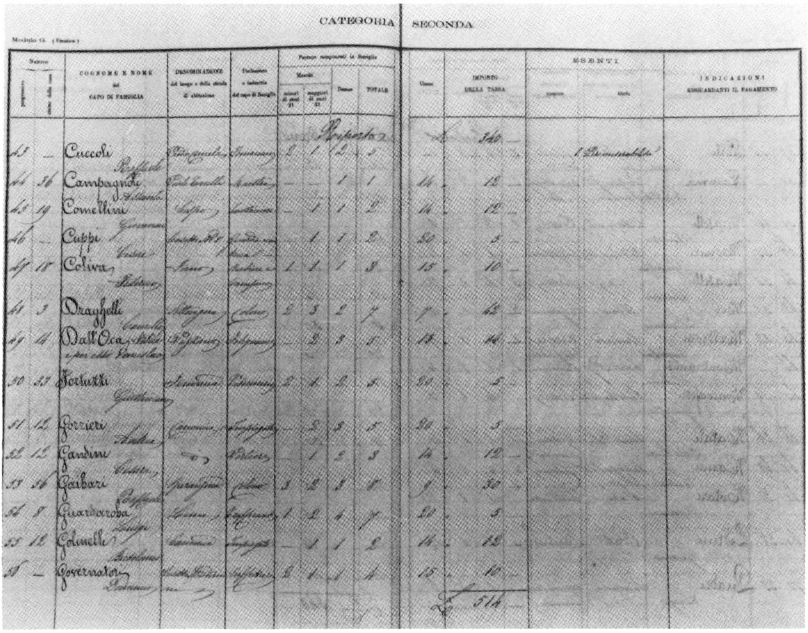

Document 8

F. Church records. These are of two principal kinds:

1. Religious marriage records were kept by each parish, covering all marriages celebrated in that parish. Unlike the civil register records, parish records were not exchanged between parishes. Thus, a religious marriage of a Casalecchio man to a woman of a different commune (religious marriages were almost always celebrated in the parish of the bride) would normally not be recorded in any Casalecchio parish. The data base contains information on all religious marriages celebrated throughout the 1865–1921 period in Casalecchio's largest parish, San Martino, which contained the majority of Casalecchio's population. Information on all religious marriages celebrated between 1865 and 1904 in Casalecchio's second largest parish, Sant'Antonio, was also entered. However, research was affected by diocesan restrictions on scholarly access to parish individual-level data, preventing us from copying the marriage records after 1904 for Sant'Antonio and the records of the small parishes of San Giovanni Battista and San Donino for the entire period. As a result, the data base does not contain all religious marriage information (roughly 20–25 percent is missing, although the proportion of missing records is smaller for 1865–1905.

2. Baptism of Casalecchio infants was largely performed in the central Bologna church of San Pietro until 1917, when local Casalecchio churches were given the right to baptize their parishioners. Indeed, by ecclesiastical edict in that year all parishes were required to provide baptism for their parishioners. These records were used to double check civil information regarding (presumed) stillbirths and (civilly registered) illegitimate births until 1900. More recent baptismal records have been closed to researchers by the church authorities.

The Record System

Overview

A longitudinal perspective informs this study, and the basic unit of analysis is the individual. We had to be able to follow each individual's life course continuously throughout the time he or she lived in Casalecchio. In order to do this we assigned a unique identification number to each individual, and used that number to bring together all data sources providing information on that person. Identification numbers were assigned not only to the individuals who resided in Casalecchio during the period under study (1865–1921), but also to other individuals who stood in significant relationship to the Casalecchio residents. These include parents of Casalecchio residents and deceased spouses who themselves never lived in the commune. In all, approximately 19,000 Casalecchio residents and 14,000 people who did not reside in Casalecchio in the years 1865–1921 were assigned identification numbers. Use of identification numbers for these significant others was crucial to the tracing of kinship relations among Casalecchio residents.[2]

Individual identification numbers consist of six digits, the sixth of which is a control digit computed through a formula based on the position of each of the first five digits. The control digit was particularly useful in catching data errors involving the transposition of digits in the identification number when coded data were entered into the computer. Given the importance of the identification number for bringing together different kinds of information for the same individual, this allowed us—through use of a simple error-detection program—to catch computer entry errors and correct them.

Assigning identification numbers was one of the most time-consuming aspects of data coding, and certainly the trickiest. In the first phase of the research this was done manually by a team of research assistants. For each record source, beginning with the first manuscript census, a card was compiled for each individual and arranged alphabetically. Later, all cards for the same individual were identified and a single identification number assigned. This also involved compiling one card for every mention of an individual in someone else's record (e.g., a father). Although computer-assisted record linkage methods had already been pioneered before the start of this research in 1979, the limited computer availability in Bologna where this process was conducted, and problems in confidently assigning an identification number in a setting where illiteracy was high (and hence names varied in spelling from one source to another) and different people had the same name, led to adoption of the manual approach.[3] As most documents provided not only the name of the individual but also the father's name and often the mother's (including maiden name), linkage was facilitated. Use of birth date, birthplace, and other information also aided linkage. In later stages of the research, conscription-register data and annual household tax information were added at Bowdoin College and computer programs were written to assist the assigning of identification numbers. However, where a firm assignment could not confidently be made by the computer, research assistants used all available records (again, assisted by the computer) to assign the proper identification number.

All individual input forms follow a similar format in providing in the first two columns the code for the type of input form, with the following six columns identifying the individual in question. Individual input record forms are of the types listed in table A.1.

Each individual who was ever officially resident in Casalecchio during the period of observation must have at least three input records: 01, 02, and 04. If the person never married while in the commune, no form 03 would appear. Even in the case of stillbirths born to Casalecchio residents, the stillborn child is recorded and has forms 01, 02, and 04. People who lived in Casalecchio at some time, but who were official residents of another commune, had no *anagrafe* entry. The most important category consists of foundlings lodged in Casalecchio homes and considered official residents of the foundling home in Bologna. As there were no more than a handful of these living in Casalecchio at any one time, this has no serious impact on the data base. Since our calculation of rates of births, deaths, migrations, and so forth is based on the officially resident population, the fact that these individuals do not have their vital events registered in Casalecchio is not a problem.

The record system is designed to document the coresidential experiences of all individuals over the portion of their lives spent in Casalecchio. This is done by making use of the numbering system devised by the communal officials in compiling their population-register household forms. It may be recalled that all individ-

Table A.1. The Casalecchio Data Base

File Name	Description	No. records	Characters/record
	Individual-Level Records		
F01	Identification	19,052	54
F02	Migration	20,290	52
F03	Marriage	2,490	97
F04	Coresidence	22,342	66
F06	1861 Census	2,373	45
F07	1865 Census	2,470	57
F08	1871 Census	2,810	47
F09	1881 Census	2,860	49
F10	1911 Census	4,420	56
F11	1921 Census	5,990	57
F12	Legitimation	315	35
F15	Numerario (Name)	32,916	57
F17	Household head	3,868	38
F18	Annual household tax	18,882	64
F19	Conscription	2,007	30
F20*	Marriage analysis	3,302	80
F21*	Marital status	9,809	26
	Household-Level Records		
F91	Household head	3,868	38
F92	Household composition	7,769	20
F93	Coresidence	22,342	64
F98	Annual household tax	18,882	64

*These records have been created from other individual-level records.

uals not only had individual population-register record forms compiled by the commune, but were also registered on household forms. These household forms were regularly updated to note changes in who was living there, along with the date of any entry to, or exit from, the household. In the course of residing in Casalecchio, an individual could move from one of these administratively defined households to another; the entire time the person spent in the commune should be recorded as a continuous series of dated entries in different household forms. By giving an identification number to each of these administratively defined households, we were able to follow these movements and determine who lived with whom continuously through time.

Record input form 04 is organized in this way, with one such form compiled for each individual for the period of time the person spent in a given numbered household. The time periods recorded in form 02, showing dates of residence in Casalecchio, are covered by a series of 04 forms starting at date of entry into the commune and ending with date of exit. Of course, for individuals who were always recorded in a single household folder in the population register, just one 04 input record was compiled (assuming continuous residence in Casalecchio). In fact, less than 15 percent of Casalecchio residents moved from one household to another within the commune and hence had more than one 04 form.

Thus, just as there are individual identification numbers, there are also household identification numbers. By using form 04 we are in a position to determine who was residing with whom at any point in time, following the changing constellation of individuals with whom a person lived over his life course and relating this to various events. The household identification numbers, then, are used as instrumental means of tracing the coresidential experience of individuals. The household units are those distinguished by the municipal officials who kept the population register. The primary criteria employed in defining the household unit were (1) sharing lodging in the same housing unit and (2) sharing a kitchen. It should be borne in mind that the household was an important municipal unit of annual taxation and that the precise definition and recording of the household unit were therefore of considerable importance to the local officials.

Introduction to the Data Input Record System

Before turning to the format used in the various data input forms, it should be stressed that many of these forms are repeatable for the same individual, for they refer to events that are repeatable.

Form 01. This provides the basic identifying information for each individual who ever officially resided in Casalecchio during the period under study. Information includes father's and mother's identification numbers, sex, date and commune of birth, vitality and legitimacy at birth, and date and commune of death. This form is not repeatable.

Form 02. This provides dated information, based on the population register, on the communes that the individual immigrated from and emigrated to. In the current data file this involves periods of residence in Casalecchio, providing, for each period the individual lived in Casalecchio, date of immigration, commune immigrated from, date of emigration, and commune emigrated to. Information is also provided on cause of entry and cause of exit. An individual may enter observation by being born in Casalecchio, immigrating into Casalecchio in the period under study, being already a resident of Casalecchio in 1865 when observation began, or being entered in the population register upon appearance in a census (municipal officials used the manuscript censuses to check their population-register data). An individual may exit from observation by dying while resident in Casalecchio, emigrating, being still resident in Casalecchio in 1921 at the end of observation, or being removed from the population register upon checking with the census (emigration).

While every resident in Casalecchio has at least one form 02, some have more than one. This is the case for those who lived in Casalecchio for a period, left, and then returned to the commune. The chronological ordering of these various forms, along with the indication of periods of residence outside Casalecchio (i.e., between one emigration and the subsequent re-immigration), is provided through subsequent computer manipulation.

Input form 02 also provides information on the marital status of individuals who enter observation. This is important because the marriage form 03 is compiled only for individuals who married while they were resident in Casalecchio. To have marital information on the immigrants, form 02 is used, giving the immigrant's marital status at the date of immigration and providing the identification number of his or her spouse (including deceased spouse in the case of widows and widowers).

Form 03. This provides data on each marriage contracted by a Casalecchio resident during the period of study. The forms pertain to two kinds of marriages—religious and civil—with a code indicating to which kind the record refers.

For each marriage of two Casalecchio residents, a separate form 03 was compiled for each individual, for in addition to joint information on the wedding (type, date, commune of celebration), individual information is provided (commune of residence, occupation, literacy, whether previously married, and identification number of previous spouse). In the case of a marriage between a Casalecchio resident and a nonresident, only one form 03 was compiled (that for the resident), with a special section of this form devoted to assembling all possible detail on the background of the nonresident spouse. This is because we do not have such information as date and commune of birth and identification numbers of parents for marriage partners who never lived in Casalecchio.

Form 03, then, is repeatable for each individual. A person who celebrates a religious and a civil marriage to X, and then marries Y religiously and civilly after the death of X, would have four 03 forms.

Form 04. This allows us to know who lives with whom over time. As discussed above, each individual has as many 04 forms as the person has continuous periods of residence in a municipally defined household. All residents of Casalecchio have at least one form 04.

Each form 04 indicates the identification number of the household entered, the date of entry, and the relationship of the individual to the household head at that date. Subsequent changes in relation to household heads are generated electronically, making use of the 91 form—which gives dated changes in the identity of the household head—along with the genealogical and marital data available in the file. This procedure is accomplished through use of our kinship tracing program (see below).

The Census Forms (06–11). Each individual who appears in a census has a record form for that census. An individual thus has a number of such forms (up to six), equal to the number of censuses in which the person resided in Casalecchio. A persistence code, electronically tagged onto each individual record, indicates the combination of censuses in which the individual was found. Censuses contain information on the individual's sex, age, relation to household head, marital status, literacy, occupation, place of birth, and so forth. They also provide data on household context (e.g., occupation of household head and household composition code).

Form 15. With the exception of form 15, all the data record forms are composed entirely of numeric entries. This file provides the alphabetic name (last, first, middle) of each individual who has been assigned an identification number. One of its primary uses has been in permitting us to print out identifying names for records having errors or missing data. In correcting such errors we had to consult data record forms and archival sources based on names rather than on our identification numbers.

Form 17. This provides a record for each individual who ever was a household head in Casalecchio, with one record for each continuous period of headship. It contains the same information as form 91, which is based on household identification number.

Form 18. From 1869 through 1914 an annual household tax was assessed and a ledger of this tax (*focatico*) kept. Form 18 records this information, which provides a listing by household head each year for each household in Casalecchio. The record is based on the identification number of the household head, but has subsequently been tagged with the household identification number as well. The same household number could have entries for each year throughout this period. Each record gives information on the number of individuals in the household (by sex and, for males, by age group), tax category (a measure of social class), tax class (a measure of income), and tax assessed.

Form 19. This contains information from the conscription register. Based on the identification number of the registrant, it gives the year of the registrant's birth, whether the registrant's father and mother were alive at the time of registration, and the occupations of the registrant and his father.

Form 20. Because the same couple could have more than one marriage record (one religious and one civil), a combined marriage-analysis record was electronically generated, bringing together all information on the marriage(s) of those for whom we have at least one marriage record (i.e., at least one 03 form). For most purposes, use of form 20 obviates need for use of the multiple 03 forms in data analysis, making retrieval simpler. Of the 2,142 couples with form 20 records, 222 include information on religious marriages only, 991 on civil marriages only, and 929 on both religious and civil marriages.

Form 21. Given the emphasis on our ability to follow any individual continuously through time, data on marriages (as found in forms 02, 03, and 20) must be complemented by information on the dissolution of marital states, enabling us to determine the marital status of any Casalecchio resident at any point in time. Thus, form 21 was created electronically by linking information on the initiation of a particular marital status with information on the end of that marital status in Casalecchio. A form 21 was compiled for an individual at the first indication that the person lived in Casalecchio in a married or widowed state. In the case of an immigrant arriving married or widowed (noted in form 02), the corresponding 21 form gives the date of arrival as the beginning of observation in that married state (the latter indicated by a code).

The closing date was found by checking to see, for a married person, if there was a record of the spouse's death (from the spouse's 02 form) before the end of observation of the individual in question in Casalecchio (again found in the person's 02 form). If there was not, the closing date of the 21 form was the same as the closing date of the individual's 02 form. If there was a record of a previous death of a spouse, this death date was used as the closing date of the person's 21 form, and a new 21 form was compiled, for widowed status, using the date of the previous spouse's death as the beginning date of this new form. The end date of such a widowhood form was provided by marriage date in the case of remarriage, date of departure from Casalecchio, or own death. Thus, once an individual appeared in Casalecchio in a married or widowed state, he or she would have one or more 21 forms covering the entire period of residence in Casalecchio.

Form 91. Each municipally defined household has at least one form 91, providing the dated succession of its household heads. This was compiled on the basis of the population-register household forms. There is a separate form 91 for each individual who was ever head of the household.

Form 92. Form 92 was created electronically, based on forms 01, 02, 03, 04, and 91. Employing a 51-value code, it characterizes the household composition of each municipally defined household continuously through the time it existed in Casalecchio. The household code is first assigned based on the initial membership of the household and then the program is rerun every time a new member is added or an old member leaves. The result is a succession of 92 forms for each household number, providing information on the composition of the household throughout its existence from 1865 to 1921.

Form 93. This provides the same information as form 04 but is based on the household identification number rather than on the individual identification number. Its use facilitates examination of coresidence.

Form 98. This contains the same annual household tax information found in form 18, but here it is based on household identification number.

Coding Kin Ties

The coding system used for kin ties reflects the importance to our research of providing rich detail in tracing kin relations. Vague categories such as aunt or cousin are avoided, for these conceal distinctions that may be crucial to interpreting the kinship and coresidential systems (e.g., the difference between father's sister and mother's sister). Using a highly analytical code also allows flexibility for subsequent aggregations, as these become theoretically specified by the particular problem at hand. For example, we can group together all patrilateral relatives, or all relatives at the ascendant generation.

Kinship tie to household head was manually coded for all census entries and for the initial status of each individual in each of the numbered households in which he or she was listed in the population register (this was placed in form 04). Subsequent changes in relation to household head, using the same kinship code, are dealt with electronically by our retrieval system, as are queries concerning any other kin ties. In other words, we can ask the kin relationship between any two people and retrieve the proper kin code.

The kin-tie code follows standard anthropological genealogical procedures in tracing the full path of kinship relation between any two given individuals. In the following discussion, the example used is that of the individual's relationship to the household head, as found in the censuses and in the 04 coresidential forms.

However, the same coding and kinship tracing system is employed in a variety of kinship analyses not limited to those involving a household head.

The household head is assigned the code 011. In the census forms and form 04, the code of each kin-related member of the household is assigned by tracing the kin tie from the household head to the individual in question. This is a three-digit code which allows for up to two kinship intermediaries between the two individuals in question. It may be useful to think of this procedure as tracing the relationship between two people through a genealogical diagram. The basic elements of this coding system are the elementary forms of kinship relation:

1	wife	5	mother
2	son	6	brother
3	daughter	7	sister
4	father	8	husband

Where the relationship between the household head and the other individual falls into one of the above categories, the appropriate digit is placed in the first column, followed by two zeros. Thus, the code given to the wife of the household head is 100. A sister of the household head is coded 700.

More distantly related kinsmen are coded by tracing their relationship to the household head through the intermediary, more closely related kinsmen of the head. For example, the wife of a son of the household head is coded by beginning with the household head and tracing first through the intermediary relative (son = 2) and then the relationship of the individual to that intermediary kinsman (wife = 1). If this can be done, as in this case, by using just one intermediary, the third digit is coded 0. Hence, the code for son's wife is 210.

Illustrating the use of this system for tracing more distantly related kinsmen, we can use the example of the brother of the son's wife. Such an individual is linked to the household head through two kinship intermediaries, his son and the son's wife. The relationship is son's (2) wife's (1) brother (6), coded 216.

This system has been limited to three digits for practical reasons. Rarely is analytical use made of specific categories of kin traced through more than two intermediaries. When more than two kin intermediaries link two individuals, just the first two are specified, and the summary code of 9 is provided for the third digit. For example, if the brother of the son's wife in our above example had a wife, we would not use the required four digits (2161) to fully specify that relationship, but would just retain the first two digits (21), adding a 9 (219) to indicate a more distant kin relation. We would then know that the individual in question was related to the household head by being an indirect kinsman of the head's son's wife.

Where more than one kin path can be traced between two individuals, the shorter path is used. Thus, if we find the code 120 (wife's son), we must be dealing with a child of the wife from before the current marriage.

Insofar as we are interested in looking at the relationship of any individual to the household head, we must also deal with people who have no kin relationship to the head at all. In the Bologna area the most frequent coresident nonkin were the servants, but a variety of other coresidential relationships were found as well (e.g., apprentice). Thus, in coding tie to household head, codes are provided to identify such individuals and their relationship to their coresidents. A first digit of 9 was assigned to such individuals, to distinguish them from kinsmen of the head. There are 23 such codes.

Data Cleaning and Data Quality

The value of the Casalecchio data base is no greater than the quality of the data it contains, and a great deal of effort has been put into locating missing data and finding and correcting errors in the early version of the data base prepared in Bologna. Special emphasis was placed on examining the data that came from the population register, for along with the advantages of this complex, longitudinal data source come a number of problems associated with coverage and completeness. It was important to make sure that the dates of appearance and exit of each individual in Casalecchio, and in each household in Casalecchio, were present and accurate. It was also crucial to ensure that the entire population resident in Casalecchio appeared in the population register and, hence, in the data base.

Data quality-control procedures may be divided into two phases: those that took place during the original compilation of the data records, and those that took place after initial creation of the data base. The first phase was carried out largely in Bologna by Giancarlo Bernabei and a group of research assistants under the supervision of Andrea Schiaffino. This involved manual comparisons of different archival data sources when the data source in use gave contradictory information or no information at all regarding a variable.

Certain data sources were always double-checked, given known incidence of errors. Most notable here were the cases of infants who died in the first few days of life. Many of these infant deaths were not entered into the relevant household population-register folder, and, for these cases, no individual population-register card was compiled. Hence, rather than relying entirely on population-register documents (which, theoretically, should contain these data), we consulted the civil birth and death records to identify all cases of infants who died in their first days of life. This information was then checked against the population-register data and, where necessary, the appropriate data forms were compiled.

There was likewise a problem in identifying stillbirths as opposed to infants who died very soon after birth. Since civil registration generally took place a few days after birth, civil authorities were not always careful to distinguish between stillbirths and infants who died before having their births registered. Consequently, all cases of civilly registered stillbirths were checked against the baptismal records in Bologna to see if the more accurate (in this regard) church records indicated if the infant were in fact alive at birth. As a result, several births civilly recorded as stillbirths were recorded instead in our data base as live births.

Once the data forms were compiled, a comprehensive error-detection and correction program was written by Shawn McDermott at Bowdoin College. This program checks for legal values for each variable, for missing data, for compatibility of data within individual data records, and for compatibility of data among the different records for the same person. For example, for every 02 (migration) entry date, there must be an 04 (coresidence) record having the same entry date for that individual (i.e., at the same time as an individual enters Casalecchio, the person must be recorded as entering a particular household in Casalecchio). More generally, for each individual 02 period, there must be one or more 04 forms covering that period from beginning date to end date (but not extending beyond these in either direction unless the individual has additional 02 forms showing re-immigration).

The error detection program checks for dozens of errors of range, compatibility, and completeness. The program was designed not only to identify but also to correct errors. The research assistants went through all 19,000 people's records, person by person, examining the results of the error-checking program on the screen. For each individual, the screen presents the person's name and identification number at the top, followed by a listing of types of errors or gaps found and where they occur in the person's records. Below this all the records for that individual are listed, with the data fields containing the possible errors highlighted (boldfaced and blinking). Below these records are the identification numbers and names of the person's father and mother.

By examining both the error detected and the other data forms for the individual, many errors could be corrected or missing data filled in (e.g., if birth date were missing in the population-register-based 01 form, it could often be filled in there from a census-based form). This required establishing, for each variable, a decision-making system for determining which value to use where different sources gave different values. For birth date, for example, if no two sources gave the same date, the earliest source was employed.

An additional feature of the error-correction program is its ability to retrieve the records of other related individuals (e.g., all others who lived in the same household at any specific time period) and exhibit them quickly on the screen. Hence, for example, if a man's emigration date were missing, the wife's emigration date could be quickly checked and some decision made as to the adequacy of this date for the man's departure. In addition, information from the *focatico* (form 18) was frequently helpful in determining the date that any individual entered or left a household or left Casalecchio by himself or with other family members.

The program not only identifies possible errors and missing values and permits retrieval of records to facilitate determining correct values, but also allows the operator to make the necessary additions and changes in the data.

Intensive use of the program lasted from the fall of 1984 through August of 1985, involving approximately 2,000 hours of research-assistant time, plus the time put in by the programmer. Thousands of corrections and additions were made to the data base which had been received from Italy, mostly by the cross-checking of data deriving from different archival sources.

At the end of this procedure, we were left with a much reduced number of cases of missing or inconsistent data. One of the most common remaining problems was missing birthplace and missing father's identification (the latter sometimes unknown to the individual as well). In such cases, the fields were left blank.

However, in order to determine the population at risk of any event occurring at any given time, it was necessary to have completed dates of entry and exit for all individuals. Therefore, where dates of entry or exit from Casalecchio (form 02) or from any household (form 04) were not found, an estimated date was assigned. Estimates were based on all available data (e.g., censuses present and absent, *focatico* information, or if a male, whether present at age 19 from conscription register), along with a knowledge of overall rate of migration and the specific migration rates of people by age, sex, occupation, and mode of entry into Casalecchio (i.e., birth or immigration). When an estimated date was given (typically 1 July of the year in question), a special code was assigned. This code allows us to exclude these cases for certain types of analysis. In all, estimated dates were thus assigned for 100 dates of entry (0.5 percent) and 714 (3.4 percent) dates of exit.

Population-Register Coverage

Not only are we concerned that the people registered in our data base have complete and accurate records, but we also want assurance that our population-register data cover the entire population. In order to estimate the undercount of the population register, for each year in which a national census took place we identified from the 02 forms who was (according to the population register) living in Casalecchio, comparing them to the censused population. As a result of these checks, we determined that the proportion of people enumerated as Casalecchio residents in the census but not recorded in the population register was 1.3 percent in 1871, 1.9 percent in 1881, 3.4 percent in 1911, and 2.5 percent in 1921. Examination of just who these missing individuals were reveals that a substantial proportion (50–74 percent) were servants and other individuals living in households as nonkin (particularly apprentices and foundlings). This supports what we always knew: that the population register underenumerates servants, who were notoriously mobile. Generally speaking, though, servants who lived in a household for a full year were entered into the population register, while those who stayed for but a few months were often not.[4]

Data-Base Management System (CASA)

A data-base management system (CASA) was designed by Nancy Karweit of Johns Hopkins University to store and retrieve data from the Casalecchio data base. In this system, the data files (form 01, form 02, etc.) are stored separately and a record-linkage and data-retrieval system merge data for an individual, household or other unit of analysis. The CASA system solves two complex data-management problems in analysis of the Casalecchio data: (1) the need to store and retrieve data pertaining to events and (2) the need to store and retrieve data according to different views.[5]

Event Histories

Event histories record changes in a variable continuously through time. For example, migration histories record episodes of residence in particular locations. For any given history, such as marriage or fertility or residence, individuals differ in the "eventfulness" of their lives. Thus, the data arrayed for different people may appear quite different not only in their content, but in the number of episodes as well. This variability in the number of entries is not permitted in most standard statistical packages, which expect the usual one record per person encountered in cross-sectional data. Therefore, an interface, or data-base management system, was devised for efficient storage and flexible retrieval of data in a form acceptable to standard statistical routines. In the CASA system, this task is accomplished by storing the data as separate events or static files and by divising a record-linkage and retrieval system for flexibly merging records together.

Alternative Views

The CASA package was designed to retrieve data about individuals, about transitions between states (events), and about collections of individuals. This flexibility in design permits different sorts of analysis according to the research question being posed. The CASA system accomplishes this by employing a flexible record-linkage system.

In the simplest case—retrieval of static data in separate files for individuals—the retrieval entails joining records by a unique identification code. When the goal is joining event histories or time-varying data on various states together at a particular point in time, the record system must be accessed by identification number and date. The type of retrieval becomes more complex when the date is indirectly determined as the occurrence of another variable, such as retrieval of years lived in Casalecchio at the birth of the first child or at the date of the first marriage.

Transition files, which indicate the value of an attribute at two adjacent stages, comprise another view of the data. This type of retrieval may also require joining together data from other event files. For example, one may want to retrieve years lived in Casalecchio at the date of marriage or at the date of becoming a widow.

Retrievals from aggregates of individuals, such as for household or kin groupings, comprise a third type of view of the event-history data. Here interest focuses on two types of measures: it is possible to detail the coresidential or kin situation for individuals as well as for households.

The storage and retrieval capability of the present system allows for flexible definition of retrieval requests, producing standard files which may then be used as input to SPSS-X, BMDP, or other statistical packages. Each session with CASA produces several output files in addition to the standard data file. Global statistics for the retrieved variables are computed. The statistics presented depend upon what was requested. For requests pertaining to values and durations, averages and standard deviations across the sample are presented. For counts, frequencies are presented. For sample paths (which trace the entire event history), transition matrices and rates, describing the movement of the first ten states and the transition from the first to the last state, are presented.

Selected Archival Sources Used in Compiling the Casalecchio Data Base

Population-Register Household Folder. This consists of an outside sheet (1) which gives the name of the household head (Bergonzoni Ferdinando), the address, and the name of the landlord. It also provides a unique identification number (1781) that is used to link the individual population-register entries to their household folder. The oversized inside double sheet (2) provides information on each household member (here seven are listed), including their date of entry (5 November 1900 for Ferdinando and his wife Enrica, for example) and their date of exit (12 October 1916) and destination (Bologna).

Population-Register Individual Record. This consists of a double-sided card (the example refers to Giuliani Medea). The front (3) lists name, father's and mother's name, date and place (Casalecchio) of birth, name of spouse (Fanti Alberto) and date of marriage, occupation (nonagricultural worker), literacy, date of emigration (29 August 1906), and place emigrated to (Bologna). It also gives cross-reference to the household folder (865) of the household in which the person lived. The back (4) lists the sequence of addresses within Casalecchio at which the person resided (in this case, she lived at five different addresses from the time of her birth until her move to Bologna at age 27, three years after her marriage).

The Immigration Register. Shown here (5) is the internal double sheet characteristic of the immigration register. The immigrating group in this case was a sharecropping family of twelve, headed by Gubellini Paris. They arrived in 1878, coming from the neighboring rural community of Praduro e Sasso. The form lists, for each immigrant, sex, name, father's and mother's names, occupation, literacy, date and place of birth, marital status, conscription status, and kin tie to household head.

The Emigration Register. Comparable to the immigration register, this document (6) is based on information sent by officials at the commune of immigration. Here we have the case of the four-member family headed by Pasciuti Enrico, who left for Bologna in 1891.

The Census Form. Typical of the decennial census manuscript forms is this one (7) from the 1911 census, listing all members of the household headed by Vincenzi Severino. This provides name, father's name, relation to household head, date and place of birth, marital status, occupation (here sharecropper), and permanence of residence.

Annual Household Tax Register (Focatico). Each year's household tax register was divided into three sections, according to class. The double-sided page shown here (8) is taken from the second class section of the 1872 *focatico.* Each line represents a separate household, giving name of household head, address, occupation of head, number of males under and over age 21, number of females, tax category, amount of tax assessed, and notation for tax exemption (note that the household listed first, that of Cuccoli Raffaele, was exempted from the tax on grounds of poverty).

Notes

Chapter One. Demographic Transformation and Social Change

1 Of course, people did not bear as many children as they were biologically capable of in most societies, due to a variety of social controls on fertility.

2 Among those warning of the dire implications of this nuclearization was LePlay (1871). Goode (1963) has provided the classic modern sociological view of this process.

3 A similar argument is made by Anderson (1978).

4 In this attempt to identify the interaction between these political economic factors and Western family life in this period of modern industrialization, our work joins that of Hareven (1982); Katz, Doucet, and Stern (1982); Gillis (1985); Levine (1987); and Ruggles (1987). For earlier studies, see Anderson (1971) and C. Tilly (1979).

5 See Smith (1982) for an insightful account of demography in social history.

6 Of Levine's groups, Casalecchio lacks only full-fledged capitalist farmers.

By choosing a community during a time in which the newly-formed Italian state was taking actions affecting a variety of dimensions of people's lives (establishing schools, regulating work conditions for women and children, intervening in family social welfare, and slowly providing improvements in public health), we can further evaluate the role of state intervention in the ongoing demographic and socioeconomic change (Levine 1986).

7 On the use of a life-course approach in family history and historical demography, see Elder (1978), Kertzer and Schiaffino (1983), and Hogan (1985).

Chapter Two. The Political Economy of Bologna

1 On the history of Bolognese agriculture, see Landi (1977), Faina (1905), Bruno (1923), Sereni (1957), Poni (1969), Finzi (1980), Evangelisti (1980), and Dal Pane (1969). On landowners' views regarding the wisdom of retaining a sharecropping system, see Commissione per lo Studio sulle Condizioni della Colonia (1883), Tanari (1881) Goretti (1883), and Pasolini (1891).

2 Kertzer (1984) provides further detail on the sharecropper contracts. See also

Commissione Mista della Società Agraria (1874); Comizio Agrario del Circondario di Bologna (1905); Poni (1969); Ministero di Agricoltura, Industria e Commercio (1891); and Carrara (1896). On the price of farmland in nineteenth-century Bologna, see Tanari (1881:439).

3 A fuller analysis of sharecropper household organization in the Bologna area is found in Kertzer (1984). Sources used for our discussion here include Goretti (1882, 1883); Ministero di Agricoltura, Industria e Commercio (1891); Nardi (1957); Toscanelli ([1861] 1976); Pasolini (1891); Anselmi (1978); Broccoli (1979); Jacini (1882); Faina (1905); Pagani (1930); Comizio Agrario del Circondario di Bologna (1881); Tanari (1881); Istituto Nazionale di Economia Agraria (INEA) (1930); Livi (1915); Perdisa (1935); Cazzola (1980b); Bissoli (1979); Finzi (1980); Martelli (1854); Conenna (1980); Rabbeno (1895); and Biagi (1935).

4 The size of the woman's dowry was linked to her status. The dowry consisted of furniture, household furnishings, clothes, and, among the more prosperous, cash. In the nineteenth century, the value of the sharecropper's dowry ranged between four hundred and five hundred lire, equal to about a year's income for the poorer *braccianti* families. See Goretti (1882:145), Pasolini (1891:21), Priore (1906:618), INEA (1931:70), Marangoni (1948:12, 87), and Broccoli (1979:249).

5 For details on the lives of *braccianti,* see, in addition to those sources cited in n.2 above, Sezioni di Agricoltura ed Amministrativa (1889), Schiavi (1904), Pasolini (1892a, 1892b), and Cazzola (1980a, 1980b). For examples of the complaints of landowners about the immorality of the *braccianti,* see Scarselli (1890), Grabinski (1892), Ramponi (1892), and Urtoller (1898).

6 The argument that many young sharecroppers saw the move to *bracciante* status as liberating them from the suffocation of patriarchal family rule is made by Evangelisti (1980) and others. To date, no convincing evidence has been adduced that such a move was common.

7 On the economic history of Bologna industry, see Dal Pane (1969), Bergonzini (1953), and Bellettini (1978).

8 Figures for Casalecchio and the province of Bologna are found in the *Annali di Statistica* (1887:40). For the best discussion of protoindustrialization in Bologna, see Poni and Fronzoni (1979). Figures on home weaving throughout Italy in 1876 can be found in Romani (1982). For recent discussions of the role of protoindustrialization in rural European society, see Mendels (1972, 1984) and Kriedte, Medick, and Schlumbohm (1981).

9 See Gerschenkron (1955) and Del Panta (1979) on national economic developments. For Bolognese industrial statistics for this period, see Ministero di Agricoltura, Industria e Commercio (1887, 1899).

10 See Masulli (1980) and Palazzi (1982) on industrial developments in Bologna at the turn of the century.

11 Statistics on industrial employment by sex and adult status may be found in Merli (1972) and Romani (1982).

12 For an account of child and female industrial labor in Emilia-Romagna, see Palazzi (1982).

13 The effects of the agrarian crisis on Italy as a whole are discussed by Clough (1964) and Luzzatto (1968), and its impact on the Bologna area by Evangelisti (1980) and Masulli (1980). Evidence for Bologna is also found in Camera di Commercio ed Arti di Bologna (1888).

14 For discussion of the proletarianization of Bolognese agriculture, see Masulli (1980), Pagani (1931), Ramella (1977), and Sereni (1968).

15 Economic changes in Italy at the turn of the century are described by Cafagna (1976) and Preti (1955). Masulli (1980) and Arcari (1936) discuss Bologna's economic conditions in this period.

16 The historical role of the city of Bologna is discussed by Dal Pane (1969).

17 For population figures on Bologna and its environs from the sixteenth through the nineteenth centuries, see Bellettini (1978) and Sonnino (1982). Regarding the lack of urban growth in Emilia-Romagna in the eighteenth and nineteenth centuries, see Cazzola (1980a) and Bellettini (1985).

18 On the natural decrease in the urban Bologna population, see Bellettini (1978) and Natale (1982).

19 Fabbri (1980), Masulli (1980), and Ministero di Agricoltura, Industria e Commercio (1887) discuss the development of the Bologna railway in the nineteenth century.

20 The development of the tram network centered in Bologna, including Casalecchio, is chronicled in Bezzi (1983).

21 The destruction of Bologna's wall is chronicled in Cristofori (1981). Figures on the size of the commune's population are found in Comune di Bologna (1974). Ricci (1985) provides a good historical overview of Bologna's urban development.

Chapter Three. Economic and Political Change in Casalecchio

1 The history of the Reno canal is described in Chierici and Tabarroni (1980).

2 See Calindri (1781).

3 See the discussion in chap. 5.

4 The stability in the age structure of the population during these years of sharp population growth can be attributed in part to the age characteristics and volume of the immigrant stream in this period.

5 Examination of the annual municipal records on crop production through the 1879–1903 period bears out this view of unchanging agricultural productivity in these years (see Archivio Comunale di Casalecchio di Reno (ACCR), pos. spec. 32). Moreover, the yield of wheat to seed increased only marginally from the second half of the eighteenth century to the end of the nineteenth century (from roughly 6:1 to 6.5:1).

6 This discussion of agriculture in Casalecchio is based primarily on archival sources found in the Archivio Comunale di Casalecchio di Reno. Among these are not only annual tax rolls of various kinds, but also the manuscript copy of the mayor's report to the Agrarian Inquest, dated 17 October 1879.

7 Information on the wage scale of the many different positions at the hemp factory is provided for the 1862–1882 period in Romani (1982:473). Other wage data are found in the Casalecchio municipal archives.

8 Despite trying various avenues, ranging from Milan to Rome, we have not succeeded in locating the archives of the company that owned the hemp factory, if they still exist. However, much information on the factory has been located in the communal archives of Casalecchio. In addition, information has come from a variety of archival sources from the Archivio di Stato di Bologna (Archivio della Camera di Commercio, 1835–1862 and 1863–1927). Printed sources include: *Rapporto sulle industrie e commercio della provincia di Bologna nel 1864,* Bologna, 1865; "Esposizione agraria ed industriale della Provincia di Bologna nell'anno 1869," *Relazione della Commissione,* Bologna, 1870; "Esposizione Universale di Parigi nel 1867," *Relazione dei giurati italiani,* vol. 2, 1867; *Atti del Comitato dell'Inchiesta Industriale* 1:5–8, 2:9–10, 1874; "Notizie sulle condizioni industriali della Provincia di Bologna," *Annali di Statistica,* ser. 4, *Statistica Industriale,* no. 5, Rome, 1887; and Camera di Commercio ed Arti di Bologna (1884, 1888, 1897).

9 These figures are taken from the archival copy of the mayor's response to a questionnaire sent by the Camera di Commercio di Bologna in 1883, found in the Archivio Comunale del Comune di Bologna. Wages generally ran from 1.5 to 2 lire per day for adult male workers.

10 The 1914 regulations of the Ronzani brewery are found in the ACCR, titolo XI, rub. 2 (1914).

11 ACCR, Stabilimento Mauro Rappini.

12 Statistics on the impact of the war on Casalecchio may be found in Provincia di Bologna (1919). To give one example of wartime industrial conversion in Casalecchio, the silverware factory, established just before the war, was transformed into a manufacturer of weaponry.

13 With no other skills, these people called themselves *braccianti* even though many were unemployed and sought other, nonagricultural forms of employment.

14 These differences in employment by age are, of course, not only due to life-course patterns, but also to cohort effects, since men in the older age groups had come of age at a time when there were fewer nonagricultural opportunities available. However, cohort effects alone do not explain this age pattern, as demonstrated in subsequent analyses.

15 The conscription lists for the twentieth century have also been used in our study, but, unfortunately, father's occupation was no longer registered after 1900. The *lista di leva* for Casalecchio is found in the Archivio di Stato di Bologna.

16 See Featherman and Hauser (1975) on these methods. The occupational categories used here are (1) sharecropper, (2) agricultural wage laborer, (3) servant, (4) other agricultural worker, (5) elite, (6) artisan and merchant, (7) construction worker, (8) hemp worker, (9) other wage worker, and (10) not in the labor force.

17 Including those cases where the father and/or the son were not in the labor force, fathers' and sons' occupations were strongly associated ($\chi^2_{LR} = 1{,}963.3$, $df = 8$). Excluding cases involving people not in the labor force, this strong association persists ($\chi^2_{LR} = 1{,}702.0$, $df = 64$). and direct inheritance of father's occupation by son accounts for a significant proportion of it ($\chi^2_{LR} = 1{,}601.3$, $df = 9$).

18 The log linear models of occupational mobility provide parameters measuring the strength of association between each pair of father's and son's occupations. A tau parameter of 1.0 indicates no effect; a tau parameter larger than 1.0 indicates the extent to which sons from particular occupational origins held particular jobs at age 19 beyond what would be expected on the basis of chance. These tau parameters indicate that sons of sharecroppers were 371.5 times more likely than predicted by simple chance to be sharecroppers themselves. Those few young men who did leave sharecropping were more likely to become servants than anything else (tau = 3.2). Sons of *braccianti* were most likely to become *braccianti* themselves (13.6) or to become servants (tau = 2.0). Sons of other agricultural workers most often remained in that occupation (tau = 31.7) or became servants (tau = 3.1). Sons of artisans and merchants (tau = 14.1) and the elite (tau = 21.0) tended to follow their fathers' occupations. Sons of construction workers, hemp workers, and other nonagricultural wage workers tended to follow the same occupations as their fathers or to move to one of the other nonagricultural wage jobs.

19 $\chi^2_{LR} = 2{,}325.8$, $df = 81$.

20 $\chi^2_{LR} = 2{,}136.5$, $df = 10$.

21 $\chi^2_{LR} = 5.1$, $df = 10$. The tau parameters for these models demonstrate the stability of life as a sharecropper (tau = 70.0). Figures for the elite (tau = 36.2), artisans and merchants (tau = 38.7), and construction workers (tau = 30.5) indicate that each of these occupational categories retained their workers at a rate thirty times or more above chance. Other jobs also showed patterns of persistence well above that expected by simple chance, but at more modest levels. There was little systematic movement among workers who changed jobs. Sharecroppers who gave up their sharecropping jobs disproportionately became either *braccianti* (tau = 2.6) or other agricultural workers (tau = 5.1). In other words, those who left sharecropping tended to go into other occupations in the agricultural sector. The move from sharecropping to the other agricultural category could involve a relatively minor change in the contract without even changing farm or daily routine.

Men leaving artisan and merchant positions tended to become nonagricultural wage laborers (tau = 2.4). Other than these regularities, men who changed jobs were fairly randomly distributed in the types of jobs they found. Further statistical tests for age differences in these processes indicated that the young (men under 25 at the earlier census) were more likely to change jobs, and were especially likely to leave agricultural wage labor and hemp worker jobs.

22 Since we could not follow individuals who left Casalecchio between censuses, we do not know what occupations sharecroppers who left the commune found. It is likely that some of them ended up in the city and thus left the agricultural sector altogether.

23 Figures for literacy at marriage are found in Benini (1911:43) and Raseri (1906). Corridore (1908) has written a comprehensive study of illiteracy in Italy in this period, using census, marriage and conscription records.

24 On the history of schooling in the decades before Unification, see Fantini (1971:

238–39). For some notes on the Casalecchio schools after 1860, see Polvani (1985).

25 This was the Coppino Law, passed 15 July 1877 (law no. 3961).

26 On the many agricultural tasks assigned to children in sharecropper households, see Malaguti (1981).

27 On the decline of religion in the rural population of Bologna, see Scarselli (1890), Grabinski (1892), Ramponi (1892), and Urtoller (1898). The landowners' growing fear of the *braccianti* is evident in Tanari (1881), Goretti (1883), and Pasolini (1891). The role of the *osterie* is discussed by Arbizzani (1977:234).

28 The report of the Bolognese commission on sharecropper theft is found in Bandera (1875). The declining morality of the Bolognese sharecroppers is lamented in Goretti (1882) and Rabbeno (1899).

29 Cammelli (1981) reports on resistance to conscription in Bologna in the 1860s, and mentions the role of the parish priest of Casalecchio (90n).

30 On the popular protests over the grist tax in the Bologna area, see Cammelli (1981).

31 Zangheri (1957) and Romanelli (1979:156) examine the impact of the grist tax and the revolts it sparked. The reaction of the rural population of Bologna to the tax is discussed in Tanari (1881:444–45). The 1874 armed march on Bologna is described in Berselli (1980).

32 For a discussion of the role of rural immigrants in the rise of urban labor militancy in Bologna, see Masulli (1980).

33 See Graziadei (1913) for a discussion of these organizing attempts and the reasons for their failure.

34 On problems of socialist organizing among the sharecroppers in this area, see Preti (1955) and Evangelisti (1980). On sharecropper debt and political organizing, see Cattini (1978).

35 Lotti (1980) is among those claiming that Emilia-Romagna was the area of greatest class conflict and socialist organization in Italy in the early twentieth century. On the spread of the *case del popolo* in rural Bologna in this period, see Arbizzani (1977). On peasant protest in the Po valley in the late nineteenth century, see Arbizzani, Cazzola, and Esposto (1985).

36 This is detailed in the report of the mayor of Casalecchio to the Prefect and Police Headquarters of Bologna (ACCR, 1902, cat. XV, class 5).

37 The history of labor unrest in turn-of-the-century Casalecchio has been documented by Segredin (1982).

38 These figures closely follow the more general pattern in Emilia-Romagna (Ballini 1985:186–87).

39 Casalecchio municipal vote results are found in Segredin (1982).

Chapter Four. Life in Casalecchio

1 See Herlihy and Klapisch-Zuber (1985). For a more general review of household composition in Italy, Spain, and Portugal in the past, see Kertzer and Brettell (1987). In southern Italy, such high proportions of complex-family households were much less common, although considerable range is found in the

community studies conducted to date. For southern Italian household composition, see Da Molin (1987), Delille (1977, 1985), and Douglass (1980).

2 For example, in 1881, in San Giovanni in Persiceto (province of Bologna), 65 percent of the 344 sharecropping households were of a multiple-family type and another 15 percent extended families. In the commune of Ferrara, as late as 1911, 46 of the 63 sharecropper households were multiple-family units (Barbagli 1984:76–77). Della Pina (1987:5), in a study of the countryside of Prato (Tuscany) in 1786, found 76 percent of the 870 sharecropper households to be complex.

3 There have now been hundreds of studies, largely spawned by the work of the Cambridge Group (Laslett 1972), which have produced figures on household complexity in European communities of the past. Only some of the eastern European communities can rival the high proportion of multiple-family households found in the rural areas of central and northern Italy in the nineteenth century.

4 The distinction between measurements based on household units and measurements based on people must always be kept in mind. For example, in a community in which half of all households are multiple and half nuclear in composition, we would expect at least two-thirds of the population to be living in multiple-family households (and even more if the average number of simple-family units in the multiple-family households is greater than two).

5 Comparative data on household composition among Italian sharecroppers are provided in Kertzer (1984) and Barbagli (1984). The figures on the rural parishes surrounding the city of Bologna in 1847 are found in Angeli and Bellettini (1979).

6 Figures on *braccianti* households in rural Bologna in 1847 are provided by Angeli and Bellettini (1979). Further comparative data are provided in Barbagli (1984).

7 Of the people living in multiple-family households in 1871, 90 percent lived in patrilateral households, as did 88 percent in 1921. Of the people living in extended-family households in 1871, 74 percent lived in patrilateral households, 15 percent in matrilateral households, and 11 percent in mixed patrilateral/matrilateral households. A half century later these proportions were little changed: 72 percent, 19 percent, and 9 percent respectively.

8 In fact, there are few differences in age and sex distributions between 1871 and 1921, with most change involving the occupational composition of age and sex groups.

9 In order to ensure that the differences between occupational categories and within categories across years were not due to differences in the age and sex composition of each category, we performed an age-sex standardization. Comparing the standardized and unstandardized distributions (i.e., computing an index of dissimilarity) showed differences of no more than 3 percent for any occupational category in either year.

10 The actual Bolognese proverb is "Quand un puvràtt magna una galénna, o l'é amalè lo, o l'é amalè la galénna" (Menarini 1975:41).

11 See Toscanelli (1861), Comizio Agrario del Circondario di Bologna (1881), Goretti (1882, 1883), INEA (1931), and Broccoli (1979:59).

12 "Al bon véin al fà bon sanghv" (Malaguti 1981:48).

13 On the diet of the *bracciante,* see Tanari (1881:233–34, 443). An example of a household budget for a *bracciante* family in the Ravenna area in 1890, not far from Bologna in Emilia-Romagna, shows 73 percent of all expenditures being devoted to food, with two-thirds of the food budget going to cereals (Nardi 1980:173).

14 Data on the diet of the urban workers of Bologna is taken from the 1885 questionnaire on sanitary conditions; see n. 16.

15 For a discussion of the sanitation problems in the city of Bologna during this period, see Della Peruta (1980).

16 Health information for Casalecchio and Bologna is taken from the manuscript text of the responses of each commune to the questionnaire of the national Inchiesta sulle Condizioni Igienico-Sanitarie of 1885. These are found in the communal archives of Casalecchio (28 February 1885) and Bologna (Archivio di Stato di Bologna, St. comunale; Igiene tit.; anno 1885).

17 Tanari (1881:10). For the housing of the sharecroppers, see Nardi (1957).

18 The report of the Casalecchio sanitation officer may be found in ACCR (pos. spec. 111; 10 April 1895).

19 The regulation governing the *focatico* tax was issued by royal decree on 9 September 1869. Its application, with modification, to the province of Bologna was approved on 2 May 1875. A copy is found in the Archivio di Stato di Bologna, Prefettura Generale, ser. 1, cat. 24, Amm.ne Provinciale, Affari generali, anno 1875. All manuscript tax lists for Casalecchio for the years 1869 through 1914 were photocopied and later entered in coded form into the Casalecchio data base (see the Appendix).

20 The regulation governing the disbursement of free medicines is no. 466, promulgated on 19 July 1906. Lists of the poor of Casalecchio eligible to receive free medicines in 1910–1913 are found in ACCR, II, 4, 1.

21 For example, the crude death rate increased substantially during the cholera epidemic of the 1880s and the influenza epidemic of 1918.

22 These death rates have been directly standardized to control for the small changes that occurred in the age and sex compositions of Casalecchio during these years. The average age and sex composition for the entire period was used as the standard population.

23 Data on mortality in Italy and its provinces are drawn from Santini (1974:36) and Gini and Galvani (1931:190).

24 The proportion of all deaths in Italy accounted for by children five and younger fell from 48 percent in the early 1870s to 33 percent by the early 1920s.

25 The annual number of births ranged from 66 to 151 over this period, averaging 86 in 1865–1874, up to 111 in 1912–1921.

26 The infant mortality rate we discuss here is the number of infants out of 1,000 born who die before their first birthday.

27 Infant mortality in the Bologna area reached highs of around 400 per 1,000

during some decades of the seventeenth century in which a variety of epidemics raged, but by the mid-eighteenth century declined to roughly 250, a rate that would continue for a century. It was only in 1840 that the beginning of the definitive decline in infant mortality could be discerned (Bellettini and Samoggia 1982:11, 1984:200–202). Italian infant mortality declined from a rate of 229 in the early 1870s to 126 by the early 1920s (Santini 1974:41; Poulain and Tabutin 1980:153). These declines were sharpest in the northeast (including Emilia-Romagna), where the rate dropped 63 percent from 1870–1872 to 1930–1932, while in the mainland south the rate dropped 46 percent (Del Panta 1979:227).

Excepting the low infant mortality rate in the initial years of the population register, the recorded declines in infant mortality in Casalecchio parallel those recorded for Italy, with the same pattern of sharper decline recorded for Casalecchio as for the rest of Emilia-Romagna.

28 Nationally, the European influenza epidemic caused a sharp but temporary hike in infant death (L'Eltore 1974:44).

29 This analysis of trends in social differentials in mortality is based on the *focatico* and population-register data. All persons recorded as present in the population register on the date of each *focatico* were matched to their household on that date. Social stratum was assigned to each person based on the occupation and tax category of the household head recorded in the *focatico.*

Using the population-register data on cause of exit, each person matched to the *focatico* was classified according to whether he or she died during the twelve months following the *focatico,* or emigrated during that period. Person-years of exposure for each stratum (the denominator for the death rate) were calculated by assigning one year to persons who lived throughout the year, and one half-year to those who died or emigrated during the year. The number of persons who died during the year is the numerator for the death rate.

This analysis of trends is restricted to the 1869–1905 period, during which a substantial proportion of the population is recorded in the *focatico.* The age-sex specific death rates for each period were calculated based on the aggregated experiences of the person-years lived during the period. The age-sex specific death rates for each stratum in each period were used to calculate a summary death rate for the stratum directly standardized for age and sex. The average distribution of the population by age and sex during the years 1865–1921 was used as the standard population.

This procedure underestimates the total annual mortality rate of each stratum. Infant deaths are underrepresented because deaths to persons under age one are concentrated in the first days of life. Very few of the infants recorded in the *focatico* files would have been in their first week of life; most infants included in this analysis would already have survived this dangerous period. Consequently, the rates reported in fig. 4.3 should be interpreted as the post-neonatal mortality rates for the total population.

In chap. 6 we present economic differences in infant and child mortality based on matching mothers (rather than the infants themselves) to the *focatico.* This analysis indicates that there were only relatively small differences in the infant mortality rates among the strata. Consequently, fig. 3.4 accurately represents economic differentials in mortality, even though the magnitude of the mortality rates is biased downward by the underrepresentation of infant deaths.

30 In 1869–1880 the mortality rate of infants and children under 10 was 44 per 1,000 among wage earners and 21 per 1,000 among sharecroppers. By 1881–1892 the mortality rate among wage earners was down substantially (to 35), but that of sharecroppers was virtually unchanged (20). By 1893–1905, the child mortality rate of wage earners was 21, compared to 15 among the sharecroppers. As discussed above, these rates are somewhat low because infant deaths are underrepresented. The differences recorded here are, therefore, attributable to improvements in the survivorship of children who live at least one year.

While we can bring no direct evidence to bear on this issue, we believe that this pattern may be explained by improvements in the diets of wage-earner families between the mid-nineteenth and early twentieth centuries (an effect that would be observed only after an age at which breast-feeding ceased to be a major source of nourishment). It was during this time that wage-earners were more likely to be literate, have their children enrolled in school, and begin limiting family size. Caldwell (1979) has argued that this combination of factors may be important in assuring adequate provision of familial resources to children in poor patriarchal families.

See chap. 6 for a more complete discussion of infant and child mortality differences among the strata.

Chapter Five. On the Move

1 For prior studies of migration using the Casalecchio data, see Kertzer and Hogan (1985) and Hogan and Kertzer (1985b). Since these articles were written the population-register data used in this chapter have been more fully edited for missing dates of entry and exit and places of origin and destination. This data cleaning was done using other archival sources unavailable at the time of the earlier analyses. Also, this chapter uses information from the *focatico* (annual tax registers) to provide insights into the relationship of migration to the family economy.

2 In the census of 1911 45 percent of the population was native-born.

3 For data on population mobility see Schofield (1971) and Tilly (1978b). On land inheritance and the assumption of lack of geographic mobility, see Berkner (1972). For a critique similar to ours, but regarding political relations and the assumption of geographic stability, see Stephenson (1979). Studies that have taken exception to these inaccuracies include Hochstadt (1981), Sabean (1970), and Sharlin and Sammis (1982).

4 See Ravenstein (1889) and Jansen (1970) for statements of the stage model. See Crew (1979), Sharlin and Sammis (1982), and Hochstadt (1981) for empirical evidence calling into question the assumptions of the stage theory of migration. Da Molin (1980) and Laslett (1977) discuss high peasant mobility, and Czap (1983) examines serfdom and migration.

For related evidence on the United States see Thernstrom and Knights (1970); Thernstrom (1973); Stephenson (1979); and Katz, Doucet, and Stern (1982).

5 Moch (1983:24–25), in this context, writes of the necessity of examining migration systems rather than simple movements between countryside and city.

6 Lequin (1977) and Moch (1983) use cross-sectional data on nativity. Studies by Anderson (1980) and Friedlander and Roshier (1966) distinguish place of birth among non-natives. Matched data from successive censuses were used in the studies by Katz (1975); Lehning (1980); and Pouyez, Roy, and Bouchard (1981).

7 The limitations of conventional data on migration and the advantages of residential histories are discussed in Taeuber (1961) and Shryock and Larmon (1965). Hogan and Kertzer (1985a) discuss these issues in relation to historical research.

8 Use of the population register for detailed migration analyses was made widely known to the demographic community through the work of Goldstein (1964). However, Goldstein used the Danish population register to examine twentieth-century migration. Few demographers have followed his lead to use these data to shed light on nineteenth-century migration in Europe.

9 See discussions in Di Rienzo (1957) and Cariani (1977).

10 For a detailed description of these procedures, see the appendix to the Casalecchio handbook (Kertzer 1985), written by Roger Bertsch.

11 In theory, we could use information on date of migration and destination to follow the individual through his or her stay in that other commune using its population register. This is at best a long and expensive process. Moreover, some communal registers have been destroyed and others are uncatalogued. Our study is therefore limited to following the portion of people's lives lived in Casalecchio, including return migrations, making use of data on places of origin and destination to provide insight into the geographical dimensions of migration.

12 While census data on occupation are available for individuals present during a census year, they provide a biased source of information for economic differentials in migration because those groups in the population that are most migratory are underrepresented.

The lack of population register data on economic activity and the biases inherent in using the census data on occupation precluded a discussion of economic differentials in migration in earlier analyses of these data, which did not have the benefit of the annual tax records (Kertzer and Hogan 1985; Hogan and Kertzer 1985b).

13 The *focatico* begins in 1869 with records for 415 households. The number of households enumerated in the *focatico* varied from one year to the next, but was always between 409 and 489 for the years 1869–1886. In 1887 the number increased to 544, and climbed progressively for the rest of the period, with between 659 and 706 households recorded in the *focatico* of 1900–1905. Interannual changes in the number of households was 10 percent or less, except for the years 1890, 1891, 1893, and 1897, which had 30–40 percent fewer households than in the years immediately before or after. Except for these four years,

the *focatico* appears to have been administered consistently from 1869 to 1905. It continued to be administered from 1906 to 1914, but with dramatically fewer households (0 in 1908 and 129–206 in other years). Therefore, we did not attempt to use the *focatico* data collected after 1905.

Household heads recorded in the *focatico* could usually be matched to individuals recorded as household heads in the population register. In 1869 (the first year of the *focatico* and fifth year of the population register) 93 percent of the *focatico* heads of households appeared in the population register. By the next year, the match had increased to 97 percent, and remained in the 94–99 percent range until 1905.

14 Relatively complete information on the occupation and/or social strata of the household head was obtained by the *focatico* in these years. Only 0.4 percent of the persons recorded in the *focatico* lived in households that could not be classified into one of the economic strata used in this analysis.

See the Appendix for a discussion of the type of occupation and social-strata information collected, and for problems with the completeness of the *focatico* information on household economic activities in years subsequent to 1905.

15 The number of immigrants and emigrants varied greatly from year to year. These temporal variations may relate to sudden shifts in the economic opportunities available in Casalecchio as well as to random variations associated with the town's relatively small size. Underlying long-term trends in migration rates resulted from large-scale changes in the Casalecchio political economy, as well as from demographic changes in the age and sex composition of the population. The immigration and emigration rates displayed in fig. 4.3 remove the effects of demographic structure by directly standardizing the rates for the age and sex composition of the population (using the average composition for the entire period as the standard population). We have attempted to reduce random fluctuations in the annual rates of migration by presenting three-year moving averages.

16 Unfortunately, we could not use precisely the same groupings of years for analyses of the *focatico* data. The *focatico* covers only the period from 1869 to 1905, which we arbitrarily divided into three equal periods (1869–1880, 1881–1892, and 1893–1905). The immigration and emigration rates for the years differently classified (1881–1882 and 1893–1896) in the population register and *focatico* analyses suggest that these years were not turning points during which major changes in migration behaviors occurred. Thus, despite some differences in the exact cutting points between periods, these three periods can be roughly viewed as corresponding to times of agricultural prosperity, agricultural crisis, and the beginning of the period of increased commercial and industrial linkages between Casalecchio and Bologna.

17 The virtual absence of international migration in this area can be illustrated with figures for the period 1880–1885. In those years the rate of such emigration from the province of Bologna was just 8 per 100,000 population, compared to a national rate ranging between 421 and 594 in those same years (Ministero di Agricoltura, Industria e Commercio 1887:4). For discussion of

the geographical mobility of the rural population of the Po valley in the late nineteenth century, see Dalle Donne (1986).

18 There were few marked age or sex differences in places of origin or destination. During the earliest period, young females were more likely to come from or move to the commune of Bologna and young men were more likely to move between rural communes.

Census data for Casalecchio in 1861, 1881, and 1921 show a secular increase in the proportion literate, regardless of birthplace. In 1861 Casalecchio residents born in Bologna were somewhat more likely (32 percent vs. 20 percent) to be literate, but this difference disappeared by 1881. Immigrants from remote regions were much more likely to be literate than other Casalecchio residents (77 percent vs. 20 percent in 1861), with this advantage persisting until literacy became widespread in the population of the province of Bologna.

19 See Hogan and Kertzer (1985b, table 1) for previous research documenting the changing family and household situations of men (age 10 and older) who immigrated to Casalecchio. We focus on males to simplify the analysis. In general, the migration of females is directly related to the migration decisions of their fathers or their husbands. Females were much less likely to migrate as servants, since the agricultural servant market was largely male. Important differences in the mobility of females during the ages of marriage are discussed below.

20 The remaining 4–5 percent of immigrants were widowed at the time of migration to Casalecchio.

21 Our data base lacks information on economic activity of men at the time of entry. (Although this information was available on the immigration-register forms, we decided not to enter it into the data base because of the relatively weak quality of the information and the attendant expense for its coding and editing.) We do, however, have direct information on whether the men were servants at the time of their arrival in Casalecchio and have used this information in this analysis.

22 This indicates that boarding, so characteristic of North American communities of this period, was rare in central Italy.

23 This analysis requires data on the population at risk of migration, classified according to these demographic and socioeconomic characteristics and their subsequent migration experience. Data on the population at risk of migration are available for the study of emigration rates from Casalecchio, since we have complete representation of people who resided in Casalecchio during this period. We lack similar data on the population at risk of immigration to Casalecchio (since persons who are at risk of immigrating to Casalecchio but do not immigrate never appear in the Casalecchio population register).

24 The hazard rate of emigration indicates the proportion of native-born persons still in Casalecchio on a given birthday who emigrate within the next year.

25 That is, we classify every individual according to the economic activity of the head of the household in which he or she lives.

26 These calculations control for the differing age and sex composition of the

various strata. Recall that the middle stratum consists of the middle category assigned by the keepers of the household tax register (*focatico*) minus the sharecroppers, for whom we have created a separate category. The middle stratum includes merchants, artisans, clerks, and professionals, although the first two occupations dominate.

27 These observations are based on a complex analysis of the *focatico* data. Each person matched to a household registered in the *focatico* during a given year was classified according to economic stratum, age, and sex. Each person was further classified according to whether emigration from Casalecchio occurred during the twelve-month period following the *focatico* (excluding persons dying during the year).

The 92,650 person-years of experience recorded in the *focatico* and population register were then analyzed using log linear modified multiple regression procedures, in which emigration during the year (yes/no) was treated as the dependent variable. See Goodman (1978) for a discussion of this methodology.

We used reverse stepwise procedures to determine which of the many possible associations between the independent variables and emigration needed to be considered in order to present a complete picture of the migration process. We found that certain associations significantly improved the fit of the model and could not be omitted from consideration. For example, taking into account the association between the independent variables (stratum, time period, age group, and sex), there are differences between males and females in the effects of strata on the likelihood of migration ($\chi^2_{LR} = 11.2$, $df = 3$, $p < .01$). Strata differences in the changing age pattern of migration are statistically significant ($\chi^2_{LR} = 47.0$, $df = 30$, $p < .02$). There are gender differences in the age pattern of migration ($\chi^2_{LR} = 18.5$, $df = 5$, $p < .01$). Together, these three factors provide an adequate account of the associations of the independent variables with migration. The fit of the model including these factors is quite good ($\chi^2_{LR} = 53.0$, $df = 63$, $p = .82$) and no additional factors result in a further statistically significant reduction of the chi-square test statistic. (For example, the gender differences in the age pattern of migration did not vary by strata [$\chi^2_{LR} = 8.6$, $df = 15$, $p = .94$].)

The results of this complex statistical analysis were used to guide our discussion of the descriptive statistics presented in the text of this chapter.

28 During 1869–1880, sharecropper household residents (male and female combined) aged 10–17 had annual emigration rates of 92 per 1,000, compared to 42 per 1,000 among the wage earners. By 1893–1905 these rates had declined to 38 and 35, respectively.

29 See Greewood (1975) and Goldstein (1976) for discussions of the research opportunities created by migration histories. See Gross and Clark (1975) and Tuma and Hannan (1984) for expositions of methods of survival analysis. Sandefur and Scott (1981) use the methods advocated by Tuma and Hannan to analyze migration histories of contemporary American males. See Hogan and Kertzer (1985a) for a complete discussion of the uses of survival methods in the historical study of migration.

30 For persons born in Casalecchio, age is equivalent to duration of residence, and the hazard rates can be interpreted as age-specific rates of emigration (as in fig. 5.7). For immigrants, duration of residence and age are two distinct variables. We use more elaborate survival techniques to identify the independent effect of age on the duration-specific hazard rate of emigration among immigrants.

31 In doing this analysis we calculated annual hazard rates of emigration for relevant comparison groups, but such data are extremely cumbersome to present. By way of summary we present data on the percentages of persons emigrating from Casalecchio within five years of arrival. More detailed investigations of the complete survival distributions indicate that the use of this summary measure does not produce a misleading picture of differentials in the rate of emigration. Our discussion of these summary data are also guided by statistical tests of significance for overall differences in the survival distributions of the groups.

32 One method for the multivariate analysis of the determinants of the hazard rate of emigration uses the maximum likelihood estimation of a continuous-time semi-Markov model. This model exactly specifies the form of the hazard rate, which, in the case of migration, is best fit by a negative exponential (see Sandefur and Scott 1981). Other authors have noted the possibility of using methods for the analysis of contingency tables to estimate determinants of the hazard rate (Trussell and Hammerslough 1983). We use the well-established partial likelihood technique developed by Cox (1972, 1974) to identify the effects of life-course characteristics at the time of immigration to Casalecchio on the subsequent rate of emigration.

As noted by Menken, Trussell, Stempel, and Babakol (1981), such a model is analogous to calculating a multivariate life-table model, in which the effects of particular independent variables are assumed to be proportional at each point in time, but the overall form of the hazard function is left unspecified. This assumption of proportionality was tested by inspecting the hazard rates produced in the initial survival analysis of the total effect of each variable. This inspection indicated that the hazard rates of emigration of the comparison groups analyzed here remain proportionately different for at least the first five years of postimmigration experience, and tend toward proportionality, but are subject to large standard errors, thereafter.

33 This analysis of differences in the migration experiences of individuals over their life course is based on the population-register data on dates of entry and exit. These analyses were done using methods of survival analysis. These calculations provide unbiased estimates of emigration over the life course, since they include the relevant periods of experience of persons who were exposed to the risk of emigration from Casalecchio, but who died or were still present when the population register ended in 1921.

34 In survival calculations of this sort we use 1915 (rather than 1921) as the closing date for entry into observation in order to allow some years of exposure to the risk of migration before the closing date of observation at the end of 1921.

35 This sex differential widens slightly, to 8 percent, among immigrants of ages

10–17, because male immigrants of these ages were more likely to come as short-term servants.

36 In 1865–1882, 54 percent of male immigrants left Casalecchio within five years. By 1883–1896 this figure had dropped to 49 percent, and by the time of urban expansion, only 38 percent of male immigrants to Casalecchio stayed less than five years. The trend toward a decreased rate of emigration was more gradual for female immigrants, 47 percent of whom emigrated from Casalecchio within five years in the earlier period, the proportion declining to 45 percent during the agricultural crisis and going down to 36 percent in the period of urban expansion.

37 The proportion of immigrants aged 10–29 emigrating within five years declined from 58 percent of those immigrating in 1865–1882 to 38 percent of those immigrating in 1897–1915.

38 Some of these "return" migrants to the remote provinces may have been migrating to another province than the one from which they came.

39 Servants who emigrated from Casalecchio were actually somewhat less likely to choose Bologna as their destination. But they were much more likely than other immigrants to emigrate to Bologna because their overall rates of emigration were so high. (The overall emigration rate of servants was 100 percent higher than that of household heads, while their emigration rate to Bologna was 78 percent higher; see table 5.3, models 3 and 4.)

40 It is likely that the higher rate of emigration to Bologna among the elite migrants to Casalecchio is associated with the greater likelihood of these men coming to Casalecchio from Bologna and the strong tendency of immigrants from Bologna to return to the city.

Chapter Six. Children and the Family Economy

1 Quoted in Nardinelli (1980:739).

2 See also Mendels (1972, 1984) and Kriedte, Medick, and Schlumbohm (1981), on protoindustrial family systems. A rare glimpse into the human side of these conditions for children is provided by Grafteaux (1986).

3 These historians have not been without their critics. See, for example, Pollock (1983).

4 See Samoggia's (1985) study of infant mortality in the rural area surrounding the city of Bologna.

5 See the discussion of trends in infant mortality in chap. 3. In other analyses we have shown that the usual demographic differentials in infant mortality were observed in Casalecchio (Hogan and Kertzer 1986). Males had consistently higher infant death rates than females, and were especially subject to death from infectious diseases (such as the influenza epidemic of 1918–1919). Infants born to mothers under age 25 had higher rates of infant death (associated with first births), and children born to mothers 35 and older were subject to somewhat higher rates of infant death (in part due to such births being higher parity).

6 The Lee-Desu test for measuring the statistical significance of differences between survival distributions indicated that the differences in infant and child

morality discussed here are statistically significant ($p < .05$). In 1869–1880, the elite and sharecroppers had rates of infant and child death that were significantly different from those of wage earners. The elite had lower rates of mortality compared to each of the other groups from 1881–1905. The infant and child mortality rates of sharecropper and artisan and merchant families were significantly lower than those of the wage earners during this time. At no time did the sharecropper and middle group have rates of infant or child mortality that differed significantly from each other.

7 Obviously, no population has an infant mortality rate of zero. What these figures demonstrate is that for the very small elite group in Casalecchio the rate of infant death was quite low. Had the rates of infant death that applied to the elite group in 1869–1880 continued during the subsequent periods, 8 of the 55 children born would have died before reaching their first birthday. Instead, as soon as public-health measures brought the worst infectious diseases under control, medical care purchased by the elite further enhanced the survival chances of their children.

8 In other analyses of infant mortality we used census data on father's occupation to address the question of economic differentials (Hogan and Kertzer 1986). This analysis suggested that there were no significant differentials between the elite, sharecroppers, and agricultural wage laborers in 1867–1886. However, the infant mortality probability was .202 among families headed by nonfarm wage workers, compared to .148 for other families (a difference that is statistically significant: ($\chi^2 = 7.6$, $df = 1$, $p < .01$).

By 1907–1916, the census-based analysis showed that the infant death probabilities of all other groups had converged on the low rates (.070 probability of death in the first year) that (according to the *focatico*) had characterized the artisans and merchants earlier in the century.

9 The subsequent survival chances of children who lived to age five were reasonably good in each period (about 97–99 percent), and did not differ by economic class.

10 This interpretation is consistent with the widening of child mortality differentials between sharecroppers and wage earners during the agricultural crisis, when living conditions for wage earners were particularly bad. By contrast, the economic class differential in infant mortality remained stable between the periods of agricultural prosperity and the agrarian crisis.

Note, also, that this argument relates to differentials in child mortality. Levels of child mortality in every group declined somewhat during the agricultural crisis as improvements in public health and infectious-disease control occurred.

11 For the claim that the extended-family past is simply a myth of Western nostalgia, see Laslett (1965, 1972, 1977). Laslett (1983) has recently recognized that complex-family households were historically common in parts of Mediterranean Europe.

12 In 1892, five Bologna foundlings were entrusted to Casalecchio wet nurses. That number declined to one in 1893, four in 1894, one in 1897, four in 1898, and two in 1899. On the history of child abandonment and the institution of found-

ling homes in Italy, see Corsini (1976), Da Molin (1984), and Della Peruta (1979). See also Ministero di Agricoltura, Industria e Commercio (1888).

13 For an excellent study of service as a life stage in rural England in the early modern period, see Kussmaul (1981).

14 In Parma, for example, the proportion of households having servants declined to 18 percent in 1851.

15 Data on servants in urban Italy in the 1545–1850 period are taken from Barbagli (1984:216–33).

16 See Tittarelli (1985) on the domestic servants of Perugia. Unfortunately, no similar study exists for Bologna.

17 Using the population register, we have been able to trace the background of 571 individuals who worked as servants for sharecropping households and who arrived after 1865. Just 23 (4 percent) of them came from other households in Casalecchio where they lived as kin of the household head. Ninety-six percent joined households where they worked as servants upon their arrival in the commune. An unfortunate implication of this pattern is that we are unable to provide direct data on the economic characteristics of the households that were *providing* the servants (but see our discussion of the data from the conscription register below).

18 In all, 65 servants registered for the military draft in Casalecchio in this period. Of these, 36 gave a father's occupation, with the following breakdown: 23 *braccianti,* 4 sharecroppers, 3 other agricultural work, 2 servants, 2 hemp workers, 1 construction worker, and 1 other wage laborer.

19 It should also be noted that the decline in the practice of service came disproportionately from the males. By 1921, just 25 percent of Casalecchio's servants were males, down from 71 percent sixty years before. The actual numbers of servants living in Casalecchio at the census dates were 98 in 1861, 111 in 1871, 115 in 1881, 84 in 1911, and 63 in 1921. These figures and those in the text do not include people who worked as servants but who lived at home.

20 This letter, written by the socialist deputy A. Celli, is quoted in Merli (1972: 240).

21 See Merli (1972:177, 212) on the conditions of factory labor in the wake of Unification.

22 It should be recalled that many of the children who worked in the hemp factory came from neighboring communities. The data provided in this paragraph refer only to those resident in Casalecchio households.

23 Separate analyses of the data for the 1871 and 1881 censuses yield very similar patterns. We combine the data here, given the relative smallness of our numbers (71 children were hemp workers in 1871 and 66 a decade later). Of these 137 children, 111 are female.

24 While 13 percent of the Casalecchio children aged 8–19 lived in households headed by other wage laborers, 19 percent of the children working in the hemp factory came from such households. Similarly, 14 percent of all children came from *bracciante*-headed households, with 20 percent of the children working in the hemp factory coming from such households.

25 The report quoted here is found in the *Annali dell'Industria e del Commercio* (1880).
26 See note 25.
27 This law is the *legge sul lavoro dei fanciulli* (law no. 3657), issued on 11 February 1886.
28 On the effect of Italy's child labor laws in the late nineteenth century, and on comparison with other European countries, see Merli (1972:244, 337, 350).
29 Article 7 of *Legge sul lavoro delle donne e dei fanciulli* (law no. 242), issued 19 June 1902, and published in the *Gazzetta Ufficiale del Regno* on 7 July 1902.
30 This source, the *Registro comunale dei libretti rilasciati ai fanciulli operai (o alle donne minorenni)* for the commune of Casalecchio, was found in the ACCR, Archivio Generale, cat. XI, class 1, 1927.

Chapter Seven. Getting Married

1 The Napoleonic directives cited here are dated 1 April 1806, 31 December 1808, and 8 October 1810, and are found in Ministero pel Culto del Regno d'Italia (1808:140, 1813:18–21, 101–3).
2 This letter was reproduced in the socialist newspaper *La Squilla,* published in Bologna on 31 March 1906, under the title "The Cursed House." For a discussion of the tension between civil and religious marriage during the Napoleonic period in Florence, see Gozzini (1984). Regarding the reaction of the Church to the 1866 marriage law, see Rocchi (1893).
3 Although the state officially recognized the civil validity of church marriages with the Concordat in 1929, the battle between church and civil marriages has continued in recent decades in Italy in a different form, with the refusal to celebrate church marriage seen as a symbol of allegiance to the political Left. See Kertzer (1980).
4 This example is provided by Galassini (1874:6–7).
5 These cases are discussed by Rocchi (1893) in an article that shows the continuing concern over the problems occasioned by the dual marriage system almost three decades after its inception.
6 See Benini (1911:60–61) for precise figures on the extent to which people anticipated the dates of their marriages in 1865 to avoid the new marriage law. In 1863 and 1864, the marriage rate per 1,000 in the region was 7.4.
7 For regional differences in illegitimacy rates, see Ministero di Agricoltura, Industria e Commercio (1888:86). See Raseri (1906, table 41) for the national pattern during this period.
8 As part of the Casalecchio study, information from all of the 2,020 marriage entries in the civil marriage register was employed, together with information from the parish records of 1,151 church weddings in Casalecchio in the 1865–1921 period. We have 100 percent coverage of civil weddings, but only an estimated 75–80 percent coverage of the religious marriages. The latter gaps are due to restrictions on access to some of the parish archives which especially affect the period after 1905. Hence, for the more crucial nineteenth-century period the proportion of church marriages recorded is on the order of 90 per-

cent. We were able to obtain all marriage records for the entire 1865–1921 period from the main church of Casalecchio, and all records for the 1865–1904 period for the Ceretolo parish, Casalecchio's second largest. Records of later years for that parish as well as all records for the small rural parishes of San Giovanni Battista and San Donino were unavailable to us due to diocesan restrictions.

The greater number of civil marriages for which we have records is also because church weddings were traditionally celebrated in the parish of the bride. In cases where a Casalecchio man married a woman from elsewhere, no church record of the marriage was made in Casalecchio. Fortunately, this is not the case for civil records, since communes in which marriages were celebrated were obliged to send a copy of the marriage-register entry to the commune of the nonresident spouse.

Another problem is that we are unable to follow couples who moved away from Casalecchio, other than knowing the commune to which they moved. Since religious marriage generally preceded civil marriage, this means that we have quite a few cases (222) where we have religious-marriage data but no record in Casalecchio of a civil marriage. Given the pattern of patrilocality, this should not be surprising, for while the church marriage of a Casalecchio woman to a non-Casalecchio man would be celebrated and recorded in Casalecchio, their subsequent civil marriage would be celebrated in the commune in which the groom was living. If this marriage took place after the bride had officially changed her residence from Casalecchio to her husband's commune, there would be no civil record of their marriage in Casalecchio.

The result of all these factors is that we have civil-marriage records corresponding to 81 percent of all our church-marriage records, whereas we have church records for only 46 percent of those for whom we have civil-marriage records. However, our matching rate is higher in the nineteenth century than in the twentieth, which is fortunate for our purposes. While the precise figures we present in analyzing the relationship of civil marriage to religious marriage must be seen only as indications of tendencies and trends, they provide some of the first empirical historical data on this issue. However, we cannot know how many couples celebrated only a religious marriage or only a civil marriage. The great majority of couples in fact celebrated both, however, and it is this population that we examine here. Of course, the longer the gap between religious and civil marriage, the more likely it is that the couple moved in the interim. Our data, based on Casalecchio alone, are hence biased against those who waited longer times between religious and civil marriage.

Our marriage records for Casalecchio consist of the following: for 1865–1882, 50 percent both civil and religious, 31 percent only civil, 19 percent only religious, $N = 484$; for 1883–1896, 48 percent both civil and religious, 38 percent only civil, 14 percent only religious, $N = 500$; and for 1897–1921, 39 percent both civil and religious, 56 percent only civil, 5 percent only religious, $N = 929$.

9 Among the nobility, it could be argued, there may have been countertendencies

due to the opposition of segments of the nobility to the new regime and the close ties many had with the Church hierarchy. Unfortunately, Casalecchio does not provide us with enough cases of marriage to shed much light on the behavior of the elite.

10 Unfortunately, as noted earlier, we have no direct data on cases where people celebrated a civil marriage only, since we could never be sure that a couple had not celebrated a church marriage. On the leadership role in patriotism, anticlericalism and "free thinking" played by the artisans and merchants of this part of Italy—with a focus on the mountainous zone—see Sarti (1985).

11 The central demographic role of age at marriage is argued most forcefully in Wrigley and Schofield (1981). Netting (1981:135) observes a similar relationship in a Swiss village in the eighteenth and nineteenth centuries.

12 On the relationship between proletarianization and a lowered age of marriage, see Anderson (1971:132–34) and Levine (1977:146).

13 One environmental factor that should also be emphasized is sex ratio of the population, as suggested by the comparison of coal-mining and textile communities. Where women are in short supply they tend to marry at earlier ages, and where they outnumber men they tend to marry later. See Wrigley (1961:145–46) and Anderson (1976). On the historical demography of British coal miners, see Haines (1979). Sex ratio is not a significant factor in accounting for Casalecchio marital age (see chap. 3).

14 Derouet's (1980) study of four rural French villages in the eighteenth century is an exception to this general reliance on community-level and aggregate occupational data.

15 See Saller (1987) for a discussion of age at marriage in the Roman Empire.

16 On marital age in Italy from the early Middle Ages through the medieval period, see Herlihy (1985).

17 Of Italian women, 17 percent were married by age 20, compared to 21 percent in France and 14 percent in England at this time.

18 See also Hajnal (1965:111).

19 For a comparison of Italian age at marriage with that of the rest of Europe, see Bellettini (1982:775). National age-at-marriage figures for both sexes, by marital status, are found in Somogyi (1965:360), with regional breakdowns for female mean age at first marriage found in Livi-Bacci (1977:107). Livi-Bacci (1977:118) also gives figures on marital ages in some of the largest cities around 1900.

20 Our earliest nineteenth-century data for Casalecchio are from the Napoleonic period, when, in 1811–1812, mean age at marriage was 27 for men and 24 for women, identical to the means for the Bologna hills as a whole. In the plains marriage was only slightly earlier (by a year), while marriage in both the city of Bologna and in the mountains was at later ages: 30 for men and 26 for women in the city, and 29 for men and 26 for women in the mountains (Bellettini 1965:133–35).

21 Marriage-rate figures come from Somogyi (1965:330). The marriage rate per 1,000 population for Emilia-Romagna was 7.34 in 1914, down to 3.28 in the

1916–1918 period, and skyrocketing to 12.21 in 1920. Even sharper trends are evident for Italy as a whole.

22 Again, it should be remembered that marriages were typically first celebrated in church, and thus, especially in the first period, age at civil marriage was apt to be a few months greater than age at religious marriage.

23 "L'é méi dir puvràtt me, che puvrétt no" (Menarini 1975:14).

24 Rettaroli's (1986:252–53) recent study of marital age in various Tuscan communities similarly fails to find much difference in age of first marriage between sharecroppers and *braccianti* in the mid-nineteenth century. From 1829 to 1859 her sample of communities showed a slightly higher mean male sharecropper marital age (28.2 vs. 27.0), with female age at first marriage virtually identical between sharecroppers (24.6) and *braccianti* (24.4). On the continued tendency of French proletarians to marry at a relatively late age, see Spagnoli's (1983:234) study of the Lille region in the mid-nineteenth century.

25 Compared to the attention recently lavished on the issue of bastardy in European history, the much more common phenomenon of pregnancy before marriage has received relatively little attention. This is partly due to the greater ease with which bastardy may be studied, since the basic source is a single civil register, namely, the birth register. On the other hand, in order to study bridal pregnancy, one must not only locate but also link two different vital registers: the marriage register and the birth register. Indeed, in many cases the authorities themselves prepared aggregate summaries of births by legitimacy, but nowhere did they prepare such data on bridal pregnancies. On bastardy in European history, see especially the volume edited by Laslett, Oosterveen, and Smith (1980).

26 This distinction is discussed by Laslett (1977:128–29).

27 Others who employ the seven-month definition for bridal pregnancy include Kalvemark (1980) and Watkins and McCarthy (1980). In their American historical study, Smith and Hindus (1975) provide measures on three periods: under six months, under eight and a half months, and under nine months.

28 This represents 64 percent of the 929 marriages for which we have both civil and religious records.

29 See Spagnoli (1983:240–41). For bridal pregnancy rates in England, see Hair (1966, 1970); Laslett (1980:23); Oosterveen, Smith, and Stewart (1980:108–9); and Levine and Wrightson (1980:161–62). For French rates, see Smith (1986:80–81) and Houdaille (1987:661).

30 The case of La Hulpe, in Belgium, is discussed in Watkins and McCarthy (1980); Kalvemark (1980) has studied the Swedish community of Julita; and Caspard (1974) has examined nine Swiss parishes.

31 Here it would be comforting to have more direct testimony on the values associated with premarital pregnancy. Unfortunately, little such evidence is available. Indeed, it seems to be a topic that was either deemed so common as to be hardly worthy of attention or best not discussed publicly. However, the social acceptance of sexual relations between single men and women (as the couple were prepared to marry should the woman become pregnant) has been posited by a number of scholars for various areas further north in Europe. See Gillis

(1985:52, 126–27), Robin (1986:123–24), and Smith (1986:91–92) for England, and Kalvemark (1980:330) for Sweden.

32 For age data on prenuptial pregnancy in England, see Smith (1986:91) and Robin (1986:121–22); for France, see Houdaille (1987:661); and for Sweden, see Kalvemark (1980:335).

33 Robin (1986:121) has made a similar observation with regard to the English village of Colyton in the period 1851–1881.

34 Data in the "Other" category of table 7.8 are contaminated by the fact that some women likely left their employment because they were pregnant. Hence, their occupation at marriage would be listed as "housework" rather than the occupation they might have had at the time they got pregnant. This might account for the generally higher proportion of such women who were pregnant at marriage.

35 The multiple classification analysis model we estimate is a form of ordinary least-squares regression model in which all independent variables are categorical. In this case, the dependent variable is a dichotomy (pregnant at marriage/not pregnant at marriage). While ordinary least-squares regression procedures can produce biased results when the dependent variable is dichotomous, the estimation procedures are quite robust when the event of interest is not rare. Since 44 percent of all Casalecchio women included in this analysis were pregnant at marriage, the results of the multiple-classification models are unlikely to be biased.

The proportion of variance explained by these models is quite low. This situation is not unusual when a deterministic model is used to predict an event that is dichotomous and stochastically distributed. The critical item of interest in such cases is the between-group differentials in bridal pregnancy, not the proportion of variance explained.

This model of differentials in bridal pregnancy is intended to be descriptive. We are not attempting to infer a causal model of the determinants of bridal pregnancy. Limitations in population coverage mean that the results of the tests for statistical significance should not be interpreted inferentially. Also, some variables in the model (such as age at marriage) are as much a result of an out-of-wedlock pregnancy prompting a marriage as the reverse, precluding statements of cause and effect.

36 That is, husbands and wives tend to be from similar economic backgrounds, both relatively young or relatively old, and both literate or illiterate. Problems of multicollinearity arise in the estimation of such models and it is difficult to come up with plausible interpretations of such "net" effects. We did, however, consider interactions between the wife's and husband's characteristics, and these are reported in the text and in footnotes where relevant.

37 Another way of expressing this finding is to note that if the occupational composition of brides in 1865–1882 had continued unchanged, but the bridal pregnancy rates of each occupational group did change to the pattern observed in 1897–1921, the percentage of brides pregnant at marriage would have risen from 36 percent to 42 percent (instead of to the 50 percent actually recorded).

A similar direct standardization for the changing occupations of men at marriage indicates that the rate of bridal pregnancy would have increased only to 40 percent by the turn of the century, if the occupational distributions of men in 1865–1882 had continued unchanged.

38 Elsewhere in this chapter we note that many of the young brides who were employees of the hemp factory married men who also worked there. The courtship of these couples would have been largely unsupervised by the family of the bride, although the hemp factory itself did supervise the young women resident at the plant.

39 This differential resulted not only from the different marriage and labor markets found in the city and countryside, but also from a tendency for the never-married from the countryside to be drawn to the city (Livi-Bacci 1977:106, 119).

40 Only the elite show especially high rates of definitive celibacy, but this must be viewed with some caution, since both the clergy and school teachers fall in this small category. In 1921, when we have a sufficient number of cases, 9 percent of elite men over age 50 had never been married, compared to 6 percent of sharecroppers and artisans/merchants, 4 percent of agricultural wage laborers, and 7 percent of nonagricultural wage laborers.

41 The proportions of never-married men over age 50 in Casalecchio at the census years are 7.3 percent in 1861, 9.1 percent in 1871, 7.0 percent in 1881, 10.0 percent in 1911, and 7.4 percent in 1921.

42 "L'é méi un trésst maré, ch'an fa un ban fradèl" (Menarini 1975:16).

43 "Bisugnarév che quand la dona nas, l'omen zapàs" (Menarini 1975:15).

44 The minimum legal age for marriage for women was 15 (Taglioni 1866:175).

45 Netting (1981:181) has observed a similar relationship between marriage age and the age differences between spouses among Swiss alpine peasants.

46 In Laslett's English village of Ealing in 1599, 21 percent of the wives were older than their husbands, while in his French village of Longuenesse in 1778, 27 percent were. In contrast, the Serbian case of Belgrade in 1733–1774, presumably representing the Mediterranean, showed just 0.5 percent of its marriages involving wives older than husbands (Laslett 1977:26–27). The English sample consisted of 62 married couples, the French of 48, and the Serbian of 192. It does not appear, moreover, that remarried widows and widowers were eliminated in these calculations. Yet, on the basis of these tiny samples, members of the Cambridge Group could summarize the findings as showing a "mean age gap in favour of husbands of about 3 years in the west and 10 in the east. A fifth of wives were older than husbands in the west, almost none in the east" (Wall 1983:461, referring to Laslett's findings).

47 We here refer to the whole fifty-seven year period, as analysis of various subperiods shows no significant changes in the proportion of wives older than their husbands. In 1865–1882, 21 percent of husbands were younger than their wives, while in 1897–1921 this proportion stood at 20 percent.

48 Rettaroli (1986:263) finds a similar pattern in rural Tuscany in 1820–1859, where 15 percent of the sharecroppers, but 22 percent of the *braccianti,* married women older than they.

49 In 1865–1896, in 741 civil marriages uniting never-married individuals, the age differences were as follows: in 3 percent husbands were over 10 years younger than their wives, in 2 percent 5–9 years younger, in 5 percent 2–4 years younger, and in 9 percent under 2 years younger; in 18 percent husbands were less than 2 years older, in 26 percent 5–9 years older, and in 11 percent over 10 years older than their brides. In 1897–1921, in 1,025 such marriages, 2 percent of the grooms were over 10 years younger than their brides, 2 percent were 5–9 years younger, 4 percent were 2–4 years younger, and 12 percent were less than 2 years younger; in 22 percent the husband was less than two years older, in 31 percent 2–4 years older, in 22 percent 5–9 years older, and in 7 percent of the marriages the groom was ten or more years older than the bride.

For a discussion of contemporary international comparisons in age differences between spouses and their implications, see Casterline, Williams, and McDonald (1986).

50 In cases where the civil marriage followed the religious marriage by a substantial amount of time, it is possible that the occupational status of the bride actually reflects her occupation after the religious marriage. Insofar as women quit their jobs at marriage, this probably inflates the proportion of brides listed as outside the labor force.

51 We first looked separately at the 1865–1882 and 1883–1896 periods. However, as the pattern was largely the same for both and the numbers in some categories (especially the elite) were small, we have combined them in our presentation.

52 Rettaroli's (1986:266–67) study of rural Tuscany in 1820–1859 produced similar results, with 75–80 percent of the sharecroppers marrying other sharecroppers and 62–65 pecent of the *braccianti* marrying other *braccianti.*

53 This is the coresidential transition at marriage that Laslett suggests for the traditional Mediterranean pattern.

54 For a study of marriage patterns in the rural periphery of Bologna in the eighteenth century, see Angeli (1985).

55 These figures actually underestimate the proportion of brides who joined preexisting households headed by an extended kinsman, since some had already moved into independent households by the time of the census.

56 On industrialization without family change in turn-of-the-century Holland, see Janssens (1986). Laslett (1983) also discusses the conservatism of norms of postmarital residence.

57 In the case of sharecroppers, having a surviving father at the time of marriage is less crucial in providing an opportunity for patrilocal marriage, since the household is commonly headed by a paternal uncle or married (or older) brother. Having a widowed mother is not sufficient for this purpose, as, at marriage, the son generally becomes household head if there is no other married man (or man from a senior generation) present in the household. Although such cases can be considered forms of patrilocal residence, they are not counted as such for the purposes of the figures presented here.

58 See Somogyi (1965:335). For comparative German data on the secular decline

in remarriage rates, and for a discussion of possible explanations, see Knodel and Lynch (1985).

59 There were 38 cases of widower remarriage in Casalecchio in 1865–1882, 29 in 1883–1896, and 42 in 1897–1921.

60 "Maré vèc', méi che gnént" (Menarini 1975:16).

61 Data on length of time before remarriage in 1883–1886 are given in Somogyi (1965:341), by region and for Italy as a whole. In Emilia-Romagna, just 6 percent of the widowers who were remarrying did so within six months of their wives' death, with another 14 percent marrying within the following six months.

62 It would be inappropriate to infer rates of remarriage from these data since they do not, strictly speaking, refer to the same population at risk.

Chapter Eight. Falling Fertility and Social Change

1 See Notestein (1953) for this oft-cited statement on the demographic transition. Subsequent research suggests that the "high" pretransition fertility was nowhere near the biological maximum. Unspecified homeostatic mechanisms apparently regulated reproductive behavior in these societies so that fertility was kept high enough to ensure that a population reproduced itself, while its moderate levels ensured that periodic crises resulting from overpopulation could be avoided (Coale 1986).

2 See Portes (1976) for a review and critique of sociological theories of development.

3 The reciprocal effects of population growth on the pace of economic modernization were also noted (Coale 1969). Policy makers, concerned that the very high rates of population growth resulting from historically unprecedented declines in mortality and continued high fertility would hamper economic development, were led to consider ways to limit the fertility of populations (Mauldin 1983).

4 See Preston (1975, 1978).

5 For an excellent overview of the European Fertility Project and a summary of its principal findings, see Coale and Watkins (1986).

6 Anderton and Bean (1985) and others have suggested that the fertility transition may include substantial and intentional increases in birth spacing, as well as the limitation of births by higher-parity women.

7 The fertility declines occurred over half a century earlier in France (Coale and Treadway 1986).

8 This work is most associated with John Knodel (1977), who popularized the use of an index of fertility control (designated as *m*) based on the model fertility schedules developed by Coale and Trussell (1974, 1978).

9 This is not to say that fertility levels cannot increase in a population practicing birth limitation. What the birth-limitation model posits is that women will begin to have all of the children they desire immediately after marriage and will, within the biological limits on reproduction associated with current sexual and breast-feeding practices, continue to have births until they achieve their target family size. Women with a larger desired family size will still limit their fertility

once the target family size is reached, but this birth limitation will begin somewhat later in their life course since it will take somewhat longer to have a larger number of births.

10 A 10 percent decline in marital fertility typically signals the onset of the fertility reduction. This reduction occurred first in France, in 1827, but began after 1870 for the rest of Europe. The average date of initial decline in marital fertility across all European provinces was 1903. The Italian marital fertility decline began somewhat later (1913). The diffusion of family limitation was more rapid in districts that began the fertility transition at a more recent date (Coale and Treadway 1986).

11 See, for example, Knodel and van de Walle (1986).

12 Livi-Bacci (1986) reports that the fertility decline occurred as much as one century earlier among the elite population of Europe. Jews also experienced early reductions in marital fertility. But both of these populations were concentrated in urban areas and had lower mortality levels than the other groups, making it difficult to separate class, cultural, and modernity explanations of the fertility decline. See also Anderson (1986).

13 Economists would refer to this as the articulation of a demand function for fertility. Lee and Bulatao (1983) call it the transition "to demand for children," which they distinguish from a transition "in demand for children" (that is, a change in the *number* of children desired). Cleland and Wilson (1987) have been among the most vociferous advocates of the argument that ideational, rather than structural, economic change, with more favorable attitudes toward birth control, is critical in the fertility decline.

14 See Caldwell (1982, chap. 10) and Cochrane (1983). Cleland and Wilson (1987) are among the most recent advocates of literacy as a key factor in fertility control. See also Woods (1987).

15 See the excellent review by Graff (1979).

16 See Levine (1980), Handwerker (1986a, 1986b), and Lesthaeghe and Wilson (1986). Caldwell's (1982) "wealth flow" theory also explicitly takes into account the effects of formal education on the family economy.

17 See Livi-Bacci (1986) and Sharlin (1986) on rural-urban differentials in the level of fertility and the timing of fertility declines. Watkins (1986) notes the possible spillover effects of urban development on the socioeconomic structures of nearby rural communities. See Levine (1977) on the protoindustrialization argument. Tilly (1979) has tied the employment of women in textile factories to their lowered fertility, but cautions that the net effects of rural wage labor must also depend on the employability of children.

18 For a typically vague discussion of the role of cultural institutions and customs on fertility, see Levine and Scrimshaw (1983). In the European Fertility Project, culture was usually operationalized as "nonsocioeconomic variables such as religion, ethnicity, language, and region" (Anderson 1986:293). Lesthaeghe and Wilson (1986) attend more seriously to the content of these cultural elements, although their specification of critical variables has been questioned (Tilly 1986).

19 Examples include Inkeles (1969), Inkeles and Smith (1974), and Fawcett and Bornstein (1973). Caldwell (1982:269–300) discusses this issue, though his major emphasis is on the neglect of demographic processes in theories of social change, rather than on the applications and misapplications of these theories by demographers.

In the same account, Caldwell suggests that attention should be directed to "Westernization" rather than simply modernization, with an investigation of the cultural diffusion of Western ideas and values that have an effect on the value of children. However, Caldwell himself does not give primary place to this theme in his "wealth flows" theory. Empirical evidence suggests that such Western influences may indeed alter individual demographic behaviors unless modified by state intervention that mobilizes the population in pursuit of national goals (Delacroix and Ragin 1978). Moreover, it is unclear to what extent changes associated with state-sponsored institutionalization and bureaucratization of individual lives should be viewed as something uniquely Western.

20 As described by Levine (1986) in his review of the summary volume of the European Fertility Project, "At the heart of each essay is an unbending belief that fertility behavior before the demographic transition was nonrational in the sense that it was largely the product of 'tradition'; thus, group norms are held to play a larger role than do individual strategies. It is these unexamined group norms that are deemed to reflect 'tradition.' . . . These connections between modernization theory, on the one hand, and schooling and literacy and rationality and secularization, on the other, have a long lineage that has now become transparent in its usage" (336).

Equally surprising is demographers' adoption of an innovation-diffusion theory with little attention to the literature on diffusion. A major exception is the review by Retherford and Palmore (1983).

21 See Andorka (1986) for a discussion of this issue. Carlsson (1966) explicitly advances a model of fertility control as an adjustment, rather than an innovation, process. For rural population control in preindustrial France, see Derouet (1980).

22 Hull (1983) astutely comments on cultural explanations: "[The fertility] decision-making environment is cultural, including language, belief systems, technology, social institutions, and individual environment. Decision making is both a product and a determinant of this framework. Societies undergoing cultural change are likely to be changing with regard to the way fertility decisions are made" (399).

23 An important exception is the account of Sicilian demographic change by Schneider and Schneider (1984).

24 This is not to say that many of the demographers involved in the European Fertility Project were unaware of these limitations. As Livi-Bacci (1977) remarks at the beginning of his book: "A fourth set of problems was posed by the need —deeply felt by the author—to link the results of demographic analysis with the pace and patterns of the cultural modifications in the Italian society. Unfortunately, we have done little more than acknowledge a need for a higher

level of knowledge in this field. Fertility changes are the consequence of deliberate and conscious decisions taken at the individual level by couples. They imply complex modifications in the systems of preferences and values attached by individuals to the children and to the family. These preferences and values are part of a more general system involving the relations between individuals and between individuals and society. In this respect, we do not know very much about our contemporaries, but we know far less about our ancestors" (5–6).

25 In his reconstitution study of the women of Verviers, Belgium, in the mid-nineteenth century, Alter (1988) skillfully demonstrates the flip side of this phenomenon. It was the women who had lived in the city from childhood who first began limiting their births, not the women who had migrated to the city from rural areas.

26 See discussion in Watkins (1986). Livi-Bacci (1986) tries to address these questions with aggregate data. Schneider and Schneider (1984) combine archival, ethnographic, vital, and oral historical data to provide an informative study of social-class differences in the fertility declines of persons in a rural Sicilian town. In cases where direct information on contraceptive use is available, this issue is much more readily addressed (Hogan and Frenzen 1981).

27 These hypotheses are informed by the "wealth flows" theory advanced by Caldwell (1982). Lehning (1984) has drawn attention to the economic value of children in understanding the decline of marital fertility in rural villages in the French department of La Loire. However, McQuillan (1984) reports no clear link between the mode of production and marital fertility in nineteenth-century French departments.

28 For a recent discussion of the northern Italian artisanal traditions in this period, see Bell (1986).

29 Tilly (1979a) has characterized this dilemma: "Family fertility strategy in early textile towns had to deal with deep and painful contradictions. . . . On the one hand, there were many jobs for children. Under these conditions, did families choose to send wives out to work or to have more children? In fact, fertility was high in early industrialized textile cities" (385–86).

30 There is considerable evidence that the opportunity costs of childbearing and child rearing (in terms of lost female wages) are an important consideration in fertility decisions (for example, see Schultz [1985] on the Swedish fertility transition). These associations have sometimes been interpreted as being the result of opportunities that compete with traditional wife and mother roles (Oppong 1983) or that result from the emancipation of women (Shorter 1973, 1975). Tilly, Scott, and Cohen (1976) argue that the association between factory labor and fertility results from economic necessities imposed on wage-earning families as the net value of children declined (see, additionally, Tilly and Scott [1978]). Also, see Tilly (1979b) for a description of similar changes in the value of children and the costs of women's labor in Roubaix during this same period. A careful review of research on the status of women and fertility is found in Mason (1983).

31 Becker (1960), Schultz (1973), and Leibenstein (1974).

32 See Graff (1979) for a superb critical review of the literature on literacy, education, and fertility.
33 See Knodel and van de Walle (1986), Lehning (1984), Levine (1980), and Cochrane (1983) for evidence about the literacy/education and fertility linkage.
34 Lehning (1984) shows that villages that were closer to urban areas had an earlier decline in marital fertility in the French department of La Loire.
35 On this point, see Livi-Bacci (1986) and Schneider and Schneider (1984).
36 Caldwell (1982) has been one of the foremost proponents of this hypothesis. See Mason (1983) for an evaluation of the logic of this idea and the empirical evidence supporting it. As Mason notes, this hypothesis assumes that the costs of childbearing are greater for the wife than for other household members, so that the net value of children is less for women. These women will elect to have fewer children than desired by other household members, once the decision is theirs to make.
37 Strictly speaking, this was not a province but a department (the Dipartimento di Reno) under the Napoleonic territorial system that prevailed at the time.
38 Statistics are from Livi-Bacci (1977). In reviewing these figures Livi-Bacci remarks: "The birth rate of Italy started declining at the end of the nineteenth century, about a century later than that of France, a few decades later than that of other western European countries, and a few decades earlier than that of other Mediterranean populations. The timing of the decline is in agreement with the place and role of Italy in Europe and with her double soul, Continental and Mediterranean at the same time" (3).
39 A similar pattern is found in central Italy, but not in the south, where the urban-rural difference remained minimal. See Del Panta (1979:201–2) and Natale (1982).
40 Bellettini (1965, 1971), as cited in Livi-Bacci (1977).
41 The European Fertility Project was forced to classify as legitimate births that were recorded as illegitimate because of the discrepancies between social and legal marriage arising in the dual religious and secular marriage systems (discussed in chap. 6). Because we have individual-level data, such gross adjustments were not necessary. In this fertility analysis a woman is classified as married if she has been married in either a religious or a civil ceremony.
42 The European Fertility Project had to work with limited data for many times and places. A set of indexes was developed that needed only the count of women by marital status and age and the number of legitimate and illegitimate births. Coale and Treadway (1986) describe these: "There are three indexes of childbearing: I(f), the rate of childbearing by all women regardless of their marital status; I(g), the index of the rate of childbearing by married women; and I(h), the index of the rate of childbearing by women not currently married. All three indexes incorporate the same concept: each relates the number of births produced by the women in question to the number they would have produced had they experienced the highest set of birth rates by age of mother that has been reliably recorded" (33).

Our analysis of fertility differentials and trends can be much more sophisticated than that permitted by these indexes of fertility control because we are able to associate births with particular mothers and fathers. In the multivariate analyses we look at differentials in birth probabilities and birth rates for women in the population; these analyses do not use a natural fertility population as the standard for comparison. To maintain comparability between the analysis of changes in the overall fertility rate and differentials in those changes, we use the marital general fertility rate (rather than I[g]) to describe fertility trends in Casalecchio. The five-year moving average marital general fertility rate and I(g) for the years 1867–1919 are correlated at .93.

43 Again, for these years of Napoleonic rule, the actual territorial unit uniting the city of Bologna and its rural hinterland was the Dipartimento di Reno.

44 For the 1867–1877 period the average I(g) was .706. Thus, the fertility of married women in Casalecchio prior to the fertility decline was about 70 percent of the maximum natural fertility level. This is somewhat higher than the I(g) of the marital fertility of women in the entire province of Bologna, which was .625 in 1864 and .597 in 1871 (Coale and Treadway 1986:127), a reflection of the rural character of Casalecchio. From 1878 to 1888 the Casalecchio I(g) averaged .662. The I(g) first declined by 10 percent below its pretransition level (from .706 to below .635) in 1889 (when I(g) was .630), and to just under .500 in the early part of the twentieth century. The I(g) showed considerable variability during the 1900–1919 period (ranging from .364 to .551), but it never again returned to its pretransition high.

45 The marital fertility rates shown in fig. 8.1 are based on five-year moving averages, which dampen the apparent magnitude of the fertility disruptions during the War years. The actually recorded single-year marital fertility rates indicate the dramatic nature of the fertility changes induced by the War. The annual marital fertility rate ranged between 186 to 203 for each year from 1908 to 1915. The rate dropped to 129 in 1916, 116 in 1917, and 104 in 1918. Postponed fertility recovered after the war, but not to its prewar highs, with the marital fertility rate increasing to 157 in 1919, 172 in 1920, and 178 in 1921.

46 See the Appendix and chap. 5 for descriptions of the *focatico* and its uses in this study.

47 See chap. 5 for an explanation of log linear modified multiple regression models.

48 These *focatico* and population register-based marital fertility rates are determined by calculating the marital fertility rate for each year from 1869 to 1905, and averaging the annual rates for the periods to which they refer.

49 We analyzed data for the 1881 and 1921 censuses, but do not present the results here. The coverage of the 1881 census for purposes of fertility analysis proved inferior to both the 1871 and the 1911 censuses. (The fertility rate recorded for women represented in the 1881 census was 19 percent lower than the rate recorded in the population register for the same period, whereas the rates for the women in the 1871 and 1911 censuses were only 11 percent and 12 percent too low, respectively.) The 1921 census data are not analyzed here because the 1919–1921 fertility rates were so heavily influenced by recovery from wartime fertility interruptions.

50 The dates represented include 1 January 1870 to 31 December 1874 (for the

1871 census), and 1 January 1909 to 31 December 1913 (for the 1911 census).

51 Random variations are less of a problem with the *focatico*-based analyses since we examine person-years of experience aggregated over long periods of time.

52 This analysis includes all women who were resident in Casalecchio within ninety days of marriage (to guarantee complete coverage of the birth history) and who were still present after one year (to exclude women who married in Casalecchio and then migrated elsewhere).

53 Fewer than one hundred women were in each higher-order parity progression, beginning with the eighth to the ninth birth interval. In light of the small sample size, we have excluded consideration of ninth and higher-order parity progressions.

54 See chap. 5 for a description of such models.

55 There is some evidence that the higher fertility of sharecroppers relative to agricultural wage laborers may antedate the late nineteenth-century fertility decline, thus suggesting the use of family limitation methods before the fertility decline. Angeli and Bellettini (1979:165–67), using an 1847 census covering 3,074 married women aged 15–49 in the rural belt surrounding the city of Bologna, computed the ratio of children aged 0–4 to these women, pooling on the basis of occupation of household head. They found a child-woman ratio of 0.973 in sharecropper households, compared to a ratio of just 0.727 in *braccianti* households. Unfortunately, though, this inferential method is tainted by the higher infant mortality that likely prevailed among the *braccianti* as well as their greater tendency to abandon children at birth (leaving them at Bologna's foundling home).

56 Although the general contour of the fertility decline among the elite is reasonably clear from these data, the small size of the Casalecchio elite makes even the five-year averages very unstable.

57 This finding is consistent with the claim by Stokes, Schutjer, and Bulatao (1986: 306) that operational holdings, not land ownership, exert a positive influence on fertility.

58 Very few women have more than one birth in any twelve-month period. (For all years from 1869 to 1905, only 1 percent of the 2,465 women who gave birth to at least one child had two children during the year.) For all practical purposes, then, this analysis of the probability that a woman has a birth during the year (ignoring whether she had one or two births) is the equivalent of an analysis of differential birth rates.

59 Nor was there a significant difference in the average age pattern of fertility contrasting only women aged 15–34 and 35–49 ($\chi^2_{LR} = 0.09$, $df = 3$, $p = .95$).

60 The relative birth rates of women 15–34 and 35–49 did not change between the periods ($\chi^2_{LR} = 0.6$, $df = 2$, $p = .76$).

61 To provide further confirmation of the accuracy of these results, we analyzed the *focatico* fertility data using model fertility schedules (Coale and Trussell 1974, 1978). These calculations were done using the GLIM statistical package, which provides statistical tests of significance for intergroup differences in the estimated model schedule parameters (Alter 1984).

The *m* parameter of the model fertility schedules provides an index of the departure of age-specific fertility rates from natural fertility to a fertility regime in which older women are substantially limiting their fertility. The *m* index is approximately 0–0.2 where there is no age-dependent fertility limitation, with larger numbers indicating increasing age-dependent fertility limitation. The *m* index in 1869–1880, 1881–1892, and 1893–1905, respectively, was −.068, .240, and 1.651 among the elite; .393, .659, and .575 among the middle strata; .298, .435, and .321 among sharecroppers, and .327, .286, and .442 among wage workers and the poor. The trend in the *m* index of fertility control was statistically significant ($p < .10$) only for the elite ($\chi^2_{LR} = 5.8$, $df = 2$). There were no statistically significant differences between strata in the *m* index in any of the three periods.

62 This model explains virtually all of the association between strata, time period, age, and birth probability ($\chi^2_{LR} = 64.2$, $df = 66$).

63 In the case of the poor and wage earners, the distinction is between those who had a sufficient income to pay 3.0 lire for the annual household tax and those who were assessed the minimal tax of 1.5 lire.

64 $\chi^2_{LR} = 9.1$, $df = 8$, $p = .396$. An inspection of the logged effect parameters for the model indicates that the lower and higher income groups within each of the strata displayed quite similar patterns. The one exception is that the marital fertility of the poorest wage earners was low relative to other wage earners. This difference may be a reflection of less complete coverage in the *focatico* of the poorest households (since these would be largely irrelevant for tax collection purposes). In any case, this early difference in the marital fertility of the poorest wage earners and those able to pay a tax is not statistically significant.

For a discussion of fertility differences between richer and poorer working-class families in England in this same period, see Levine (1985:191–92).

65 The census also includes birthplace for all women, and we used this as an indicator of urban experience. However, it is a crude variable insofar as women in this highly migratory population may well have had urban experience even if they were not born in Bologna, and they might have been born in Bologna but spent virtually their entire lives living in rural communities. Hence, the migration data from our *focatico*-based study are superior, for they use the population register to identify the woman's place of residence immediately before Casalecchio.

66 Similar categories of social strata are included, but these are based on the husband's occupation rather than on that of the household head (as in the *focatico*).

67 Women younger than age 35 are scored according to their years of age on the first age variable, and are scored 0 on the variable indicating number of years beyond age 35. Women older than age 35 are scored as 35 on the first variable, with the number of years of age beyond 35 being entered as the value of the second age variable. (For example, a woman aged 37 at the start of the birth interval is scored 35 on the first age variable and 2 on the second age variable.)

This functional specification allows for the biological deterioration in capacity to bear children experienced by women as they age beyond their mid-thirties.

68 This variable includes a separate category for those women who were religiously married but for whom no civil marriage record was available.

69 Alternatively, one could say that the parity progression rate declined by 49 percent from its 1865–1882 level.

70 This means, for example, that the rate of next birth of women 40 years of age was only 25 percent as high as the parity progression rate of women who were 35 at the start of the interval.

71 It should again be recalled, however, that we were not able to measure women's wage employment during the course of their marriage, and thus no firm conclusions can be reached about the relationship between women's postmarital wage work and their fertility behavior on the basis of this analysis. However, we do have evidence that continued wage labor provided no strong bar to childbearing by the twentieth century, when governmental legislation protected the employment security of pregnant women. Like other communes, Casalecchio kept a register (*Registro Comunale dei Libretti Rilasciati in Esecuzione alla Legge sulla Cassa di Maternità*) listing the names of pregnant factory workers having the right to go on leave and have their job back a month after giving birth. The number of such workers so registered in Casalecchio averaged 27 per year from 1913 to 1917. These registers are found in the Casalecchio communal archives.

Chapter Nine. European Social History and Demographic Theory

1 Most notable here is the argument that proletarianization brought about a lowering of the marriage age as young people no longer needed to depend on their parents for access to the resources to support a family. See Tilly (1978a) and Levine (1977) for discussions of this issue.

2 The decline in male age at first civil marriage may be illusory, insofar as it was common in the early period to celebrate a civil wedding several months after the religious wedding, as discussed in chap. 7.

Appendix. Archival Sources and the Casalecchio Data Base

1 Much of the initial work involved in the creation of the data record and coding system and the unedited data files was done by Andrea Schiaffino, as described in our preface. Schiaffino and Kertzer jointly authored an initial description of the data base in August 1982. However, since Schiaffino and Kertzer began working separately in the spring of 1983, both the data files described in this appendix and the data-base management system have been greatly altered and further developed. Therefore, Schiaffino should not be held responsible for the current data base and data-base management system described here.

2 Andrea Schiaffino had primary responsibility for the design of the original record system and for overseeing the work of the coders in Bologna.

3 Among the earlier attempts to use computers in record linkage, see Skolnick

(1973); Hershberg, Burstein, and Dockhorn (1976); Guth (1976); Kelly (1974); Akerman, Johansson, and Juslin (1978); and Skolnick et al. (1978). Since our research began, numerous other procedures have been discussed. See, for example, Roy, Pouyez, and Martin (1980); Bouchard and Pouyez (1980); Winchester (1980); and Weiss et al. (1980).

4 An appendix to the Casalecchio History Project handbook, available on request from David Kertzer, provides a more detailed account of the data-cleaning procedures used in compiling the Casalecchio data base.

5 The theory behind the data-base management system briefly described here is more fully presented in Karweit and Kertzer (1986). Technical documentation for CASA is available in Karweit (1988).

References

Akerman, Sune, Egil Johansson, and Kari Juslin. 1978. Computerized family reconstruction. In *Chance and change: Social and economic studies in historical demography in the Baltic area,* ed. Sune Akerman et al., 283–87. Odense, Sweden: Odense University Press.

Alter, George. 1984. Memorandum of the estimation of fertility indices with GLIM. Indiana University.

Alter, George. 1988. *Family and the female life course: The women of Verviers, Belgium, 1849–1880.* Madison: University of Wisconsin Press.

Anderson, Barbara A. 1980. *Internal migration during modernization in late nineteenth-century Russia.* Princeton, N.J.: Princeton University Press.

Anderson, Barbara A. 1986. Regional and cultural factors in the decline of marital fertility in western Europe. In *The decline of fertility in Europe,* ed. Ansley J. Coale and Susan C. Watkins, 293–313. Princeton: Princeton University Press.

Anderson, Michael. 1971. *Family structure in nineteenth-century Lancashire.* Cambridge: Cambridge University Press.

Anderson, Michael. 1976. Marriage patterns in Victorian Britain: An analysis based on registration district data for England and Wales 1861. *Journal of Family History* 1:55–79.

Anderson, Michael. 1978. *The family and industrialization in western Europe.* St. Louis: Forum Press.

Anderton, Douglas L., and Lee L. Bean. 1985. Birth spacing and fertility limitation: A behavioral analysis of a nineteenth-century frontier population. *Demography* 22:169–83.

Andorka, Rudolf. 1986. The decline of fertility in Europe: A symposium. *Population and Development Review* 12:329–34.

Angeli, Aurora. 1985. Dinamica matrimoniale e mobilità territoriale della popolazione. In *Popolazione ed economia dei territori bolognesi durante il settecento,* ed. Istituto per la Storia di Bologna, 115–54. Bologna: Istituto per la Storia di Bologna.

Angeli, Aurora, and Athos Bellettini. 1979. Strutture familiari nella campagna bolognese a metà dell'ottocento. *Genus* 35:155–72.

Annali dell'Industria e del Commercio. 1880. *Sul lavoro dei fanciulli e delle donne*. Rome: Ministero di Agricoltura, Industria e Commercio.

Annali di Statistica. 1887. *Notizie sulle condizioni industriali della provincia di Bologna. Annali di Statistica,* ser. 4, vol. 2. Rome: Ministero di Agricoltura, Industria e Commercio.

Anselmi, Sergio. 1978. *Mezzadri e terre nelle Marche*. Bologna: Patron.

Arbizzani, Luigi. 1977. Ideali ed istituti nuovi nella cultura contadina post-unitaria (1859–1945). In *Cultura popolare nell'Emilia-Romagna,* ed. Giuseppe Adani and Gastone Tamagnini, 219–41. Milan: Silvana Editoriale d'Arte.

Arbizzani, Luigi, Franco Cazzola, and Attilio Esposto. 1985. *Campagne e società nella valle padana di fine ottocento*. Casalecchio di Reno: Grafis Edizioni.

Arcari, P. M. 1936. Le variazioni dei salari agricoli in Italia dalla fondazione del Regno al 1933. *Annali di Statistica,* ser. 6, no. 36.

Ariès, Phillippe. 1962. *Centuries of childhood*. Trans. Robert Baldick. New York: Knopf.

Ballini, Pier Luigi. 1985. Le elezioni politiche nel Regno d'Italia: Appunti di bibliografia, legislazione e statistiche. *Quaderni dell'Osservatorio Elettorale,* no. 15, 141–220.

Bandera, Ulisse, et al. 1875. Rapporto della Commissione incaricata dalla Società Agraria e dal Comizio di proporre provvedimenti contro la illecita contrattazione delle canape e stoppe. *Annali della Società Agraria di Bologna* 13:140–47.

Barbagli, Marzio. 1984. *Sotto lo stesso tetto: Mutamenti della famiglia in Italia dal XV al XX secolo*. Bologna: Il Mulino.

Becker, Gary S. 1960. An economic analysis of fertility. In *Demographic and economic change in developed countries,* 209–40. Universities-National Bureau Committee For Economic Research. Princeton, N.J.: Princeton University Press.

Bell, Donald H. 1986. *Sesto San Giovanni: Workers, culture, and politics in an Italian town, 1880–1922*. New Brunswick, N.J.: Rutgers University Press.

Bellettini, Athos. 1965. *La popolazione del Dipartimento del Reno*. Bologna: Zanichelli.

Bellettini, Athos. 1971. *La popolazione delle campagne bolognesi alla metà del secolo XIX*. Bologna: Zanichelli.

Bellettini, Athos. 1978. La popolazione di Bologna nel corso dell'ottocento. *Storia Urbana,* no. 5, 3–23.

Bellettini, Athos. 1982. Alcuni aspetti della transizione demografica nel primo periodo post-unitario. In *Studi in memoria di Luigi Dal Pane,* ed. Istituto di Storia Economica e Sociale, Università di Bologna, 769–806. Bologna: CLUEB.

Bellettini, Athos. 1985. Le tendenze demografiche dei territori bolognesi nel corso del XVIII secolo. In *Popolazione ed economia dei territori bolognesi durante il settecento,* ed. Istituto per la Storia di Bologna, 9–22. Bologna: Istituto per la Storia di Bologna.

Bellettini, Athos, and Alessandra Samoggia. 1982. Premières recherches sur les tendances de longue periode de la mortalité infantile dans la campagne de Bologne (XVIIe siècle). *Genus* 38:1–25.

Bellettini, Athos, and Alessandra Samoggia. 1984. Evolution differentielle e mouvement saisonnier de la mortalité infantile et enfantine dans la banlieue de Bologne (XVIIe–XIXe siècles). In *Annales de Démographie Historique 1983,* 195–207. Paris: Mouton.

Benini, Rodolfo. 1911. *La demografia italiana nell'ultimo cinquantennio.* In *Cinquant'anni di storia italiana,* vol. 1, bk. 3. Milan: Hoepli.

Bergonzini, L. 1953. Il mercato del lavoro nell'industria emiliana. In *Commissione parlamentare d'inchiesta sulla disoccupazione,* 158–200. Rome.

Berkner, Lutz. 1972. The stem family and the developmental cycle of the peasant household: An eighteenth-century Austrian example. *American Historical Review* 77:398–418.

Berselli, Aldo, 1980. Primi decenni dopo l'Unità. In *Storia della Emilia Romagna,* ed. Aldo Berselli, 257–304. Bologna: CLUEB.

Bezzi, Gabriele. 1983. La costruzione della rete tramviaria (1880–1900). In *Bologna: Città e Territorio tra '800 e '900,* ed. Pier Paolo d'Attorre, 117–61. Milan: Franco Angeli.

Biagi, Bruno. 1935. Norme consuetudinarie per la divisione delle famiglie coloniche nel bolognese. *Archivio 'Vittorio Scialoja'* 1:42–50.

Bissoli, Renzo. 1979. Lavoro e rendita in un'azienda agraria bolognese del XVIII secolo. *Quaderni Storici* 40:389–413.

Boselli, Alfredo. 1904. Sullo stato igienico delle abitazioni povere di Bologna. *Bullettino delle Scienze Mediche di Bologna,* ser. 8, 4 (2): 45–59.

Bouchard, Gerard, and Christian Pouyez. 1980. Name variations and computerized record linkage. *Historical Methods* 13:119–25.

Broccoli, Armide. 1979. *Chiamavano pane il pane.* Bologna: Edagricole.

Brugnoli, Giovanni. 1881. Delle malattie epidemiche e popolari che hanno dominato nella provincia di Bologna negli anni 1879 e 1880. *Bullettino delle Scienze Mediche di Bologna* 7:233–53.

Bruno, Salvatore. 1923. *La mezzadria.* 2d ed. Turin: Biblioteca di Ragioneria Applicata.

Cafagna, Luciano. 1976. The industrial revolution in Italy 1830–1914. In *The Emergence of Industrial Societies, Part One,* ed. Carlo M. Cipolla, 279–328. Vol. 4 of the Fontana Economic History of Europe. London: Harvester.

Caldwell, John C. 1979. Age as a factor in mortality decline: An examination of Nigerian data. *Population Studies* 33:395–413.

Caldwell, John C. 1982. *Theory of fertility decline.* New York: Academic Press.

Calindri, Serafino. 1781. *Montagna e collina nel territorio bolognese.* Bologna.

Calzi, A. 1866. *Il matrimonio cristiano. Notificazione per la Quaresima dell'anno 1866 al clero e al popolo della città e diocesi di Bologna.* Bologna.

Camera di Commercio ed Arti di Bologna. 1888. *Notizie sulle condizioni industriali e commerciali della provincia di Bologna.* Bologna.

Camera di Commercio ed Arti di Bologna. 1897. *Statistica industriale, provincia di Bologna 1895–1896.* Bologna.

Cammelli, Stefano. 1981. Prima del macinato. Proteste contadine nel bolognese nel primo decennio unitario. *Società e Storia,* no. 11, 67–93.

Cariani, Giovanni. 1977. Il calcolo della popolazione residente e le statistiche del movimento migratorio interno. In *Cinquanta anni di attività 1926–1976,* ed. Istituto Centrale di Statistica, 135–44. Rome: ISTAT.

Carlsson, Gosta. 1966. The decline of fertility: innovation or adjustment process. *Population Studies* 20: 149–74.

Carrara, Mario. 1896. Feudalismo rurale: Il patto colonico in Galizia e nell'Emilia. *La Critica Sociale* 6:123–27.

Caspard, Pierre. 1974. Conceptions prénuptiales et développement du capitalisme dans la Principauté de Neuchatel, 1678–1820. *Annales, E.S.C.* 29:989–1008.

Casterline, John B., Lindy Williams, and Peter McDonald. 1986. The age difference between spouses: Variations among developing countries. *Population Studies* 40:353–74.

Cattini, M. 1978. In Emilia orientale: Mezzadria cinquecentesca e mezzadria settecentesca. Continuità o frattura? *Quaderni Storici,* no. 39, 864–79.

Cazzola, Franco. 1980a. La formazione del bracciantato agricolo di massa in Emilia Romagna. In *Il proletariato agricolo in Emilia Romagna nella fase di formazione,* ed. Franco Cazzola, 19–63. Bologna: CLUEB.

Cazzola, Franco. 1980b. La formazione di una popolazione marginale in agricoltura: Alcune ipotesi di lavoro. *Annali dell' Istituto "Aldo Cervi"* 2:79–86. Bologna: Il Mulino.

Chierici, Giovanni, and Giorgio Tabarroni. 1980. Il canale di Reno, passato e presente. In *Il Canale Navile,* ed. Comune di Bologna, 61–75. Bologna: Comune di Bologna.

Cleland, John, and Christopher Wilson. 1987. Demand theories of the fertility transition: An iconoclastic view. *Population Studies* 41:5–30.

Clough, Shepard B. 1964. *The economic history of modern Italy.* New York: Columbia University Press.

Coale, Ansley J. 1969. Population and economic development. In *The population dilemma,* 2d ed., ed. P. M. Hauser, 59–84. Englewood Cliffs, N.J.: Prentice-Hall.

Coale, Ansley J. 1973. The demographic transition. In *International Population Conference,* ed. International Union for the Scientific Study of Population, 53–72. Liège: IUSSP.

Coale, Ansley J. 1986. The decline of fertility in Europe since the eighteenth century as a chapter in human demographic history. In *The decline of fertility in Europe,* ed. Ansley J. Coale and Susan C. Watkins, 1–30. Princeton, N.J.: Princeton University Press.

Coale, Ansley J., and Roy Treadway. 1986. A summary of the changing distribution of overall fertility, marital fertility, and the proportion married in the provinces of Europe. In *The decline of fertility in Europe,* ed. Ansley J. Coale and Susan C. Watkins, 31–181. Princeton, N.J.: Princeton University Press.

Coale, Ansley J., and T. James Trussell. 1974. Model fertility schedules. *Population Index* 40:185–258.

Coale, Ansley J., and T. James Trussell. 1978. A new procedure for fitting optimal values on the parameters of a model schedule of fertility rates. *Population Index* 44:203–11.

Coale, Ansley J., and Susan Watkins, eds. 1986. *The decline of fertility in Europe.* Princeton, N.J.: Princeton University Press.

Cochrane, Susan H. 1983. Effects of education and urbanization on fertility. In *Determinants of fertility in developing countries,* vol. 2, ed. Rodolfo Bulatao and Ronald D. Lee, 587-626. New York: Academic Press.

Comizio Agrario del Circondario di Bologna. 1881. *Monografia del podere bolognese.* Bologna.

Comizio Agrario del Circondario di Bologna. 1905. *Capitolato generale per la conduzione a mezzadria dei fondi rustici nella provincia di Bologna.* Bologna.

Commissione Mista della Società Agraria, del Comizio Agrario e dell'Accademia dei Ragionieri. 1874. Modulo di nuova scritta colonica e capitolato agrario. *Annali della Società Agraria di Bologna* 11:22-37.

Commissione per lo Studio sulle Condizioni della Colonia. 1883. Adunanza del 22 gennaio 1882. *Annali della Società Agraria di Bologna* 22:87-97.

Comune di Bologna. 1974. *Annuario Statistico 1974.* Bologna.

Conenna, Lucia Bonelli. 1980. Mezzadria senese: Dimore rurali e vita economica nel XVIII secolo. *Annali dell'Istituto "Aldo Cervi"* 2:121-50. Bologna: Il Mulino.

Corridore, Francesco. 1908. *L'istruzione in Italia (dal 1871 in poi).* Turin: G. B. Paravia.

Corsini, Carlo. 1976. Materiali per lo studio della famiglia in Toscana nei secoli XVII-XIX. Gli esposti. *Quaderni Storici* 33:998-1052.

Cox, David R. 1972. Regression models and life-tables. *Journal of the Royal Statistical Society* B34:187-202.

Cox, David R. 1974. Partial likelihood. *Biometrika* 62:269-76.

Crew, David F. 1979. *Town in the Ruhr: A social history of Bochum, 1860-1914.* New York: Columbia University Press.

Cristofori, Franco. 1981. *Bologna: Immagini e vita tra ottocento e novecento.* Bologna: Edizioni Alfa.

Czap, Peter, Jr. 1983. A large family: The peasant's greatest wealth. Serf household in Mishino, Russia, 1814-1858. In *Family Forms in Historic Europe,* ed. Richard Wall, Jean Robin, and Peter Laslett, 105-51. Cambridge: Cambridge University Press.

Dalle Donne, Giancarlo. 1986. La mobilità della popolazione rurale nella bassa padana di fine ottocento. Il caso di Argenta. *Società e Storia,* no. 32, 341-80.

Dal Pane, Luigi. 1969. *Economia e società a Bologna nell'età del Risorgimento.* Bologna: Zanichelli.

Da Molin, Giovanna. 1980. Mobilità dei contadini pugliesi tra fine '600 e primo '800. In *La popolazione italiana nel settecento,* ed. Athos Bellettini, 435-76. Bologna: CLUEB.

Da Molin, Giovanna. 1984. Les enfants abandonnés dans les villes italiennes aux XVIIIe et XIXe siècles. *Annales de Démographie Historique 1983,* 103-24. Paris: Mouton.

Da Molin, Giovanna. 1987. Strutture familiari nell'Italia meridionale (sec. XVII-

XIX). Paper presented to the Primo Congresso Ispano-Luso-Italiano di Demografia Storica, Barcelona, Spain.

Davis, Kingsley. 1963. The theory of change and response in modern demographic history. *Population Index* 29:345–66.

Delacroix, Jacques, and Charles Ragin. 1978. Modernizing institutions, mobilization, and Third World development: A cross-national study. *American Journal of Sociology* 84:123–50.

Delille, Gerard. 1977. *Agricoltura e demografia nel Regno di Napoli nei secoli XVIII e XIX.* Naples: Guida.

Delille, Gerard. 1985. *Famille et propriété dans le Royaume de Naples, XVe–XIXe siècle.* Rome: Bibliotheque des Ecoles Françaises de Rome et d'Athenes.

Della Peruta, Franco. 1979. Infanzia e famiglia nella prima metà del ottocento. *Studi Storici* 20:473–91.

Della Peruta, Franco. 1980. Sanità pubblica e legislazione sanitaria dall'Unità a Crispi. *Studi Storici* 21:713–59.

Della Pina, Marco. 1987. Famiglia mezzadrile e celibato: Le campagne di Prato nei secoli XVII e XVIII. Paper presented to the Primo Congresso Ispano-Luso-Italiano di Demografia Storica, Barcelona, Spain.

Del Panta, Lorenzo. 1979. Italy. In *European demography and economic growth,* ed. W. R. Lee, 196–235. London: Croom Helm.

Del Panta, Lorenzo. 1984. *Evoluzione demografica e popolamento nell'Italia dell'ottocento (1796–1914).* Bologna: CLUEB.

Del Panta, Lorenzo. 1985. Le manifestazioni differenziali della mortalità nella città di Bologna e nel suo suburbio. In *Popolazione ed economia dei territori bolognesi durante il settecento,* ed. Istituto per la Storia di Bologna, 23–67. Bologna: Istituto per la Storia di Bologna.

DeMause, Lloyd. 1974. The evolution of childhood. In *The history of childhood,* ed. Lloyd DeMause, 1–74. New York: Psychohistory Press.

Derouet, Bernard. 1980. Une démographie sociale différentielle: Clés pour un système auto-régulateur des populations rurales d'ancien régime. *Annales, E. S. C.* 35:3–41.

Di Rienzo, Pilade. 1957. Movimento anagrafico. *Annali di Statistica,* ser. 8, vol. 6. Rome: ISTAT.

Douglass, William A. 1980. The south Italian family: A critique. *Journal of Family History* 5:338–59.

Elder, Glen H., Jr. 1978. Approaches to social change and the family. *American Journal of Sociology* 84:S1–S38.

Evangelisti, Valerio. 1980. Forme di produzione agricola e caratteristiche generali del bracciantato emiliano-romagnolo (1800–1914). In *Il proletariato agricolo in Emilia Romagna nella fase di formazione,* ed. Franco Cazzola, 65–108. Bologna: CLUEB.

Fabbri, Paolo. 1980. Il territorio e la popolazione. In *Storia della Emilia Romagna,* vol. 3, ed. Aldo Berselli, 127–59. Bologna: CLUEB.

Faina, Eugenio. 1905. Dei guadagni e dei consumi dei contadini nei paesi di mezzadria. *Nuova Antologia* (Rome) 40, no. 802:263–92.

Fantini, Rodolfo. 1971. *L'istruzione popolare a Bologna fino al 1860.* Bologna: Zanichelli.
Fawcett, J.T., and M.H. Bornstein. 1973. Modernization, individual modernity, and fertility. In *Psychological perspectives on population,* ed. James T. Fawcett, 106–31. New York: Basic Books.
Featherman, David L., and Robert M. Hauser. 1975. *Opportunity and change.* New York: Academic Press.
Finzi, Roberto. 1980. Controllo sociale e organizzazione del lavoro in un'impresa del bolognese agli inizi del secolo XVII. *Annali dell'Istituto "Aldo Cervi"* 2:87–100. Bologna: Il Mulino.
Friedlander, Dov, and R. J. Roshier. 1966. A study of internal migration in England and Wales, Part I. *Population Studies* 19:239–79.
Galassini, Girolamo. 1874. Sul matrimonio civile e religioso. In proceedings of *Memorie della R. Accademia di Scienze di Modena,* vol. 14. Modena.
Gerschenkron, Alexander. 1955. Notes on the rate of industrial growth in Italy, 1881-1913. *Journal of Economic History* 15:360–375.
Gillis, John R. 1985. *For better, for worse: British marriages, 1600 to the present.* New York: Oxford University Press.
Gini, Corrado, and L. Galvani. 1931. *Tavole di mortalità della popolazione italiana. Annali di Statistica,* ser. 6, vol. 8. Rome: ISTAT.
Goldstein, Sidney. 1964. The extent of repeated migration: An analysis based on the Danish population register. *Journal of the American Statistical Association* 59:1121-32.
Goldstein, Sidney. 1976. Facets of redistribution: Research challenges and opportunities. *Demography* 13:423–34.
Goode, William J. 1963. *World revolution and family patterns.* New York: Free Press.
Goodman, Leo A. 1978. *Analyzing qualitative/quantitative data.* Cambridge, Mass.: Abt Books.
Goretti, Cesare. 1882. Sunto della monografia della tenuta detta Minerbio. *Annali della Società Agraria di Bologna* 21:129–95.
Goretti, Cesare. 1883. Sulle mutate condizioni agricole del territorio bolognese. *Annali della Società Agraria di Bologna* 22:54–64.
Gozzini, Giovanni. 1984. Matrimonio e mobilità sociale nella Firenze di primo ottocento. *Quaderni Storici,* no. 57, 907–39.
Grabinski, Giuseppe. 1892. Lo sciopero e la questione sociale nelle campagne. *Annali della Società Agraria di Bologna* 32:139–75.
Graff, Harvey. 1979. Literacy, education, and fertility, past and present: A critical review. *Population and Development Review* 5:105–40.
Grafteaux, Serge. 1986. *Mémé Santerre: A French woman of the people.* Trans. Louise A. Tilly and Kathryn L. Tilly. New York: Schocken.
Graziadei, A. 1913. *La questione agraria in Romagna. Mezzadria e bracciantato.* Milan.
Greenwood, Michael J. 1975. Research on internal migration in the United States. *Journal of Economic Literature* 13:397–433.

Gross, Alan J., and Virginia A. Clark. 1975. *Survival distributions: Reliability applications in the biomedical sciences.* New York: Wiley.

Guth, Gloria J. 1976. Surname spellings and computerized record linkage. *Historical Methods Newsletter* 10:10–19.

Haines, Michael. 1979. *Fertility and occupation: Population patterns in industrialization.* New York: Academic Press.

Hair, P. E. H. 1966. Bridal pregnancy in rural England in earlier centuries. *Population Studies* 20:233–43.

Hair, P. E. H. 1970. Bridal pregnancy in earlier rural England further examined. *Population Studies,* 24:59–70.

Hajnal, John. 1965. European marriage patterns in perspective. In *Population in history,* ed. D. V. Glass and D. E. Eversley, 101–43. Chicago: Aldine.

Hajnal, John. 1983. Two kinds of pre-industrial household formation system. In *Family forms in historic Europe,* ed. Richard Wall, Jean Robin and Peter Laslett, 65–104. Cambridge: Cambridge University Press.

Handwerker, W. Penn. 1986a. The modern demographic transition: An analysis of subsistence choices and reproductive consequences. *American Anthropologist* 88:400–416.

Handwerker, W. Penn. 1986b. Culture and reproduction: Exploring micro/macro linkages. In *Culture and reproduction: An anthropological critique of demographic transition theory,* ed. W. Penn Handwerker, 1–28. Boulder: Westview.

Hareven, Tamara K. 1976. Modernization and family history: Perspectives on social change. *Signs* 2:190–206.

Hareven, Tamara K. 1982. *Family time and industrial time.* Cambridge: Cambridge University Press.

Herlihy, David. 1985. *Medieval households.* Cambridge: Harvard University Press.

Herlihy, David, and Christiane Klapisch-Zuber. 1985. *Tuscans and their families.* New Haven: Yale University Press.

Hershberg, Theodore A., A. Burstein, and Robert Dockhorn. 1976. Record linkage. *Historical Methods Newsletter* 9:137–63.

Hochstadt, Steve. 1981. Migration and industrialization in Germany, 1815–1977. *Social Science History* 5:445–68.

Hogan, Dennis P. 1985. The demography of life-span transitions: Temporal and gender comparisons. In *Gender and the life course,* ed. Alice S. Rossi, 65–78. New York: Aldine.

Hogan, Dennis P., and Paul D. Frenzen. 1981. Antecedents to contraceptive innovation: Evidence from rural northern Thailand. *Demography* 18:597–614.

Hogan, Dennis P., and David I. Kertzer. 1985a. Longitudinal approaches to migration in social history. *Historical Methods* 18:20–30.

Hogan, Dennis P., and David I. Kertzer. 1985b. Migration patterns during Italian urbanization, 1865–1921. *Demography* 22:309–25.

Hogan, Dennis P., and David I. Kertzer. 1986. The social bases of declining infant mortality: Lessons from a nineteenth-century Italian town. *European Journal of Population* 2:361–86.

Houdaille, Jacques. 1987. Quatre villages du Morvan: 1610–1870. *Population* 42: 649–70.

Hull, Terence H. 1983. Cultural influences on fertility decision styles. In *Determinants of fertility in developing countries,* vol. 2, ed. Rodolfo A. Bulatao and Ronald D. Lee, 381–414. New York: Academic Press.

Inkeles, Alex. 1969. Making man modern: On the causes and consequences of individual change in six developing countries. *American Journal of Sociology* 75: 208–25.

Inkeles, Alex, and D. Smith. 1974. *Becoming modern: Individual change in six developing countries.* Cambridge: Harvard University Press.

Istituto Nazionale di Economia Agraria (INEA). 1931. *Monografie di famiglie agricole. VI. Contadini della valle del Panaro (Emilia).* Studi e Monografie no. 14. Milan.

Jacini, Stefano. 1882. *Atti della giunta per la inchiesta agraria e sulle condizioni della classe agricola.* Vol. 3 of *La toscana agricola.* Rome: Il Senato.

Jansen, C. J. 1970. Migration: A sociological problem. In *Readings in the sociology of migration,* ed. C. J. Jansen, 3–35. Oxford: Permagon.

Janssens, Angelique. 1986. Industrialization without family change? The extended family and the life cycle in a Dutch industrial town, 1880–1920. *Journal of Family History* 11:25–42.

Kälvemark, Ann-Sofie. 1980. Illegitimacy and marriage in Swedish parishes in the nineteenth century. In *Bastardy and its comparative history,* ed. Peter Laslett, Karla Oosterveen, and Richard M. Smith, 327–35. Cambridge: Harvard University Press.

Karweit, Nancy. 1988. *Handbook to CASA.* Baltimore: Center for Social Organization of Schools, Johns Hopkins University.

Karweit, Nancy, and David I. Kertzer. 1986. Data base management for life course family research. In *Family relations in life course perspective,* ed. David I. Kertzer, 167–88. Greenwich, Conn.: JAI Press.

Katz, Michael B. 1975. *The people of Hamilton, Canada West: Family and class in a mid-nineteenth century city.* Cambridge: Harvard University Press.

Katz, Michael B., Michael J. Doucet, and Mark J. Stern. 1982. *The social organization of early industrial capitalism.* Cambridge: Harvard University Press.

Kelly, Dennis. 1974. Linking nineteenth-century manuscript census records: A computer strategy. *Historical Methods Newsletter* 7:72–82.

Kertzer, David I. 1980. *Comrades and Christians: Religion and political struggle in Communist Italy.* Cambridge: Cambridge University Press.

Kertzer, David I. 1984. *Family life in central Italy, 1880–1910.* New Brunswick, N.J.: Rutgers University Press.

Kertzer, David I. 1985. *Handbook to Casalecchio history project.* Brunswick, Maine: Bowdoin College.

Kertzer, David I., and Caroline Brettell. 1987. Advances in Italian and Iberian family history. *Journal of Family History* 12:87–120.

Kertzer, David I., and Dennis P. Hogan. 1985. On the move: Migration in an Italian community, 1865–1921. *Social Science History* 9:1–24.

Kertzer, David I., and Andrea Schiaffino. 1983. Industrialization and coresidence: A life course approach. In *Life-span development and human behavior,* vol. 5, ed. Paul B. Baltes and Orville G. Brim, Jr., 360–91. New York: Academic Press.

Knodel, John. 1977. Family limitation and the fertility transition: Evidence from the age patterns of fertility in Europe and Asia. *Population Studies* 31:219–49.

Knodel, John. 1986. Demographic transitions in German villages. In *The decline of fertility in Europe,* ed. Ansley J. Coale and Susan C. Watkins, 337–89. Princeton, N.J.: Princeton University Press.

Knodel, John, and Katherine A. Lynch. 1985. The decline of remarriage: Evidence from German village populations in the eighteenth and nineteenth centuries. *Journal of Family History* 10:34–59.

Knodel, John, and Etienne van de Walle. 1986. Lessons from the past: Policy implications of historical fertility studies. In *The decline of fertility in Europe,* ed. Ansley J. Coale and Susan C. Watkins, 390–419. Princeton, N.J.: Princeton University Press.

Kriedte, Peter, Hans Medick, and Jurgen Schlumbohm. 1981. *Industrialization before industrialization.* Cambridge: Cambridge University Press.

Kussmaul, Ann. 1981. *Servants in husbandry in early modern England.* Cambridge: Cambridge University Press.

L'Eltore, G. 1974. Les causes de decès. In *La population de L'Italie,* ed. Comité International de Coordination des Recherches Nationales de Démographie, 41–50. Paris: CICRED.

Landi, Fiorenzo. 1977. I contratti agrari. In *La cultura popolare nell'Emilia-Romagna,* ed. Giuseppe Adani and Gastone Tamagnini, 139–45. Milan: Silvana Editoriale d'Arte.

Laslett, Peter. 1965. *The world we have lost.* New York: Scribner.

Laslett, Peter. 1972. Introduction: The history of the family. In *Household and family in past time,* ed. Peter Laslett and Richard Wall, 1–89. Cambridge: Cambridge University Press.

Laslett, Peter. 1977. *Family life and illicit love in earlier generations.* Cambridge: Cambridge University Press.

Laslett, Peter. 1980. Introduction: Comparing illegitimacy over time and between cultures. In *Bastardy and its comparative history,* ed. Peter Laslett, Karla Oosterveen, and Richard M. Smith, 1–64. Cambridge: Harvard University Press.

Laslett, Peter. 1983. Family and household as work group and king group: Areas of traditional Europe compared. In *Family forms in historic Europe,* ed. Richard Wall, Jean Robin, and Peter Laslett, 513–63. Cambridge: Cambridge University Press.

Laslett, Peter, Karla Oosterveen, and Richard M. Smith, eds. 1980. *Bastardy and its comparative history.* Cambridge: Harvard University Press.

Lee, Ronald D., and Rodolfo A. Bulatao, eds. 1983. *Determinants of fertility in developing countries.* 2 vols. New York: Academic Press.

Lehning, James R. 1980. *The peasants of Marlhes.* Chapel Hill: University of North Carolina Press.

Lehning, James R. 1984. Literacy and demographic behavior: Evidence from family reconstitution in nineteenth-century France. *History of Education Quarterly* 24:545–60.

Leibenstein, Harvey. 1974. An interpretation of the economic theory of fertility: Promising path or blind alley? *Journal of Economic Literature* 12:457–79.

LePlay, Frédéric. 1871. *L'organisation de la famille.* Paris: Tours.

Lequin, Yves. 1977. *Les ouvrièrs de la région lyonnais (1848–1914).* 2 vols. Lyon: Presses Universitaires de Lyon.

Lesthaeghe, Ron, and Chris Wilson. 1986. Modes of production, secularization, and the pace of the fertility decline in western Europe, 1870–1930. In *The decline of fertility in Europe,* ed. Ansley J. Coale and Susan C. Watkins, 261–92. Princeton, N.J.: Princeton University Press.

Levine, David. 1977. *Family formation in an age of nascent capitalism.* New York: Academic Press.

Levine, David. 1980. Illiteracy and family life during the first industrial revolution. *Journal of Social History* 14:25–44.

Levine, David. 1985. Industrialization and the proletarian family in England. *Past and Present* 107:168–203.

Levine, David. 1986. The decline of fertility in Europe: Review symposium. *Population and Development Review* 12:335–40.

Levine, David. 1987. *Reproducing families: The political economy of English population history.* Cambridge: Cambridge University Press.

Levine, David, and Keith Wrightson. 1980. The social context of illegitimacy in early modern England. In *Bastardy and its comparative history,* ed. Peter Laslett, Karla Oosterveen, and Richard M. Smith, 158–75. Cambridge: Harvard University Press.

Levine, Robert A., and Susan C. Scrimshaw. 1983. Effects of culture on fertility: Anthropological contributions. In *Determinants of fertility in developing countries,* vol. 2, ed. Rodolfo A. Bulatao and Ronald D. Lee, 666–96. New York: Academic Press.

Livi, Livio. 1915. *La composizione delle famiglie.* Florence.

Livi-Bacci, Massimo. 1977. *A history of Italian fertility during the last two centuries.* Princeton, N.J.: Princeton University Press.

Livi-Bacci, Massimo. 1986. Social-group forerunners of fertility control in Europe. In *The decline of fertility in Europe,* ed. Ansley J. Coale and Susan C. Watkins, 182–200. Princeton, N.J.: Princeton University Press.

Lotti, Luigi. 1980. La vita politica tra ottocento e novecento. In *Storia della Emilia Romagna,* vol. 3, ed. Aldo Berselli, 305–28. Bologna: CLUEB.

Luzzatto, Gino. 1968. *L'economia italiana dal 1861 al 1864.* Turin: Einaudi.

Malaguti, D. Antonio. 1981. *Il bifolco, la massaia e la famiglia contadina degli anni venti.* Bologna: Tamari Editori.

Marangoni, G. 1948. *Divisione e stime coloniche nella mezzdria, affitto e proprietà-coltivatrice dei fondi rustici e degli orti con particolare riguardo alle consuetudini dell'Emilia-Romagna.* Ravenna.

Marcolin, Massimo. 1985. The *casa d'industria* in Bologna during the Napoleonic period: Public relief and subsistence strategies. European University Institute Working Paper, Fiesole.

Martelli, Domenico. 1854. Considerazioni sul contratto di mezzadria generalmente adottato nell'agricoltura bolognese. In *Memorie lette nelle adunanze ordinarie della Società Agraria della provincia di Bologna* 7:131–42. Bologna: Società Agraria della Provincia di Bologna.

Mason, Karen O. 1983. *The status of women, fertility, and mortality: A review of interrelationships.* New York: The Rockefeller Foundation.

Masulli, Ignazio. 1980. *Crisi e trasformazione: Strutture economiche, rapporti sociali e lotte politiche nel bolognese (1880–1914).* Bologna: Istituto per la Storia di Bologna.

Mauldin, W. Parker. 1983. Population programs and fertility regulation. In *Determinants of fertility in developing countries,* vol. 2, ed. Rodolfo A. Bulatao and Ronald D. Lee, 267–94. New York: Academic Press.

McBride, Theresa M. 1974. Social mobility for the lower classes: Domestic servants in France. *Journal of Social History* 8:63–78.

McQuillan, Kevin. 1984. Modes of production and demographic patterns in nineteenth-century France. *American Journal of Sociology* 89:1324–46.

Medick, Hans. 1981. The structures and function of population-development under the proto-industrial system. In *Industrialization before industrialization,* ed. Peter Kriedte, Hans Medick, and Jürgen Schlumbohm, trans. Beate Schempp, 74–93. Cambridge: Cambridge University Press.

Menarini, Alberto. 1975. *Proverbi bolognesi.* Florence: Martello-Giunti.

Mendels, Franklin F. 1972. Proto-industrialization: The first phase of the process of industrialization. *Journal of Economic History* 32:241–61.

Mendels, Franklin F. 1984. "Des industries rurales à la protoindustrialisation: Historique d'un changement de perspective." *Annales, E.S.C.* 39:977–1008.

Menken, Jane, James Trussell, Debra Stempel, and Ozer Babakol. 1981. Proportional hazards life table models: An illustrative analysis of sociodemographic influences on marriage dissolution in the United States. *Demography* 18:181–200.

Merli, Stefano. 1972. *Proletariato di fabbrica e capitalismo industriale.* Florence: La Nuova Italia.

Ministero di Agricoltura, Industria e Commercio. 1887. Notizie sulle condizioni industriali della provincia di Bologna. *Annali di Statistica,* ser. 4, vol. 2. Rome.

Ministero di Agricoltura, Industria e Commercio. 1888. Provvedimenti a favore dei fanciulli esposti od altrimenti abbandonati dai genitori negli anni 1885, 1886 e 1887. *Statistica delle cause di morte nel 1886.* Rome.

Ministero di Agricoltura, Industria e Commercio. 1891. *I contratti agrari in Italia.* Rome.

Ministero di Agricoltura, Industria e Commercio. 1899. Notizie sulle condizioni industriali della provincia di Bologna. *Annali di Statistica. Statistica Industriale,* no. 5-A. Rome.

Ministero pel Culto del Regno d'Italia. 1808. *Decreti, regolamenti, istruzioni ge-*

nerali sopra gli oggetti appartenenti alle attribuzioni del Ministero pel Culto del Regno d'Italia. Vol. 1. Milan: Stamperia Reale.

Ministero pel Culto del Regno d'Italia. 1813. *Decreti, regolamenti, istruzioni generali sopra gli oggetti appartenti alle attribuzioni del Ministero pel Culto del Regno d'Italia.* Vol. 2. Milan: Stamperia Reale.

Moch, Leslie. 1983. *Paths to the city: Regional migration in nineteenth-century France.* Beverly Hills: Sage.

Nardi, Sergio. 1957. La famiglia mezzadrile nel comune di Ravenna. In *Le campagne emiliane nell'epoca moderna,* ed. Renato Zangheri, 267–82. Milan: Feltrinelli.

Nardi, Sergio. 1980. Il lavoro del bracciante nelle campagne ravennati di fine '800. In *Il proletariato agricolo in Emilia Romagna nella fase di formazione,* ed. Franco Cazzola, 147–84. Bologna: CLUEB.

Nardinelli, Clark. 1980. Child labor and the factory acts. *Journal of Economic History* 40:739–53.

Natale, Marcello. 1982. Les bilans demographiques des villes italiennes de l'Unité d'Italie à la première guerre mondiale. *Annales de Démographie Historique 1982,* 213–29. Paris: Mouton.

Netting, Robert McC. 1981. *Balancing on an Alp: Ecological change and continuity in a Swiss mountain community.* New York: Cambridge University Press.

Notestein, Frank W. 1953. Economic problems of population change. In *Proceedings of the Eighth International Conference of Agricultural Economists,* 13–31. London: Oxford University Press.

Oosterveen, Karla, Richard M. Smith, and Susan Stewart. 1980. Family reconstitution and the study of bastardy: Evidence from certain English parishes. In *Bastardy and its comparative history,* ed. Peter Laslett, Karla Oosterveen, and Richard M. Smith, 86–140. Cambridge: Harvard University Press.

Oppong, Christine. 1983. Women's roles, opportunity costs, and fertility. In *Determinants of fertility in developing countries,* vol. 2, ed. Rodolfo A. Bulatao and Ronald D. Lee, 547–89. New York: Academic Press.

Pagani, Aldo. 1930. *La distribuzione del lavoro umano nell'azienda agraria.* Bologna.

Pagani, Aldo. 1931. *Inchiesta sul bracciantato della valle padana.* Piacenza: Federazione Italiana Consorzi Agrari.

Palazzi, Maura. 1982. L'industria emiliana alle soglie del XX secolo. In *Studi in memoria di Luigi Dal Pane,* ed. Istituto di Storia Economica e Sociale, Università di Bologna, 893–949. Bologna: CLUEB.

Pasolini, Maria. 1891. *Una famiglia di mezzadri romagnoli nel comune di Ravenna.* Bologna.

Pasolini, Maria. 1892a. Monografie di alcuni operai braccianti nel comune di Ravenna (I). *Giornale degli Economisti* 5:311–43.

Pasolini, Maria. 1892b. Monografie di alcuni operai braccianti nel comune di Ravenna (II). *Giornale degli Economisti* 5:411–27.

Perdisa, Luigi. 1935. *La distribuzione del lavoro manuale in poderi a mezzadria della Romagna.* Faenza: Osservatorio di Economia Agraria per l'Emilia.

Pollock, Linda A. 1983. *Forgotten children: Parent-child relations from 1500–1900.* Cambridge: Cambridge University Press.

Polvani Dalmonte, Annamaria. 1985. *Casalecchio di Reno: Percorsi e immagini della sua civiltà.* Bologna: Ponte Nuovo Editrice.

Poni, Carlo. 1969. *Gli aratri e l'economia agraria nel bolognese dal XVII al XIX secolo.* Bologna: Zanichelli.

Poni, Carlo, and Silvio Fronzoni. 1979. L'economia di sussistenza della famiglia contadina. In *Mestieri della terra e delle acque,* ed. Casse di Risparmio dell' Emilia Romagna, 11–41. Vol. 3 of *Cultura popolare nell'Emilia Romagna.* Milan: Pizzi.

Portes, Alejandro. 1976. On the sociology of national development: Theories and issues. *American Journal of Sociology* 82:55–85.

Poulain, Michel, and Dominique Tabutin. 1980. La mortalité aux jeunes âges en Europe et en Amerique du Nord du XIXe à nos jours. In *La mortalité des enfants dans le monde et dans l'histoire,* ed. Paul-Marie Boulanger and Dominique Tabutin, 119–57. Liège: Ordina Editions.

Pouyez, Christian, Raymond Roy, and Gerard Bouchard. 1981. La mobilité géographique en milieu rural: Le Sanguenay, 1852–1861. *Histoire Sociale* 14:123–56.

Preston, Samuel. 1975. The changing relation between mortality and level of economic development. *Population Studies* 29:231–48.

Preston, Samuel. 1978. Causes and consequences of mortality declines in less developed countries during the twentieth century. In *Population and economic change in developing countries,* ed. Richard Easterlin, 289–360. Chicago: University of Chicago Press.

Preti, Luigi. 1955. *Le lotte agrarie nella valle padana.* Turin: Einaudi.

Priore, Gennaro Orazio. 1906. Una famiglia di mezzadri nella Media Valle del Tevere. *La Riforma Sociale* 16:602–35.

Provincia di Bologna. 1919. *Rilevazione statistica sulle condizioni del mercato del lavoro nella provincia.* Bologna.

Rabbeno, Aronne. 1895. Consuetudini rurali e divisioni dei contadini nella provincia di Bologna. *Annali della Società Agraria di Bologna* 35:59–88.

Rabbeno, Aronne. 1899. I patti colonici nei rapporti colla odierna coltura. *Annali della Società Agraria di Bologna* 39:41–58.

Radbill, Samuel X. 1968. A history of child abuse and infanticide. In *The battered child,* ed. Ray Helfer and C. Henry Kempe, 3–21. Chicago: University of Chicago Press.

Ramella, Franco. 1977. Fabbrica e società nell'Italia dell'800. *Classe* 9:41–57.

Ramponi, Agostino. 1892. La mezzadria e la coltura intensiva. *Annali della Società Agraria di Bologna* 32:95–132.

Raseri, Enrico. 1906. *Atlante di demografia medica d'Italia.* Rome: Istituto Geografico dott. G. De Agostini.

Ravenstein, E. G. 1889. The laws of migration. *Journal of the Royal Statistical Society* 52:241–301.

Retherford, Robert D., and James A. Palmore. 1983. Diffusion processes affect-

ing fertility regulation. In *Determinants of fertility in developing countries,* vol. 2, ed. Rodolfo A. Bulatao and Ronald D. Lee, 295–339. New York: Academic Press.
Rettaroli, Rosella. 1986. *Modelli di nuzialità nell'Italia rurale del XIX secolo.* Tesi di dottorato di ricerca in demografia, University of Bologna.
Ricci, Giovanni. 1985. *Bologna.* 2d ed. Bari: Laterza.
Ring, Richard R. 1979. Early medieval peasant households in central Italy. *Journal of Family History* 4:2–25.
Robin, Jean. 1986. Prenuptial pregnancy in a rural area of Devonshire in the mid-nineteenth century: Colyton, 1851–1881. *Continuity and Change* 1:113–24.
Rocchi, Gaetano. 1893. La precedenza obbligatoria del matrimonio civile rispetto a quello religioso. *La Rassegna Nazionale* 69:418–33.
Romanelli, Raffaele. 1979. *L'Italia liberale (1861–1900).* Bologna: Il Mulino.
Romani, Mario. 1982. *Storia economica d'Italia nel secolo XIX (1815–1882).* Bologna: Il Mulino.
Roy, Raymond, Christian Pouyez, and Francois Martin. 1980. Le jumelage des données nominatives dans les récensements: Problèmes et méthodes. *Histoire Sociale* 13, no. 25:173–93.
Ruggles, Steven. 1987. *Prolonged connections: The rise of the extended family in nineteenth-century England and America.* Madison: University of Wisconsin Press.
Sabean, David. 1970. Household formation and geographical mobility: A family register study for a Wurttemberg village 1760–1900. *Annales de Démographie Historique 1970,* 275–94. Paris: Mouton.
Saller, Richard P. 1987. Men's age at marriage and its consequences in the Roman family. *Classical Philology* 82:21–34.
Samoggia, Alessandra. 1985. La mortalità infantile nella campagna bolognese fra Seicento e Ottocento. In *Popolazione ed economia dei territori bolognese durante il settecento,* ed. Istituto per la Storia di Bologna, 87–114. Bologna: Istituto per la Storia di Bologna.
Sandefur, Gary D., and Wilbur J. Scott. 1981. A dynamic analysis of migration: An assessment of the effects of age, family and career variables. *Demography* 18:355–68.
Santini, Antonio. 1974. *La fecondità delle coorti: Studio longitudinale della fecondità italiana dall'inizio del secolo XX.* Florence: Dipartimento Statistico Matematico, Università di Firenze.
Sarti, Roland. 1985. *Long live the strong: A history of rural society in the Apennine mountains.* Amherst: University of Massachusetts Press.
Scarselli, Antonio. 1890. Delle condizioni morali delle nostre campagne. *Annali della Società Agraria di Bologna* 30:27–39.
Schiavi, Alessandro. 1904. *La disoccupazione nel basso emiliano: Inchiesta diretta nelle provincie di Ferrara, Bologna e Ravenna.* Milan: Ufficio del Lavoro della Società Umanitaria.
Schneider, Jane, and Peter S. Schneider. 1984. Demographic transition in a Sicilian rural town. *Journal of Family History* 9:245–72.

Schofield, Roger S. 1971. Age-specific mobility in an eighteenth-century rural English parish. *Annales de Démographie Historique 1970,* 261–73. Paris: Mouton.
Schultz, T. Paul. 1985. Changing world prices, women's wages, and the fertility transition: Sweden, 1860–1910. *Journal of Political Economy* 93:126–54.
Schultz, Theodore W. 1973. The value of children: An economic perspective. *Journal of Political Economy* 81:S2–S13.
Segredin, Graziella. 1982. *Crescita urbana e sviluppo industriale a Casalecchio di Reno all'inizio del secolo XX.* Tesi di laurea. Facoltá di Magistero, University of Bologna.
Sereni, Emilio. 1957. Note per una storia del paesaggio agrario emiliano. In *Le campagne emiliane nell'epoca moderna,* ed. Renato Zangheri, 27–54. Milan: Feltrinelli.
Sereni, Emilio. 1968. *Il capitalismo nelle campagne (1860–1900).* Turin: Einaudi.
Sezioni di Agricoltura ed Amministrativa. 1889. Riferimento sulla memoria del Cav. dott. Antonio Bernardi. *Annali della Società Agraria di Bologna* 29:53–68.
Sharlin, Allan N. 1986. Urban-rural differences in fertility in Europe during the demographic transition. In *The decline of fertility in Europe,* ed. Ansley J. Coale and Susan C. Watkins, 234–60. Princeton, N.J.: Princeton University Press.
Sharlin, Allan N., and John Sammis. 1982. Migration and urban population in pre-industrial Europe: Wurzburg in the late seventeenth and early eighteenth centuries. Paper presented to the Social Science History Association, Bloomington, Indiana.
Shorter, Edward. 1973. Female emancipation, birth-control and fertility in European history. *American Historical Review* 78:605–40.
Shorter, Edward. 1975. *The making of the modern family.* New York: Basic Books.
Shryock, Henry S., and Elizabeth A. Larmon. 1965. Some longitudinal data on internal migration. *Demography* 2:579–92.
Skolnick, Mark. 1973. The resolution of ambiguities in record linkage. In *Identifying people in the past,* ed. E. A. Wrigley, 102–27. London: Edward Arnold.
Skolnick, Mark, P. Beauchamp, Hubert Charbonneau, Carlo Corsini, Jacques Légaré, R. LeMee, and K. Lynch. 1978. *Report of the conference on methods of automatic family reconstruction.* Liège: International Union for the Scientific Study of Population.
Smith, Daniel S. 1982. A perspective on demographic methods and effects in social history. *The William and Mary Quarterly* 39:443–68.
Smith, Daniel S., and Michael S. Hindus. 1975. Premarital pregnancy in America, 1640–1971. An overview. *Journal of Interdisciplinary History* 5:537–70.
Smith, Richard M. 1986. Marriage processes in the past: Some continuities. In *The world we have gained,* ed. Lloyd Bonfield, Richard M. Smith, and Keith Wrightson, 43–99. Oxford: Basil Blackwell.
Somogyi, Stefano. 1965. Sviluppo della popolazione italiana dal 1861 al 1961. *Annali di Statistica,* ser. 8, vol. 17. Rome.
Sonnino, Eugenio. 1982. Bilanci demografici di città in Italia fino agli inizi del nostro secolo. In *La demografia storica delle città italiane,* ed. Società Italiana di Demografia Storica, 47–108. Bologna: CLUEB.

Spagnoli, Paul G. 1983. Industrialization, proletarianization, and marriage: A reconsideration. *Journal of Family History* 8:230–47.

Stephenson, Charles. 1979. A gathering of strangers? Mobility, social structure, and political participation in the formation of nineteenth-century American workingclass culture. In *American workingclass culture,* ed. Milton Cantor, 31–60. Westport: Greenwood Press.

Stokes, C. Shannon, Wayne A. Schutjer, and Rodolfo A. Bulatao. 1986. Is the relationship between landholding and fertility spurious? A response to Cain. *Population Studies* 40:305–12.

Stone, Lawrence. 1977. *The family, sex and marriage in England, 1500–1800.* New York: Harper and Row.

Taeuber, Karl E. 1961. Duration-of-residence analysis of internal migration in the United States. *Milbank Memorial Fund Quarterly* 39:116–31.

Taglioni, Giuseppe. 1866. Sulla legge del matrimonio civile, considerazioni igieniche, morali, e medico-politiche. *Bulletino delle Scienze Mediche di Bologna* 1:175–84.

Tanari, Luigi. 1881. *Atti della giunta per la inchiesta agraria sulle condizioni della classe agricola.* Vol. 2. Rome.

Thernstrom, Stephan. 1973. *The other Bostonians.* Cambridge: Harvard University Press.

Thernstrom, Stephan, and Peter R. Knights. 1970. Men in motion: Some data and speculations about urban population mobility in nineteenth-century America. *Journal of Interdisciplinary History* 1:7–35.

Thompson, E. P. 1963. *The making of the English working class.* New York: Vintage.

Tilly, Charles. 1978a. The historical study of vital processes. In *Historical studies of changing fertility,* ed. Charles Tilly, 3–55. Princeton, N.J.: Princeton University Press.

Tilly, Charles. 1978b. Migration in modern European history. In *Human migration: patterns and policies,* ed. William H. McNeill and Ruth S. Adams, 48–72. Bloomington: Indiana University Press.

Tilly, Charles. 1979. Did the cake of custom break? In *Consciousness and class experience in nineteenth-century Europe,* ed. John Merriman, 17–44. New York: Holmes & Meier.

Tilly, Charles. 1986. The decline of fertility in Europe: Review symposium. *Population and Development Review* 12:323–28.

Tilly, Louise A. 1979a. Individual lives and family strategies in the French proletariat. *Journal of Family History* 4:137–52.

Tilly, Louise A. 1979b. Occupational structure, women's work, and demographic change in two French industrial cities, Anzin and Roubaix, 1872–1906. In *Time, space, and man,* ed. Jan Sundin and Erik Soderlund, 107–32. Atlantic Highlands, N.J.: Humanities.

Tilly, Louise A., Joan W. Scott, and Miriam Cohen. 1976. Women's work and European fertility patterns. *Journal of Interdisciplinary History* 6:447–76.

Tilly, Louise A., and Joan W. Scott. 1978. *Women, work, and family.* New York: Holt, Rinehart and Winston.

Tittarelli, Luigi. 1985. I servi domestici a Perugia a metà dell'ottocento. *Quaderno dell'Istituto Interfacoltà di Statistica, Università di Perugia* 10:23–88.

Toscanelli, Giuseppe. [1861] 1976. La famiglia colonica nella mezzeria toscana. Reprinted in *Un'Italia sconosciuta,* ed. Massimo Guidetti and Paul H. Stahl, 257–64. Milan: Jaca Books.

Trussell, James, and Charles Hammerslough. 1983. A hazards-model analysis of the covariates of infant and child mortality in Sri Lanka. *Demography* 20:1–26.

Tuma, Nancy B., and Michael T. Hannan. 1984. *Social dynamics: Models and methods.* Orlando: Academic Press.

Urtoller, G. 1898. I movimenti agrari in ordine al diritto e all'economia sociale. *Annali della Società Agraria di Bologna* 38:199–229.

Wall, Richard. 1983. The compositions of households in a population of 6 men to ten women: Southeast Bruges in 1814. In *Family forms in historic Europe,* ed. Richard Wall, Jean Robin, and Peter Laslett, 421–74. Cambridge: Cambridge University Press.

Watkins, Susan C. 1986. Conclusions. In *The decline of fertility in Europe,* ed. Ansley J. Coale and Susan C. Watkins, 420–49. Princeton, N.J.: Princeton University Press.

Watkins, Susan C., and James McCarthy. 1980. The female life cycle in a Belgian commune: La Hulpe, 1847–1866. *Journal of Family History* 5:167–79.

Weiss, Kenneth M., David L. Rossmann, Ranajit Chakraborty, and Susan L. Norton. 1980. Wherefore art thou, Romio? Name frequency patterns and their use in automated genealogy assembly. In *Genealogical demography,* ed. Bennett Dyke and Warren T. Morrill, 41–61. New York: Academic Press.

Winchester, Ian. 1980. Priorities for record linkage: A theoretical and practical checklist. In *Historical social research,* ed. Jerome Clubb and Erwin Scheuch, 414–30. Stuttgart: Klett-Cotta.

Woods, R. I. 1987. Approaches to the fertility transition in Victorian England. *Population Studies* 41:283–311.

Wrigley, E. A. 1961. *Industrial growth and population change.* Cambridge: Cambridge University Press.

Wrigley, E. A. 1977. Reflections on the history of the family. *Daedalus* 106:71–85.

Wrigley, E. A., and Roger S. Schofield. 1981. *The population history of England 1541–1871: A reconstruction.* Cambridge: Harvard University Press.

Zangheri, Renato. 1957. I moti del macinato nel bolognese. In *Le campagne emiliane nell'epoca moderna,* ed. Renato Zangheri, 101–44. Milan: Feltrinelli.

Zangheri, Renato. 1969. The historical relationship between agriculture and economic development in Italy. In *Agrarian change and economic development,* ed. S. Jones and S. J. Woolf, 23–40. London: Methuen.

Zazzeri, William. 1982. L'urbanistica. *Alla Ribalta* (Casalecchio di Reno) 13 (Supplement to vol. 11/12): 17–18.

Index